The Problem of Boston

by Martin Green

A Mirror for Anglo-Saxons

Science and the Shabby Curate
of Literature

Re-Appraisals: Some Commonsense Readings
in American Literature

The Problem of Boston:
Some Readings in Cultural History

THE
PROBLEM
OF BOSTON:
Some Readings in
Cultural History

MARTIN GREEN

W · W · NORTON & COMPANY · INC · *New York*

For Bill and Mary Ann Youngren, with whom I talked over many of these ideas before they were really clear even to myself. They gave me an image of the interest this subject could have for people other than myself.

Contents

Forewords

I

SINCE I AM NOT a specialist in American history, the reading behind these essays has been in the historians themselves, not in the records they studied. When I disagree with one of them I am often therefore opposing his judgment with another's that seems on the face of it more reasonable or better substantiated; a mode of disagreement always to be conducted in a somewhat tentative and tenor voice. But I do not mean to imply by that tone any apology for discussing historical subjects or advancing historical opinions. I claim to be giving a fair account of what the historians tell us (the more accessible historians) and to be using that to discuss a problem vital to the theorist of literature. I argue, for instance, that the literary life in America in the nineteenth century seems not to have been, on the evidence given, as dismal an affair as it is painted, economically or socially. If some historian should be able to show that it *was;* that men of talent then did find it significantly harder than in other times and places to get appreciative readings, parental encouragement, substantial payments, official appointments; then I should not feel myself proved completely wrong. My argument, to be precise, is that we have *as yet* no reason (no adequate reason) to come to that conclusion. And we have of course every reason to distrust the *impulse* to believe it, in ourselves and in the historians, once we realize how much self-pity (complicated by self-dislike) gets expressed in the American intellectual's image of himself. That someone should prove that proposition, one way or the other, is very desirable. One of the kinds of usefulness I would like these protests to have is that they should provoke such an answer. That would, however, be a minor kind of usefulness; their major aims must be to use history to develop our general theories of literature and culture.

II

I have chosen two men to discuss in detail as emblems of the culture they belonged to. By an emblem I mean something pictorially and generally representative—in its limitedness as well as in its impressiveness. These men moulded the taste of their times, directing the responses of readers and the enterprises of writers, but they also learned that taste from others. I did not choose 'creative' writers as my emblems, because artists inevitably owe as much to their art and to their experience as they owe to the meaning of these for their readers' culture; critics can better represent the reasoning and moralizing, the centrally cultural, functions of their community; but even as critics Ticknor and Norton were not creative. Their strength lay in a branch of the literary life which is often not mentioned in the histories; they represented (semi-officially but also personally) the reading public and posterity to the artists of their time. They understood them, entertained them, praised them, protected them; guided, by authoritative comment and response, their efforts. This is very important work, and employs, when done on the level Ticknor and Norton did it, real literary intelligence. But they were not originators, in the important sense; they were not original minds. Consequently, though I am trying to rouse the reader's attention to their interesting and impressive qualities, I am not trying to claim the highest titles for them. They would not be so fully emblems of their culture if they were brilliant thinkers or major writers, much less if they were geniuses. I therefore want the reader to judge my account of them by asking if they seem like men of high but not original talent, profoundly participating in, as well as significantly directing, the serious mind of their times. They had not Matthew Arnold's gifts, though they filled, for want of an American Matthew Arnold, his place. But he could not be called an emblem of his culture, in this sense, just because of his gifts, his outstandingness. The interest I am asking the reader to direct at them is therefore a rather special one.

III

This subject is unfortunately another of those dense thickets of meaning where many paths of thought converge and intertwine, and where one finds oneself after a while pushing on in some near-reverse direction without having apparently taken any turning, or bursting again through the bushes into a clearing one already knows too well. Words like 'culture' refer to several classes of phenomena and orders of meaning; within each order there are stringent connections which do not apply between the orders. It is always necessary, therefore, as a part of general vigilance, to give a few key words an artificial rigidity of reference and of relationship to each other. I have used 'culture' to refer to the whole way of life of a community during a given period, all its patterns of behaviour in both labour and leisure; though I have also used it (to exclude this chance of ambiguity would require too artificial a use of language) to refer to the art, entertainment, and learning of the community, seen from a generally educational point of view, in their effects on habits of thought and imagination. Within this second meaning, I have used 'high culture' to refer to those kinds of art, entertainment, and scholarship which involve some strenuousness of thought and feeling, and 'popular culture' for those which do not. But I cannot guarantee that in some cases that distinction may not apply better to the social classes involved in the different kinds of activity. And 'humanism' I have used to refer to that conspectus of contemporary knowledge and thought which an individual rather than an institution might achieve, and which would amount to a significant participation in the mind of his time, but also to those broad and steady sympathies with which that participation enriches the individual's response to a particular idea or book.

Obviously, therefore, I do not claim to have eliminated the subject's ambiguities. To do that one would need to reconstruct half a language. I hope to have controlled them, by reducing their number and by here specifying their operation.

IV

It is one of this book's theories that the history of nineteenth-century Boston is also the history of the American mind in this period. That is, that in Boston the life of the mind was given an important and dignified place in the total culture. Poets and novelists had easy access to certain kinds of social power—at Harvard, as trustees of institutions, on popular lecture platforms —and inhabited the same world as political and administrative leaders. This did not happen to any comparable degree in most parts of America, and that fact, it is generally agreed, seriously impoverished the life of the American mind. It had no history, in the sense that it had too little continuity or reciprocity. The artists and thinkers worked too much in a social vacuum, acceding too completely to society's cruder demands on them, or rejecting its finer demands too violently. In Boston, I argue, there was such a history. Artists and scholars inherited from each other, or created for each other, various versions of the intellectual's role in society, all of which allotted him considerable dignity and effectiveness. For this reason, to dismiss the history of nineteenth-century Boston too easily as un-American (as I claim most people do) and thus to conjure up an America in which the mind *has* no history, as one's own ancestry and setting, seems to me dangerous and dishonest from several points of view. Boston is a part of American history; 'American' history is an abstraction.

I mean for instance those panoramic histories so much in vogue now, where the emphasis is on movement, change, bustle, noise: migrations and immigrations, camp-meetings and corn-huskings, Fourth-of-July oratory and Conestoga wagons through the Cumberland Gap; where each aspect of American life is presented in a context of other contrasting jostling aspects, in a great rattling kaleidoscope, and nothing is estimated in and for itself. This is a good way to avoid the painful problems of judg-

2

Foreworps 13

ment, but sooner or later the thoughtful reader is bound to ask where he (as thoughtful reader) would have belonged, what he (the man interested in history) would have counted for, in this noisy Hollywood epic. The answer must surely be Boston: that it was in those un-American, unbustling, settled areas left behind by the great caravan and left out by the historian that the history-reader would have belonged. For an intellectual to omit Boston from his map of America is to make himself a homeland so alien he must either resent and reject it or mortify himself to embrace it. (Most of the historians I borrow from seem to me to do the latter.) He must in fact give Boston a large and central place on that map, not to feel out of place there; and that is why I call this a major piece of his history. It seems to me that not only Turner's followers but Parrington's and the Beards' too—and who does that leave? *—are guilty of slighting this aspect of America.

That is the argument of the book as a whole. But I must insist here that the experience of Boston, much more the model of Boston, is not offered for any simple imitation. Indeed, an even larger argument of the book has to do with how fundamentally something went wrong there. Moreover, Boston was indeed what it is said to have been, not typically American, and too much in thrall to England, to the past, to social conservatism, and so on. Its experience is offered for a complex scrutiny and assimilation, that will include very varying degrees of acceptance and some rejection. But that scrutiny and that assimilation must be made, and made with some intensity and generosity—some fullness.

* It leaves, of course, Perry Miller, whom no-one could accuse of omitting Boston from his map. Much as nineteenth-century Boston owes to him, however (especially for his volumes on the Transcendentalists and on thought after the Civil War), I think there is room for some protest against his way of describing it. In the context of American history, 'Puritan', with all its unavoidable connotations of seventeenth-century theology and theocracy, seems to me a very confusing word and unprofitable concept. I am more conscious here than anywhere else of being presumptuous, but I must argue that nineteenth-century Boston seems to have been more like nineteenth-century London than like seventeenth-century Boston: that there were, of course, idiosyncrasies one can explain as Puritan in that sense, but that the body of life and thought owed more to generally nineteenth-century conditions and interests.

Introduction

THE NAME Boston is something of a joke; at the lowbrow level, as the home of puritanical blue laws ('The Boston Beguine'); intermediately, as the home of a queer, dowdy class-consciousness (*The Proper Bostonians*); and for serious readers, as the home of the genteel tradition in American literature, the fireside poets, the schoolroom poets. The first two are not worth thinking hard about; but the third misconception is not only unfair, it expresses at best an inattention, at worst a treachery, to an enterprise that embodied some of the best hopes of serious people in its day, and that in our day should still engage our hopes imaginatively, still command our intellectual participation. The story of nineteenth-century Boston is full of the most poignant interest for anyone who cares about literary or cultural values in a democracy. It cannot be dismissed as by and large silly, or feeble, or dull. There was something impressive in it; something very instructive; above all, something centrally relevant.

In *Culture and Society* Raymond Williams remarks, 'The image of a society organized in terms of value is recurring and inevitable.' He is talking of Ruskin's attempts with the Guild of St George, which failed, he says, like so many others, 'because the necessary social commitment could not or would not be made'. What nineteenth-century Boston meant by 'value' and 'social commitment' was always somewhat different from what Williams is getting at, and came to be narrowed down into something much smaller; but the city's leaders used a very similar vocabulary to define their aims, and an essentially similar ideology. It is hard to think of any other sizable community in the nineteenth century which meant to organize itself in terms of value. In Boston some social commitment was made, over and over again. When its record is rightly explored, it has an emotional resonance which echoes in those two sentences very stirringly.

The Problem of Boston

Chapter One

THE PROBLEM OF CULTURE

Our complaints against the society we live in, our criticisms of it, always make more or less discernible our idea of the perfect society, or, as we are more likely to say nowadays, the really healthy culture. Behind contemporary complaints from people in the humanities, the ideal is often of a society in which the different kinds of power—financial, political, intellectual, administrative—acknowledge lively mutual responsibilities; most important, since these are intellectuals speaking, the other kinds of power acknowledge the intellectual, award a high place to the life of the mind. These are responsibilities derived not from some written constitution or social contract, but from a corpus of inherited social experience, transmitted most often in the families of a particular social class, who have between them discharged all those responsibilities, and taught their value to others not born into that class. This ideal is clearly not one towards which we imagine ourselves advancing, in any predictable future; it is to be located in the past —a past from which we are ineluctably receding, retrogressing, but still a usable past, in that it offers us a vision by contrast with which to measure our actual state of affairs. This vision is of a really responsible society; not only in the sense already explained, but also in the sense that all its cultural life was responsibly administered. For instance, the average citizen's imaginative nourishment, which is mediated to him now through the mass media, was then in the hands of individuals and traditions—from the village parson and the harvest festival on up—who took it seriously, and were concerned, not to make money out of it, but to transmit it largely as they had received it. And this popular culture merged into a high culture in which the creative artists usually knew their patrons, and the reading or listening public was to be identified—to some degree—with 'society'. Writers and readers, clergymen and landowners, scholars and political leaders, formed together a body of people who knew each other, or of each other, with something like the degree of intimacy of the total academic community of the United States today, and who acknowledged a common responsibility to maintain serious standards of appreciation of the arts and learning.

This is the ideal, and though its historical accuracy is not the point, there seems no reason to call it radically false to the facts. Its most recent manifestation, in English-speaking culture, is usually said to be eighteenth-century England, and its most brilliant signs the rich intimacies, both personal and social, which Pope and Swift, Addison and Steele, Gay and Thomson, were able to maintain not only with each other and with other men of intellect, but with the men of political and social power, in both parties; which bore fruit in, for instance, the very considerable official patronage of poets. This last point is central, for this idea of cultural health focuses on the conditions that foster literature —taken to represent all the arts—not that foster any-quality writing, and not the inexplicable achievements of genius, but the best employment of a talented man's talent. It is concerned with the other forms of thought and learning, and with social conditions like housing and employment laws, but in proportion as these things depart from that central question, they become peripheral and minor. This may seem too sweeping and simple an account of some theories of culture, but I would argue that that is because so many writers on the subject have had more than one centre to their theory, more than one focus to their vision.

Let me expand that point. This general theory would not have attracted so many expounders, or have generated such intense convictions, if it did not express a multiplicity of interests. There is the concern for high culture and the concern for popular culture, the concern for education and the concern for art, the concern for critical standards and the concern for social justice, and so on. Most of the expounders share most of the interests, quite passionately, and of course there is often no contradiction or conflict necessary between those interests.* The phenomena in one area are *connected* with those in another, and a failure in one area is usually reflected, *in some way,* in performance in the others. By measuring the quality of life a society offers its members in its expression in art, and in the members' response to that art, we can hold all those phenomena together and harness all those interests. But in fact these phenomena are not connected according to any predictable or calculable necessity, and there could easily be a conflict between these interests. In a given situation the quality of cultural life could be held either to have suffered terribly (by some social injustice to the poor) or to have benefited considerably (by some discriminating patronage of the arts) by the rule of a particular class. It will not do to assert that *all* these criteria must be satisfied before we praise a culture—any more than to hope that failure in one way will *somehow* be followed by failure in all the others; if this is to be a usable theory we must admit to there being an order of importance among our criteria. And of cultural interests, the one most proper to act as primary in a theory of literature seems to me the concern for high culture—primarily as it applies to writing, of course. That is, the 'really healthy culture' from our point of view would be the one which fostered serious writing—rewarded it with discriminating praise, prestige, and payment commensurate with the rewards of professional men and politicians— while it also acknowledged some serious obligation to serve the other interests harnessed together as 'cultural values'.

What interests me in the Boston of the nineteenth century is the way it answers to that ideal. The Boston of 1900 was of

---

* In Great Britain the expounders include notably F. R. Leavis, Q. D. Leavis, T. S. Eliot, Richard Hoggart, Raymond Williams. In America the theory is less completely identified with particular writers, but it is reflected in the work of most critics.

course importantly unlike that of 1800, but the city throughout that century held by a faith which no other city I know shared with it: a vivid faith, expressing itself at many levels of individual and corporate action, in the possibility of achieving a high quality of life in a community as a whole, and of expressing that quality in a great literature. By 1900 the idea of that community had become much more partial. Actual Boston had become widely separate from ideal Boston. There were many citizens of the actual city for whom no elevation in quality of life could be hoped—at least there could be no vivid faith in any particular means to that end. But there was still a community within Boston, as Samuel Eliot Morison makes clear in his reminiscences of 1962.

> Someone explaining the decay of American cities since 1940 observed that we had no solid core of nobility and bourgeois, as in Amsterdam, Strasbourg, Bordeaux, Bristol, and Milan, who insisted on living in town, interested themselves in local politics and supported cultural activities. But Boston had just that sort of group in my childhood. Not nobility, of course, but families who endowed Harvard and other universities, founded the Museum of Fine Arts, the Symphony Orchestra and the Opera House, and took pride in supporting great charitable foundations such as the Perkins Institute for the Blind and the Massachusetts General Hospital. And Boston had something more than that. . . . When a family had accumulated a certain fortune, instead of trying to build it up still further, to become a Rockefeller or Carnegie or Huntington and then perhaps discharge its debt to society by some great foundation, it would step out of business or finance and try to accomplish something in literature, education, medical research, the arts, or public service. Generally one or two members of the family continued in business, to look after the family securities and enable the creative brothers or cousins to carry on without the handicap of poverty. Of course there were families like that in other cities, but in Boston there were so many of them as to constitute a recognized way of life. One has only to think of the Prescott, Parkman, Shattuck, Cabot, Holmes, Lowell, Forbes, Peabody, Eliot, Saltonstall and Sargent families, and what they have accomplished for the beauty and betterment of life, to see what I mean.[1]

Some of those institutions, like the Perkins Institute and the Hospital, were begun in the first half of the century, about which the point is more easily made, but others, like the Symphony

Orchestra and Fenway Court, belong to its last twenty years; and they too are quite heroic gestures of faith—in a very Bostonian way, both personal and civic faith—in communal cultural life. It might seem more natural to describe Fenway Court as a purely personal gesture, and of fantasy more than of faith, but if one reads the response of people when it was opened, one sees that it had the other character too.

Thus Barrett Wendell wrote to Mrs Gardner, in 1902.

More and more, it seems to me that the future of our New England must depend on the standards of culture which we maintain and preserve here. The College, the Institute, the Library, the Orchestra,—and so on,—are the real bases of our strength and our dignity in the years to come. . . . And what you have so quietly and so surely done seems to me not only a thing in itself beautiful and admirable beyond anything else in this country, but also a kind of public service, which would have been done by no other human being, and of which the influence must remain increasingly, incalculably good.

And later, in another letter to her, we catch the same remarkable note of patriotic, nearly religious, earnestness.

Above all, as an American of New England, I feel, as I wrote you before, glad beyond words that this work of living beauty has been wrought here, where I had felt that the glories were only of our own little past. Now that I have seen, even in these passing glimpses, what seems to me the most nearly perfect work of art which has grown anywhere in the years of our own time, there comes from it a great, measureless surge of happiness and of stimulus. One must do one's best, to merit right in a world and a time when such standards may still be.[2]

Barrett Wendell's 'world' and 'time' usually seem to us cramped and sickly. His judgment was often corrupted by a sophistication and disenchantment unimpressive in many ways. But in this situation the sophistication and disenchantment disappear, and he stands before us a true Bostonian, absolute in his earnestness about 'standards' (a key word), recalled to the faith that Boston is their most natural home and setting. We catch the same note in Mr Morison's last sentence, too. That faith was still being put into practice up to the end of the century.

The Boston that interests us flourished best during roughly the first half of the century; it is not profitable to seek more exact delimitations, because the crucial date for one aspect of city life is less apt for another equally important. The years 1836–45 are crucial for the influx of immigrants, with all the changes it brought in the social and economic life of the city, but the dates of Jackson's administration before, and of the Civil War, after, are equally important in changing the America of which Boston was perforce a part.

Moreover, the Boston of the second half of the century was a genuine continuation of the same enterprise, only under less favourable conditions, and therefore advancing more defensively, more conservatively, less hopefully. It became progressively more malformed and dysfunctional, a caricature of the earlier ideal. But it was not until after 1900 that it could be called an ordinary city in which the attempt to be extraordinary survived mainly in oddities—the city Cleveland Amory described.

We should not let ourselves take this extraordinariness for granted, as something historically inevitable. It has become habitual, partly because of the Bostonians' latter-day self-accusations, to describe them as still Puritans, as if there were a New England character independent of time or external events, or as if the Boston of the nineteenth century were the immediate heir of that of the seventeenth century. But it was Charles Chauncy who was the representative figure of Bostonian religious life before Channing, not Jonathan Edwards, much less John Cotton. Eighteenth-century Boston was a leading commercial centre, where social life modelled itself on that of London, with a miniature court around the governor, and where large fortunes and elegant manners were the normal objects of ambition. It was in its measure a worldly and epicurean city, with a worldly and rational ideology—the birthplace of Benjamin Franklin and the background of Copley's portraits—of which the nineteenth-century Bostonians were the immediate heirs.

Religious liberty had been secure since 1691. Of course New England remained devout, and with the devotion of a rather severe religion. Just as of course the disappearance of the governor, the court, and the Tories at the end of the century led to plainer manners and a higher moral tone in Boston. But to apply the term 'Puritan' to it (and thus to imply anything of the seventeenth-century meaning) is surely neither to classify nor to clarify, but to confuse and mistake. There is nothing of the seventeenth century about George Ticknor's mental habits, severe and upright as he was; it is Athens he compares Boston to, in his excited moments; he would never dream of comparing it to Jerusalem. And if we use the word 'Puritan' about both Emerson and John Cotton (or Jonathan Edwards) we should realize that we are making either a pun or a blunder. Yet the word is used quite generally and quite weightily about all Bostonians; we find Edmund Wilson using it to explain Justice Holmes, for instance. This causes many kinds of confusion and inattention, not the worst of which is to suggest that what is so labelled deserves no more serious consideration. Puritans are another biological species; they are presumably happy in their own way, and with each other; one may feel sorry for them, or dislike them; one starts from the assumption that they are 'different'. It seems to be by this simple mechanism that so many have excluded from all serious awareness a major part of their history. (Perry Miller himself of course was all the more interested in his Puritans for being Puritan. But even in his interest, the insistence on how totally unlike ourselves they were—how incapable of looking at people like us the way we look at them—is disturbing. It makes them less than fully real, and so surely indicates a failure of sympathy somewhere in the historian.)

It is easy enough to recognize the bundle of qualities in the Bostonian character which incite people to apply the word 'Puritan' to it. They are reflected in key words of the Bostonian vocabulary, like 'values', 'standards', 'responsibility', 'culture and civilization', 'moral taste', and 'education in the largest sense'. It is less easy to suggest what alternative label to give those qualities. But we can point out that this is also the vocabulary of the great tradition of British culture-critics described by Raymond Williams in *Culture and Society;* the tradition that includes Coleridge, Carlyle, Ruskin, Arnold, Lawrence, and Leavis. They have been called Puritan too (more casually); because they tried to apply moral criteria to the operations of a culture as a whole.

Boston was perhaps Puritan also in other senses of the word (psychological inhibition, conversational prudery), but if we are talking seriously we can call it Puritan only in the sense that British tradition was. That is, its 'culture' was to be achieved by 'education' in 'standards' of critical discrimination among the products of the arts, but also among styles of moral and rational discourse, and models of personal and group behaviour. These were not standards derived from theology or philosophy or any structure of theory, but from the co-operative practice of evaluation in a community—'the common pursuit'. This could vary all the way from what Carlyle meant by it to what Arnold meant by it, but these were clearly enough all variants of one big idea. This idea was not written out in essay form in Boston so brilliantly as in London; but it was translated into corporate action in Boston more effectively than in London. This is a very nineteenth-century tradition, developed in reaction against the disruption of social values by the Industrial Revolution. If we ever use the word 'Puritan' to describe this tradition, it certainly cannot be in contexts like the present one, where other meanings of the word, in theology, in history, in personal morals, are so likely to blend into it. 'Moralist' is perhaps the best substitute; the important thing is to exclude all seventeenth-century connotations.

Thus I argue that nineteenth-century Boston was not a product of continuity so much as of creativity; it came out of nowhere, or out of something else, as much as a city can. In 1776, after all, when the Tories had left, the population was under 10,000; and it was a long time since it had been the cultural capital of America. As Henry Adams put it, in 1800 Boston was the Bristol of America; Philadelphia was its London; New York was its Liverpool. It had a population of 25,000, against Philadelphia's 70,000, and Philadelphia had the publishers, the magazines, the more literary and political society. Nor was Boston growing fast. New York had only 33,000 in 1790, but in 1800 it had 60,000. Boston never began to challenge New York, in absolute numbers or in growth rate.[3]

How then did it make itself, and so long maintain itself, the cultural capital of the nation? The answers of the time are almost unanimous: because its atmosphere was favourable to writers; financially, but even more socially. This meant not only that many writers lived there, but that the non-writers respected the writers; in Boston a writer was *ipso facto* a gentleman, as Howells said.

This is one of those facts that were largely true from the beginning to end of the century, and that make it possible to discuss nineteenth-century Boston as a unit. Writing was taken seriously, as a major form of human activity there. New York had its writers and its literary society, but that was a Bohemia; writing was not taken seriously by the city as a whole, nor indeed by the writers themselves—they had their intensities about literature, but 'respectability' was an idea in which they saw mainly dangers.* Howells and Aldrich (and others) tried New York and left it for Boston. 'Bohemia was but a sickly colony,' says Howells, 'transplanted from the mother asphalt of Paris.' [4] And history has on the whole endorsed their judgment. Small as these adoptive Boston writers may loom in our lives, the people who stayed in New York (N. P. Willis, for instance, and Bayard Taylor) surely loom less. In Boston literature *was* taken seriously; and therefore writers came to live there, and magazines were founded there, and publishers flourished there, and it became a cultural centre. Boston's power of self-creation derived from its interest in literature, much more than from its economic vitality; it was as purely as can be imagined a phenomenon of the mind.

This was, then, a remarkably self-creative enterprise, and like any other act of self-creation, it was always in process and often in jeopardy, seeming about to fail, to distort itself, to dry itself up. It did not spring fully armed out of the mind of Jove in 1800. It was not until 1830, for instance, that Boston could claim to be even New England's publishing centre. Before that, as William Charvat tells us, Hartford had been quite as important; and until much later (until the emergence of Ticknor and Fields) Boston publishers catered mostly to New England tastes; it was the publishers of the Philadelphia–New York axis who were the discoverers and interpreters of American literary taste before then.[5] And once established, Boston's personality did not expand

* The society Perry Miller discusses in *The Raven and the Whale* was not simply a Bohemia; but the exception is too partial to spoil the rule.

or express itself unquestionably. So great a concentration of institutions, so great a predominance of respectability and responsibility, provoked the Transcendentalists to their radical criticism. That criticism did not, unfortunately, have the effect it deserved; Boston culture remained too institutional and respectable; but we should not assume that it was merely traditional and impervious to ideas. The Transcendental criticism could also remind us of the risky and living nature of the Boston enterprise—of the ways it might have changed—of the awareness of those institutions. For the Transcendentalists would have found any *other* city far *more* worldly and uninspired.

Like any other living fact, Boston's cultural success provoked resentments and contradictions, and if those took the form of declaring Boston culture safe or inert or a mere continuation, we have no business believing them literally. Boston *made* itself the cultural capital, and the bruises of that struggle still ache today. Thus Mr Charvat quotes this Philadelphia judgment of 1940, 'Boston once excelled in cultural achievement by the simple device of defining culture in terms of those things in which Boston excelled.' This comes from an article in the *Pennsylvania Magazine of History and Biography* (LXIV, July 1940), in which Richard H. Shryock points out that in music, painting, science, and architecture, not to mention theatre, Boston was inferior to Philadelphia in 1840. Theology and literature were the only cultural items in which Boston excelled, and the rest of the country was persuaded to regard those as the most important. This was not mere Bostonian sleight-of-hand, however, despite Mr Shryock. It was a part of the general transition from eighteenth-century to nineteenth-century culture, in England as well as in America. Boston had caught the spirit of the time better than Philadelphia. It was its contemporaneity that was its strength, not its continuity or traditionalism.

Institutions, moreover, do not merely continue, especially in America; they have to be created, and they have to be kept alive. Even Harvard, which nineteenth-century Boston did in fact inherit, and which seems now the most solid of her monuments, had moments during the century when it looked like failing or wrecking—like ceasing to be what we mean by Harvard. It was

not until late in the century what we would call a university at
all; it was, in Ticknor's words, a high school (he had been to
Göttingen) and the reforms he strove to introduce in the twenties
aimed only at making it a 'respectable' high school. And even
comparatively, it was not always pre-eminent. In the mid-thirties,
for instance, Yale, Princeton, Dartmouth, and Union, all had
higher enrollments, and the enrollments of Middlebury and Amherst were nearly as high. During the decade 1870–80, its enroll-
ment increased by only 3.7 per cent, while Yale's increased by 37
per cent, and Princeton's and Williams' by 60 per cent. Not until
1900 did it acquire its present position in graduate studies; earlier Johns Hopkins led in that field.[6]

Moreover, it had dangerous enemies. In the early years of the
century it was attacked by Calvinist preachers, who warned parents against letting their sons go there, because of its Unitarianism. Later the attackers were Jacksonian Democrats, who resented the existence of a privileged and aristocratic institution in
a democracy. In 1850 the committee report of the General Court
declared that the college did not answer to the expectations or
needs of the people of the state; that professors ought to be paid
according to the number of pupils they attracted; that the college
should be for boys seeking 'specific learning for a specific purpose', not for an aristocracy seeking a classical-literary culture.
When the Boston newspapers attacked Professor Bowen in the
fifties, the Board of Overseers fired him. They found ways to re-
instate him, and to increase their own independence, in the long
run, but they had then to yield to popular pressure. We should
not assume that such institutions were as stable and secure in the
nineteenth century as they are now. (I think we often assume
they were more so.) We should not assume that anything in
Boston was stable and strong, except insofar as particular acts of
particular men made it so.

Above all, in order to awaken our minds to this piece of his-
tory, we should remember the relevance of this enterprise to the
American enterprise as a whole. It does not matter much whether
Boston or Philadelphia was more of a cultural centre in 1840;
and it is possible to have mixed feelings about that report on
Harvard of 1850; but it was of unmixed importance that some-

where in America then there should be a society where high-cultural values could flourish. Richard Hofstadter has made it clear, in his recent book, how sparsely and feebly that happened. And high culture, in this application, does not refer only to standards of aesthetic taste. In fact, the values refer just as much to general culture; to standards of personal behaviour, and to attempts at political reform. Oscar Handlin says in *Immigration and American History*,

> In the 1840s and 1850s, for instance, the clusters of New England settlements across the country formed links in a chain that held together the reform movements of the period. One of the significant aspects of reform in those decades was precisely the effort to preserve the values of the Puritan community under the changing conditions of American society.* [7]

There was the simple philistinism that made men like Theodore Parker, for instance, contrast the fine arts with the 'coarse' arts, that 'feed and clothe people'; and consequently of course decide he would rather be Benjamin Franklin than Michelangelo. But there was also something more sinister. The various frontiers of American life generated an anti-intellectualism which influenced—increasingly as the century advanced—the rest of the culture. Richard Hofstadter makes it clear that at and near the literal frontier, cultural law and order was often at a discount. In the backwoods mountain country of Georgia and the Carolinas all professional men and men of education were distrusted and resented; and in those huge areas of the West settled from the South the same was often true. Some communities refused to have schools or churches built amongst them. Some families refused all conformity to civilized norms—even marriage —and rejected all contact with cultural objects—even a book in the house. Individuals made their careers out of drinking, gam-

---

* It is difficult to challenge Professor Handlin on such a piont, but his use of 'Puritan' here, and '*the* Puritan community', seems to encourage those confusions of thought which obscure both the essential character of Boston then, and the inventiveness of its self-creation. These people wanted to make moral sense out of their politics; if this is Puritanism, we surely need to mark off a sense of the word that will align them with contemporary English radicals rather than with seventeenth-century American theocrats.

bling, stealing, and terrorizing others. The evangelists who peri-
odically visited these communities, and who organized revivals in
the cities, were also in other ways anti-intellectual and antinomian; and increasingly so as the century progressed. Business
became another source and centre of that complex of feeling;
and Jacksonian democracy brought its forces to bear on national
politics, so that the immigrants, as their numbers became significant, delivered their votes overwhelmingly to demagogic politicians.

The presidential elections of 1824 and 1828 mark the introduction of these forces into national politics, and illustrate their
power; they also illustrate the typical American alternative, the
Bostonianism of John Quincy Adams. In the election propa-
ganda Adams was said to have learning, Jackson wisdom—a
powerful contrast, given the polarities of American culture.
'What wisdom will he bring with him from the forest?' they
enthusiastically wondered. 'What rules of duty will he evolve
from the oracles of his own mind?' [8] Naturally, those rules did
not include any duty to the national mind to foster the intellectual life of America. That was left to Adams, who in his first
annual message to Congress called for a national university at
Washington, a naval academy, a national observatory, a voyage
of discovery to the north-west, a patent-office, and federal aid to
the sciences. This was a typical Bostonian programme in national
affairs. It was never even seriously debated. His cabinet forced
him to give up the attempt, knowing that Congress was profoundly hostile. He had referred to European precedents for
these projects; he had referred to European observatories as 'light-
houses in the skies'; the phrase was taken to be exquisitely absurd. In some sense, Boston learned then that it could not mould
national policy (Adams was the last New England president for
a hundred years) and had better concentrate on maintaining its
own commonwealth, though that was indeed a lesson it learned
over and over again. Some time would pass before the temper of
Boston reached the plaintive hopelessness of *The Education of
Henry Adams*, the President's grandson. During the Civil War,
Sumner tried to prevent a tax on books, and later tried to establish national academies of literature, of art, of moral and politi-

cal science.* It was the East that supported the Morrill Act.

This is surely one of the major conflicts in American history, and one that characterizes and identifies the American psyche. It is also surely one in which the educated man of today should feel himself most engaged on one side and against the other. That is why I call this the most important of all the ways Boston history should be alive to us—should not seem mere continuity and traditionalism.

But even if our sympathies in this struggle are divided, it surely will not do to describe what Adams and Boston stood for as 'the genteel tradition', a phrase which refers only to its limitations, when it was in fact America's major intellectual tradition. But that phrase, and its cognates, are what one finds in most scholars of American culture, from Oscar Handlin to Marius Bewley. Mr Bewley [10] describes James Fenimore Cooper (a Jacksonian Democrat) as being politically in the position of a liberal today, who 'refuses to accept . . . an aristocracy of intrenched capitalists intent on augmenting their own powers and resources'. Cooper was a Democrat and not a Whig (the party we can roughly identify with Adams and Boston) because he saw that it was 'possible to be a Jacksonian Democrat without being also a Vandal, but it was scarcely possible to be a Whig without being also a philistine'.**

Gentility and philistinism were of course to be found among the Whigs, but it is hard to see them as worse enemies of high culture than Jacksonian anti-intellectualism. The cultural theory of the Whigs was no more philistine than that described at the beginning of this chapter, the theory of class cultural responsibility, to which Mr Bewley has in other places given a strong en-

---

* He of course failed. Merle Curti, after reporting this, comments, 'Plain people had no desire to set up institutions which might attempt in some fashion to tell the ordinary man what pictures to prefer, what books to venerate, what ideas to entertain.[9] In context this comment cannot be taken as simply ironical; it is one of those swerves of thought forced on the historian by his need to be both an intellectual and an American.

** The best answer to that is Henry Adams' account of New England society at the beginning of the century, a part of which I quote on p. 70. New England was the great centre of the Whig party, and it was not ruled—certainly during Cooper's lifetime—by 'intrenched capitalists intent on augmenting, etc', nor by philistines.

dorsement. We must take this, surely, as an example of that scholars' prejudice against Boston we spoke of; we must also begin here to work back towards restating that theory, connecting it with nineteenth-century Boston, and summarizing our whole argument. Bearing Mr Bewley's remarks in mind, let us quote Q. D. Leavis's definition of 'society' in *Fiction and the Reading Public*—a fair example of the cultural theory we mean. Towards the end of her book, Mrs Leavis explains that she has all along distinguished between two kinds of social force, acting on the individual, as 'society' and 'the herd'.

'Society' was to be interpreted in the 18th century sense in which, like 'the world', it meant a select, cultured element of the community that set the standards of behaviour and judgment, in direct opposition to the common people. Thus the highest definition of man was that of a social animal; the gregarious instinct he shares with sheep and wolves. The ameliorating influence of associating with the well-bred and cultivated was universally acknowledged—it accounts for the horror of being confined in the country, away from 'the world', so noticeable in the literature of the Restoration and the 18th century, until the Romantic poets discovered the superiority of solitary to social man.

If we apply these categories to nineteenth-century America, it could not be clearer that the New England Whigs and Brahmins were 'society'. And those categories were in a sense intended to apply to that situation—that is, they were derived from the experience of a very similar situation. *Fiction and the Reading Public* deals with the disruption of cultural standards in modern England, under the stress of social change. In the anti-Romantic and anti-'democratic' bias expressed in those categories, we find one of the great links between Bostonian cultural standards and those of these contemporary theorists. Mrs Leavis continues,

If one accepts the argument that 'In any period it is upon a very small minority that the discerning appreciation of art and literature depends: it is only a few who are capable of unprompted first-hand judgment. . . . [Mrs Leavis's omission] The accepted valuations are a kind of paper currency based upon a very small proportion of gold. To the state of such a currency the possibilities of fine living at any time bear a close relation', then it becomes evident that the individual has a better chance of obtaining access to the fullest (because finest) life in a community dominated by 'society' than in one protesting the superiority of the herd.[11]

The quotation Mrs Leavis makes there is from Dr F. R. Leavis's *Mass Civilization and Minority Culture,* and a little further on in the latter pamphlet we come upon a passage which expands the point interestingly.

> The minority capable not only of appreciating Dante, Shakespeare, Donne, Baudelaire, Hardy (to take major instances) but of recognising their latest successors constitute the consciousness of the race (or of a branch of it) at a given time. For such capacity does not belong merely to an isolated aesthetic realm; it implies responsiveness to theory as well as to art, to science and philosophy in so far as those may affect the sense of the human situation and of the nature of life. Upon this minority depends our power of profiting by the finest human experience of the past; they keep alive the subtlest and most perishable parts of tradition. Upon them depend the implicit standards that order the finer living of an age, the sense that this is worth more than that, this rather than that is the direction in which to go, that the centre is here rather than there. In their keeping . . . is the language, the changing idiom, upon which fine living depends, and without which distinction of spirit is thwarted and incoherent. By 'culture' I mean the use of such a language.[12]

Neither the ruling class of nineteenth-century Boston nor its literati satisfied all the criteria of that minority; but then no social group ever did. They—centres of power like the Lowell and Eliot families—did *accept* a version of those criteria, and did strive to satisfy them; they would have understood that passage. It is not easy to find another ruling class of which the same could be said. Certainly in nineteenth-century America it had few rivals.

In *Education and the University* Dr Leavis—still expounding the same theory of cultural health—indicates what is needed in the present with a quotation describing the intellectuals of the past; a quotation taken from *The New Frontier,* a Harvard-edited magazine of the thirties:

> The important point is that they represented the centre of the civilization of their age—not particular and isolated aspects of it, but the whole of it. They had, of course, their varying occupations, their

special ignorances—but they were in general aware of their world at all points. With their common *lingua franca,* their common stock of knowledge, and their common social status, they gradually developed an idea of what the truly 'educated' man should be like, what his role in society should be, and in particular what responsibility he should have for himself and his world. This class—in short—may be said to have definitely represented and been responsible for civilization in their time.[13]

The writer was thinking of eighteenth-century England, but we shall find that nineteenth-century Boston answers to the prescription quite as well. The word 'responsibility' was the sign, the device, of that ruling class, and their literati. It is perhaps no accident that Dr Leavis took his quotation from a Harvard-edited magazine. No accident because this is a subject about which England and New England have often collaborated, but even more because New England had vivid memories of such an ideal translated into practice. In nineteenth-century America, again, such an achievement was unique, and for that reason is of central historical interest.

But one of the forms this interest takes is that of a puzzle: Why was the literary product of this society so undistinguished? Boston's attitude to literature was in many ways a forerunner of the modern attitude. Its writers fought harder and earlier against the herd and for standards than any other sizable community. It tried to create a literature that would be a cultural force, aesthetically satisfying because it was also morally and socially satisfying, which would educate the community and preserve its finer values against the encroachments of vulgarity and ignorance. And the vision behind that response to that danger—the vision of traditional culture gradually succumbing to the herd, to antinomian vulgarity, to commercialised entertainment—is the largest single shaping factor behind the criticism of the Leavises and *Scrutiny* and T. S. Eliot; which shows how closely it is related to modern literary taste. Indeed, it is hard to think of any important modern criticism which does not derive from that vision to some degree. Boston was a responsible society. It tried hard to be what modern criticism says a culture should be. Its literature should surely bear *some* mark of that virtue, and in *some* way satisfy, rather than so radically dissatisfy, that taste. That is the puzzle. That is the problem of Boston.

One can of course—looking for ways out—find other theories of what constitutes cultural health. In some sense the *general* modern idea is that writers should be rebels against society, vivid and interesting personalities whose pains and virtues, whose vices and pleasures, are more picturesque than those of other people. Expressed in more guarded language, that idea is to be found in the minds of many people. And if one takes it seriously, of course there is no problem in the poverty of Boston's literature, because Boston did not encourage its writers to be picturesque or rebellious. But taken seriously—to the level of critical theory, that is—this idea is in fact rare. One of the few recent examples is Irving Howe's *A World More Attractive*. Mr Howe there does praise Bohemia and alienation and rootlessness, as symptoms of cultural health. The insistence on the artist's need for roots, he declares, veils a desire to compromise the best of the literature, criticism, and specialized knowledge of the twentieth century.

There is something attractively fresh in this theory, but there is also something unsatisfying, which becomes clear in his climax. 'The most glorious vision of the intellectual life is still that which is loosely called humanist; the idea of a mind committed yet dispassionate, ready to stand alone, curious, eager, sceptical.' [14] But if it is humanism Mr Howe wants, he will have to accept some 'need for roots', and some dissatisfaction with modernist alienated literature. Humanism needs roots to grow from and a framework to grow along. That 'committed yet dispassionate' detachment we call humanist (quite distinct from the furious or frozen disgust of the outsider) involves some acceptance of, some participation in, society's general enterprise. Mr Howe's heroes, Joyce, Prouse, Bartok, Picasso, and Kafka, Lawrence, Dostoevski, Sartre, are profoundly and powerfully (though not entirely) anti-humanist. He wants it both ways; he speaks of the early enthusiasts for Joyce as conducting a defence of traditional culture, against spokesmen for the genteel, the respectable, the academic, who were strangling it. This is too much of a paradox; just where do we locate that traditional art of the eighteenth and nineteenth centuries of which *Ulysses* and *Finnegans Wake* are the modern versions? Joyce was rebelling against that art and its cultural theory.

Mr Howe's argument seems to me to illustrate the uniformity of tendency in modern critical theory. Even he, the Bohemian, is forced to speak in terms of 'traditional culture' and 'humanism', even a man who wants to praise chiefly that modernist art which seems to be (and surely is) violently rebellious against its cultural function. For surely much great modern art sets out to be so obscure, esoteric, outrageous in its methods, and so metaphysically and religiously extreme in its message, as to defy all attempts to introduce it to the common reader, or to 'use' it in common experience. And surely 'traditional culture' and 'humanism' apply much better as categories of art—forgetting for the moment evaluation—to the art of nineteenth-century Boston. Mr Howe's theory is insufficiently different from the Leavises'. It offers us no real alternative.

Paradoxically, it is a good deal the challenge of modern art that drives critics back to this first 'cultural' theory; because that art's failures so often derive from an exaggerated rebelliousness and experimentalism, an inadequate sense of tradition and culture. Van Wyck Brooks complained in *The Writer in America* that the whole idea of art as culture is dying today; that ambitious artists now always attempt in their work some illumination of a great problem, metaphysical, psychological, what you will; and since art as culture solves no such problems, it seems a waste of time. The idea of culture centres in the social uses of art; cultural art is that kind (Jane Austen, typically, but also Dickens) which entertains, delights, inspires, fortifies, man in the daily round of his social duties—the kind nineteenth-century Boston produced. This can be great literature, but it is of a kind which most modern artists have not written. Brooks quotes from Berdyaev on Dostoevski.

> There is no general culture in Russia, no cultured society, and almost no cultural tradition. In this matter nearly all Russians are nihilists. Why? Because culture does not resolve any ultimate problems. . . . [Brooks' omission] For 'the Russian boy' (a favourite expression of Dostoevski), absorbed in the solution of metaphysical questions, God, immortality, or in the organization of mankind on a new model, as

well as for any atheist, socialist, or anarchist, culture is an obstacle in the way of their impetuous rush towards a consummation.[15]

What has happened to the more ambitious kinds of modern art is that they have responded to this mood. They have taken on such metaphysical ambitions, such anti-social enthusiasms, that they have lost their sense of themselves as related to social life, as a part of general culture, as something which *taste* could measure and estimate. They deal in *truths*—truths that shatter taste. Writers, and readers, have lost their sense of art's social function, and consequently have lost too one important set of controls over what they are doing.

That is why this corrective theory (the Leavises' and others') of the necessary relationships between art and culture is so useful today. It guides us immediately to what is wrong with so much modern nihilism, in the pseudo-metaphysical extremist modes: the hysteria, the thinness, the emptiness of, for instance, Edward Albee's plays. Once we see the full complexity of the best art of the past, in which intensity of personal emotion co-operated with strenuousness of thought and breadth of experience, and even more with a sense of responsibility to one's society as well as to oneself, then these nightmare expressions of self-hatred and reader-hatred lose their power to impress. We would not be impressed for long, whatever our critical theory, but this one guides us to the relevant truths immediately. Similarly, this theory leads us directly to those concerns in D. H. Lawrence which conflict with, interact with, his impulses to pure freedom, rebellion, self-assertion, and make him the endlessly interesting and valuable writer he is. (Consider a story like 'England, My England', and the complex contrast Lawrence draws between the independent artist, Egbert, and his businessman father-in-law.) I offer these as typical cases, and the theory has many other advantages: it connects literary values with other kinds; it makes literary values morally serious; it shows us what is wrong with our advertising, our education, our culture as a whole. This criticism is, after all, an integral part of that tradition of cultural prophecy we discussed before; the tradition of Coleridge, Carlyle, Ruskin, Arnold, Leavis; the tradition which serves so many of our deepest interests, and satisfies, better than anything else, the humanist in us. That, above all, is why we are forced back to seeing literature in terms of this theory, whatever the problems it brings.

On the other hand, some of those problems, and the historical case this book discusses is one of them, are very puzzling. It is surely implicit (though rarely explicit) in such a theory, that 'healthy cultural conditions' will be favourable to the creative artist as well as to the total community. But if an active cultural conscience in him, and a responsible reading public, and an integrated society, and a powerful image of 'the educated man', are valuable, why is the work of nineteenth-century Boston in literature so unvaluable, so feeble? I trust it is possible to agree that it is feeble. There are exceptions (literary achievement is not entirely a matter of cultural conditions) but Longfellow, Lowell, Holmes, Whittier, the fireside poets, surely give the impression of failure, and *cultural* failure. Literary talent in the narrow sense they had—Longfellow most notably. Energy and cleverness and every possible stimulus to write, Lowell had in abundance. But what they wrote failed, and failed because of the directions their culture gave them—as to what subject to choose to write about, what tone to take, what to make explicit and what implicit, what kind of experience to call literary, and what to call 'too personal' or 'too painful'.

They were not men of the first intelligence, perhaps, but neither were Tennyson or Browning; why is Longfellow's and Lowell's work inferior to theirs? Longfellow was long considered—and in England—as good a poet as Tennyson; the *Biglow Papers* won golden opinions also abroad. By the general literary standards of their day, the American writers succeeded, brilliantly. It is time's abrasion which has revealed a failure in them, even by the standards of Victorian poetry, an insidious failure in that culture which was so much more responsible and integrated (so much less self-contradictory) than that of the Englishmen.

It is not easy, of course, to assign the fair share of the blame for a particular artist's failure—in life or in art—to the society he belonged to. A case like Poe's, for instance, is dominated by such powerful forces making for destruction in the poet's own psyche that it seems mere sentimental nihilism to blame 'society'. In a career like Melville's, even, one is bound to feel that the writer scarcely gave his society a chance; he did not recognize the best intelligences in it, or what they wanted from him. But the Bostonian writers did know the best of their society, and it was one dedicated, energetically dedicated, to high standards of culture, and primarily to high literary standards. They accepted their society's high standards as their own, and devoted long healthy lives to meeting them; they were intelligent, talented, serious, vigorous men; what went wrong?

Chapter Two

BOSTON: THE CITY OF CULTURE

NINETEENTH-CENTURY Boston was an adventurous attempt to create an ideal total community; not of course in the sense of the phalansteries, nor, it is more worth insisting, in the sense of the Puritans' Boston; but in the sense of a city from which the most shameful kinds of vice and lawlessness and disease would be excluded, where decent living conditions would be available to all, and where good sense, good behaviour, and good taste would be the norms—a city with a high quality of life.

This attempt met with considerable success in the first part of the century, and in certain remarkable ways was sustained throughout the second. Self-confidence faded during the fifties, but was revived by the Civil War, which seemed to renew the American vocation to act out of idealism; the nation followed where Boston led, and even her own Irish finally declared for abolition. In 1871 Godkin said Boston was 'the one place in America where wealth and the knowledge of how to use it are apt to coincide'. Holmes talked of Boston as the city of the three hills, in contrast to Rome, the city of the seven; the city of Reason and the city of Superstition— he foresaw a conflict between them. He treated them, with less of paradox in his tone than one would expect, as historical phenomena of equal dignity. And in *The American Scene* Henry James described Park Street (in the Gilded Age) as 'magnificently honnête . . . founded on all the moral, material, social solidities, instead of on some of them only—which made all the difference'.[1]

On the whole, however, it is Boston before the Gilded Age we must concentrate on to see this adventure at its most impressive. The power, as well as the pathos, of what followed can only be understood once we know what the Bostonians were trying to sustain. From the beginning of the century, *and with a sharp sense of building something new,* they created new institutions, reformed old ones, shook off old habits and inhibitions, tried new methods and experiments—in religion, philosophy, education, literature, everything. 'There was plenty of money, and the rich men of Boston really meant that here should be a model and ideal city,' said Edward Everett Hale of the twenties and thirties.[2] An example of what he meant can be found at the very beginning of the century, in the statement of the founders of the Athenaeum, that in Boston,

> the class of persons enjoying easy circumstances, and possessing surplus wealth, is comparatively numerous. As we are not called upon for large contributions to national purposes, we shall do well to take advantage of the exemption, by taxing ourselves for those institutions, which will be attended with lasting and extensive benefit, amidst all changes of our public fortunes and political affairs.[3]

We see behind such statements the same aspiration to a national high culture, checked, and redirected onto the city, as in the Adams message to Congress.

Hale continues with a description of the 'March of Intellect' in the New England of his childhood things like the Useful Knowledge Society his father helped found, the Round Hill School (in Northampton) founded by Bancroft and Cogswell on their return from Germany, the gymnasia, the swimming schools, the *conversazioni.*

> Briefly, there was the real impression that the kingdom of heaven was to be brought in by teaching people what were the relations of acids to alkalis, and what was the derivation of the word cordwainer.[4]

Boston was full of new theories, new experiments, new foundations. In *James Russell Lowell and His Friends* Hale comments
on the generous expansiveness of temper (most un-'Puritanical')
of the city then.

> There were still some people, and one or two teachers in the pulpit
> and in what is technically called the religious press, who believed, or
> said they believed, that all men are born in sin and are incapable of
> good. But practically, and in general, the people of Boston believed
> in the infinite capacity of human nature, and they knew 'salvation's
> free' and 'free for you and me'.

They attempted everything on a generous scale.

> If they made a school for the blind, they made it for all the blind
> people in Massachusetts. They expected it to succeed. They always
> had succeeded. Why should they not succeed? If, then, they opened a
> House of Reformation, they really supposed that they should reform
> the boys and girls who were sent to it.[5]

The economic basis for this optimism and expansiveness is
obvious enough. Real wages in America were 30 per cent to 100
per cent higher than they were in England at the beginning of
the century. The best land could be bought for only a third the
price of the worst land in Germany. And there were no servants
in the land of the free; there were hired men, but this was a
distinction with a difference. What was special about Boston
within America was that there the economic vitality and political
pride co-operated with intellectual seriousness and moral hope.
This made for a profoundly excited and exciting city. Bronson
Alcott in 1828 echoed John Winthrop two hundred years before:
'It is the city that is set on high. It cannot be hid. It is Boston.
The morality of Boston is more pure than that of any other city
in America.'[6] Foreign visitors often agreed. De Tocqueville
found in New England the best features—and the distinctively
American features—of the new society. And in his *American
Notes* of 1843 Dickens declared,

> The golden calf they worship at Boston is a pigmy compared with the
> giant effigies set up in other parts of that vast countinghouse which

lies beyond the Atlantic, and the almighty dollar sinks into something comparatively insignificant amidst a whole Pantheon of better gods.[7]

Moreover, Oscar Handlin's picture of the city, in *Boston's Immigrants* corroborates in surprising detail the accounts of the Bostonians themselves. He puts the crucial dividing line, after which the adventure was a losing cause, at 1845. Until then the city's rate of growth was slow compared with that of its rivals. It kept even that growth rate steady only because of the agricultural depression in the countryside around, which drove village people in. It maintained its trade with Russia and China, but its American hinterland was contracting. The completion of the Erie Canal in 1825 meant that the western half of Massachusetts itself found it easier to trade with New York City than with Boston. But there was a lot of money in the city, and it became a financial centre; only one bank existed there in 1790, only three in 1800, but by 1830 Boston was second only to New York City as a banking city. These resources were invested first in New England industry, and later in the railroads. However, until 1845, Boston was a city of small tradesmen and craftsmen, with an upper class of merchant princes; neither industry nor agriculture was important.[8]

This rather static prosperity was the setting for the numerous reform movements and sects and cranks so often mocked, including Transcendentalism itself, but also for a remarkable degree of community planning, in matters of architecture, land development, public health, outdoor relief, indoor institutional relief (recompensed by the state), education, and so on. Horace Mann, after studying state education in Europe, especially Prussia, opened the first American State Normal School, in 1839, in Massachusetts. He improved teachers' salaries and school buildings, and severed the connections between education and sectarian religion. (Barnard was doing similar work in Connecticut.) These programmes were often opposed by the richer and the more religious taxpayers, but they were supported by all the forward-looking citizens, and Massachusetts was very proud of its public-school system. The city Board of Health, too, set up in 1798, was very effective. There were no slums in those first decades, and remarkably little crime. This picture faded after 1845, and there were ugly features that spoiled it before then, but Professor Handlin's account should help us understand the general pride that made possible Bronson Alcott's enthusiasm. It certainly does not justify *our* dismissing that pride as largely hypocritical, Pharisaical, or blind.

What happened in 1845 was that the numbers of Irish immigrants began to become significant. Between 1835 and 1865 two and a half million people left Ireland, and owing largely to a historical accident, large numbers of them went to Boston. An average of 5,500 immigrants a year, according to Cecil Woodham-Smith's calculations, reached Boston between 1836 and 1845, and in 1847, 37,000. The city's industry immediately began to grow. Between 1837 and 1845 the number of employees in the city's major industries remained constant. Between 1845 and 1855 it doubled. The city's industry also began to compete. Until 1845 ready-made clothing from New York had sold better than Boston's. But in 1849 (owing partly to the invention of the sewing machine in 1846) the manufacturers were able to ignore a tailors' strike (rejecting the mayor's services as mediator) and hire Irishmen to run the machines. By 1860 the whole process had been largely mechanized in Boston, and a worker's annual output there was worth $1,137, against the $798 output of the New York worker, where the factory system had not been applied. Boston was meanwhile paying wages of between $4.50 and $5.50 a week, and New York wages ranged between $8 and $10.

This expansion of industry meant great prosperity, but it also meant the decay of the communal hopes of earlier times. Terrible slums developed in the city. Smallpox returned, which had died out before 1845 (there had been no epidemic since 1792); in 1849 cholera returned; tuberculosis became dangerous. Infant mortality figures rose sharply. Pauperism, drunkenness, prostitution, crime, all spread enormously. The city set on high was spoiled, and yet the citizens were individually profiting by its spoliation. They were individually richer. But their wealth came from the impoverishment, debasement, brutalization, of their fellow-citizens.

Moreover, the Irish refused to become fellow-citizens, cul-

turally. They formed a society within a society. They were opposed to the Bostonian enthusiasms—for reason, for education,
for reform. They opposed, for instance, the abolition of slavery;
out of fear of economic competition with Negroes, out of fear of
offending Catholic Louisiana and Maryland, out of a generally
reactionary temper. They opposed compulsory education and
temperance movements (which they thought ignored, contradicted, the doctrine of original sin), prison reform and women's
rights, and so on. They hated even English literature, seemingly
the most unsectarian of Boston enthusiasms. Shakespeare they
declared barbaric; his monstrous farces befouled the stage with
every abomination. Milton they described as the heretic minion
of the Drogheda monster. Politically, of course they hated England. But they hated also the movements of nationalism and
liberalism in Europe; when Kossuth and Mazzini were the heroes
of the rest of America, the Irish Catholic press reviled them.

All this presented Yankee Boston with a serious problem. She
felt entrusted with the destiny of an alien people—socially and
educationally underprivileged and so a sacred responsibility—
who refused to find that destiny in Boston's version of liberal
democracy. If she granted them full political and economic
rights, if she allowed them the control of the city, they would
move it towards reaction and ignorance and prejudice. As well as
being isolated within America, Boston was now assailed from
inside, hollowed out, materially and morally.

In 1854 the Yankee Know-Nothings won power in Massachusetts, and they ruled it for three years. Their name referred to
their refusal to reveal the secrets of their organization, and their
principles included a denial of full civic rights to all foreign-born
Americans—two powerfully illiberal traits. But some of their
domestic policies were what we would call very liberal. They did
a great deal for the school system, they abolished imprisonment
for debt, they strengthened juries, they worked for temperance
and women's rights and the abolition of slavery. This was a
Yankee reform programme, carried out in opposition to the Irish
electorate. What we mean by democratic, and undemocratic, is
not to be identified simply with either side.

Before 1845, Boston's immigrants had been largely German,

and largely intellectual and idealistic. They had been in sympathy with the society they found there, and integrated themselves into it. After 1845, things did not of course reverse themselves immediately or completely. But that confident expansiveness of temper was ruined. People continued to be proudly Bostonian; but because *they* wanted to be, not because everyone would if he could. This mood, when it showed its stiff-backed, iron-willed expression, in Colonel Higginson or Justice Holmes, was one of the things people called Puritan. But it was really always first cousin to the subtler ironic expression of that mood in Charles Eliot Norton and Santayana, which can seem exquisitely Cavalier. 'Puritan' is again a confusing term.

The great cultural institutions of the city, however, continued, were maintained, were added to, throughout the century; and they were the real strength of the enterprise. Dickens, after his enthusiastic description of Boston in his *American Notes*, says,

> Above all, I sincerely believe that the public institutions and charities of this capital of Massachusetts are as nearly perfect as the most considerate wisdom, benevolence, and humanity can make them. I never in my life was more affected.[9]

He goes on to describe the Perkins Institute, the Institution for the Insane, the House of Industry, the House of Reformation, and so on.

First of all, there were the directly charitable organizations; between 1810 and 1840 thirty benevolent institutions were founded, Cleveland Amory tells us. Let us list only those in which George Ticknor played some active part: the Massachusetts General Hospital, the Boston Provident Institution for Savings, the Massachusetts Hospital Life Insurance Company (a trust company, part of whose profits went to the Hospital), the Massachusetts Congregational Charitable Society (collecting funds to support widows and children of clergy of all denominations), the Massachusetts Farm School for Boys; and there were many more. It needs no saying, at this date, that no system of charities can transcend the limitations of charity as such, and the Boston system had also the (severe) limitations of its class, race, and time; but the contemporary habit among historians seems to be to emphasize only those limitations. Surely, compared with other contemporary cities, Boston *was* in some impressive sense charitable?

Of these institutions we will look at two in slightly more detail: the Perkins Institute for the Blind, and the Massachusetts General Hospital. In 1826 Dr Fisher brought back from his tour of Europe news of how blind people were being trained there. In 1829 a meeting of those interested was held, and was so unanimous in its enthusiasm that a school was founded on the spot; the Board of Trustees included the governor and lieutenant governor of the state, ex officio, and the state contributed a considerable sum to the project. Dr Samuel Gridley Howe was made director and was sent to Europe in 1831 to study methods there. Thomas Handasyd Perkins, the Boston merchant and philanthropist, gave a house, and the school was opened in 1832.[10]

It was the first school for the blind in America, and it seems to have maintained its leadership throughout the century. Experiments in various sorts of raised type were made from the beginning, and the kind adopted became known as Boston line lettering. In 1836 the New Testament was printed completely in that type, and in 1843 the Old. The school opened the first industrial training shop for the blind in 1840. The circulating library, opened in 1842, was another pioneer; the Howe Memorial Printing Press, founded in 1881, another; the teaching of the blind at home, beginning in 1889, another. And from the start the Boston school undertook to serve the whole of the New England area.

It is worth noting how the state government was involved in the scheme, both on the Board of Trustees, and financially, since this co-operation was a pattern in Boston charities. Dickens observed, 'It is a great and pleasant feature of all such institutions in America, that they are either supported by the State or assisted by the State.' This, with the co-operative nature of the scheme, helped mitigate the humiliating aspects of charity in Boston.

The Perkins Institute became famous, and not only in America. Dickens was very enthusiastic in his report, particularly over the education of the deaf-and-blind. Helen Keller is now Perkins' best-known deaf-and-blind graduate, but just as famous in her day was Laura Bridgman, who went to the school only five years after it opened. When Dr Howe taught her the use of language it was the first case of its kind recorded. We should think of things of this kind when we read of the atmosphere of hope and excitement then; and when we read Emerson and Thoreau urging their readers to cultivate the self and not to trust to institutions and philanthropies. We should also remember how tightly integrated this society was. Dr Howe was the husband of Julia Ward Howe, and they took their wedding journey in Europe with Horace Mann and his bride, investigating new methods of teaching. A bust of Laura Bridgman was executed by Sophia Peabody Hawthorne, and copies were distributed at the expense of Mrs Peter Chardon Brooks, wife of one of Boston's leading philanthropists, mother of Mrs Edward Everett, Mrs Nathaniel Frothingham, Mrs Charles Francis Adams, grandmother therefore of Henry Adams, Brooks Adams, and so on. All Boston was involved in its institutions.

The appeal for funds to found the Massachusetts General Hospital, signed by James Jackson and John Warren, was issued in 1810. The first patient was admitted in 1821, and for almost all the first hundred years there was a Dr John Warren on the staff. Five families, the Warrens, the Jacksons, the Bigelows, the Shattucks, and the Cabots, have supplied the majority of the physicians and surgeons, have transmitted a corporate responsibility for the hospital, a genuine family vocation, from generation to generation. Cleveland Amory tells us that Dr Shattuck and Dr Warren of Harvard Medical School are (in 1947) the fifth and sixth generations of their respective families to be there. No other of the world's great hospitals has a record like this, and it is another of the patterns of Boston institutions.[11]

The financing of the hospital, like that of the Perkins Institute, was accomplished through a combination of public and private donations, and on a much larger scale. The private subscriptions between 1811 and 1843 totalled $150,000. The state gave property valued at $40,000, which appreciated enormously as time passed. In the Hospital Life Insurance Company we see another characteristic of Boston charity, its businesslike nature. The machinery of capitalism was put to work most efficiently in the service of benevolence. And on the Board of Trustees, as we have seen, worked men like the Professor of Belles Lettres at Harvard.

The Hospital's three great medical achievements are usually considered to be the use of anaesthetics, the appendicitis operation, and the hospital social service; and of these the last is probably the most important. Dr Cabot's work in social service lies outside the period I am discussing, but out-patient service had begun in 1846, and Boston ladies had always visited the sick and the poor under the guidance of the hospital. It was no accident that hospital social service began in Boston.

When we turn to high-cultural institutions, we do not find the state contributing, but we do find a community co-operating. Let us take the Athenaeum, from the statement of whose purposes we read an extract. *The Monthly Anthology* was begun in 1804, by a group of men including Emerson's father and Ticknor's classics tutor, Dr Gardiner. In 1805 they founded the Anthology Society, and projected the library, which included an art gallery and a lecture room in its early days. It was financed by private donations, but in typical Boston fashion. In 1846 John Bromfield gave $25,000 for investment, the income to be divided—part going to buy books, part to be added to the principal. By 1906, $194,000 had been spent from that fund, and $106,000 remained. In 1853, Samuel Appleton left it $24,000; in 1867, Henry Harris $10,000; in 1879, George Bemis $20,000 and William Burley Howes $160,000. These were the large bequests; the majority were much smaller. Boston fortunes never of course reached the size of the Rockefellers' and the Carnegies'; but the smallness of these contributions also owed something to the Boston sense of community. Even the high-cultural institutions were built on the conglomeration of many people's donations, as opposed to the single enormous gift with which the great millionaires 'discharged their debt to society'.[12]

The Athenaeum was administered in equally Boston fashion. Thus John Lowell was treasurer from 1807 to 1810, vice-president from 1814 to 1815, and president from 1816 to 1819. Josiah Quincy was vice-president from 1818 to 1819, and president from 1820 to 1829. Josiah Quincy Jr was treasurer from 1837 to 1851. John Amory Lowell (the son of John Lowell) was vice-president from 1846 to 1859, and president from 1860 to 1876. (The entire collection was re-catalogued between 1862 and 1870 by Charles Russell Lowell, the cousin of John Amory Lowell.) Charles Francis Adams was vice-president in 1876, and president from 1877 to 1879. The president from 1880 to 1898 was Samuel Eliot, cousin to the Ticknors and Nortons, and to President Eliot of Harvard. And the other posts were filled by members of the same families; the secretary from 1868 to 1872 was Charles Francis Adams Jr, and from 1873 to 1879 Brooks Adams.

In 1819 there were only three libraries in America with more than 10,000 books. One was the City Library in Philadelphia, with 30,000 volumes, and the other two were in Boston: the Harvard University Library, also with 30,000, and the Athenaeum, with 18,000. In figures like these we see how private benevolence (indistinguishable in Boston from civic co-operation) made the city a national cultural centre. And the character of that culture, which is equally important, is suggested by Barrett Wendell in his essay on 'The Influence and History of the Boston Athenaeum 1807–1907'. It was never a place of severe learning, but a place where 'those who seek what they may find in the humanity of books' most surely found it. They went there not as to a laboratory or a workshop, but as to a refuge where one might confidently consort for a little while with the full humanity of the present and the past.[13]

By the time Barrett Wendell was writing, that Boston humanism was decayed. This happened most importantly for the same reasons as nineteenth-century humanism decayed elsewhere in the world: the development of anti-humanist forces in those areas of thought out of which humanism is constructed—notably the arts and the sciences. But earlier, while humanism was vigorous, Boston had been a notable centre of it. The city had no number of first-class creative minds to compare with London's (it was incomparably smaller), but it had a remarkable apparatus for disseminating the work of those minds among a whole community, for raising the general level of information, and standards of intelligence. That is why we call it a city of culture.

Barrett Wendell was distinguishing Boston humanism from that severer and more specialized scholarship which modelled itself on the German universities. (He might equally have distinguished it from New York Bohemianism and later expatriate aestheticism; this was America's middle-class, middle-brow way of taking the arts and learning.) That scholarship had its alumni at Harvard, and they included such important figures as George Ticknor, President Eliot, and James Russell Lowell. But even there, and much more in the rest of Boston, the stronger intellectual tradition remained the humanist. Ticknor's rebellion was largely a demand for efficient teaching, and his History of *Spanish Literature,* despite its enormous weight of learning, never allows itself scholarly technicalities or intensities of debate which might get between it and the general reader. Lowell's learning was always at the service of his broad aims of sympathy with the subject-matter, and the maintenance of moral standards. Indeed, in 1886 we find him attacking 'the new dry rot of learning', which is the alienation of scholarship from culture. And President Eliot made it almost his first work in office to institute various series of general University Lectures, bringing in people like Emerson and Howells, and Chauncey Wright on psychology, and Peirce on logic. The great figures in President Eliot's administration were men like Charles Eliot Norton in art history, Shaker in science, and (mostly later) Babbitt in literature; men concerned to break down barriers between branches of learning, to insist on education as opposed to training, to oppose Ph.D. pedantry. This is not to mention William James, Henry Adams, Santayana. And the whole world of learning was integrated into Boston society. The Lowells, the Eliots, the Adamses, the Quincys, the Cabots, between them ran Harvard—as trustees, as benefactors, and as scholars. Abbott Lawrence Lowell gave the university two million dollars during his presidency, and was also a scholar in political science. There was nothing like this in Germany, or in England either, and at its best such a system served to give all learning a social position and importance. These individuals served and indeed created Boston humanism, an assimilation of every kind of knowledge into a complex whole which is itself shaped into a significant relation to the individual's imagination and conscience.

This humanism was the inspiration of the last of the great

institutions to be discussed here, the Lowell Institute. This offered free lectures on science, religion, and, less importantly, literature; lectures which were the apotheosis of the great popular-lecture movement in Boston. The Fund was established in 1836, as a bequest by John Lowell Jr, who laid it down that a male Lowell was always to be trustee, and that the trustees of the Athenaeum were to be visitors to the Fund. The first trustee was the founder's cousin, John Amory Lowell, 1840–80, then the latter's son, Augustus, 1880–1900, and then *his* son Abbott Lawrence Lowell. The Fund amounted to nearly $250,000 in 1840, when lectures were first given. The fees were often higher than the yearly salary of the highest paid professor in the country— Tyndall, for instance, received $10,000 for a series. And there were many series; by 1900 five or six hundred lectures per season were being delivered. Yet by 1880 the Fund had increased to $500,000. Various subsidiary schools, and free courses at M.I.T., were established. The whole enterprise is a striking example of the all-around success of Boston's cultural institutions.[14]

The lectures were extremely popular in their early days. Eight to ten thousand people applied for tickets to a course; Professor Silliman's chemistry course was so eagerly awaited on its repetition the second season that the crowd lining up for tickets crushed in the windows of the Old Corner Bookshop, where they were being distributed. Each session of James Russell Lowell's course in the English poets in 1855-56 was repeated the day after, in the afternoon, for those who had not got in in the evening, and then printed in the paper the day after that. (Those lectures won him his appointment to Harvard, to replace Longfellow; and it was by a similar process that Agassiz went to Harvard; he came to America to lecture for the Institute, and altogether gave over a hundred lectures there.)

All accounts agree that the standards of the lectures were very high, even in scientific subjects. Cooke, the professor of chemistry at Harvard, said he had had his training at the Institute. Gray, Lyell, Wallace, Tyndall, Peirce, Geikie, G. H. Darwin, lectured in science; Everett, Sparks, Lowell, Child, Norton, Gosse, Bryce, both the Holmeses, in the humanities. Among the books made out of Lowell Institute lectures are Barrett Wendell's *English Com-*

position, books by Charles Francis Adams on railways, Justice
Holmes on the common law, James Russell Lowell on the old
English dramatists, Francis Cabot Lowell on Joan of Arc, books
by Agassiz, Norton, Lyell. On the other hand, a title like *The
Credentials of Science the Warrant of Faith* (in 1888), or even
more *The Chemistry of the Atmosphere, As Illustrating the Wisdom, Power, and Goodness of God,* shows us the weakness of this
humanism, which is the weakness of all humanism in decay: an
unwillingness to trust to the autonomy of an intellectual discipline, to risk the socially or morally dangerous. 'Crude theories
and plans for moral and political reforms are not to be found in
the Lowell lectures,' says the Institute's historian. 'The selection
of lectures and lecturers is made from a broad and comprehensive knowledge of the safe thought and intelligent study of the
time.' Thus though John Fiske could lecture on Darwin and
Spencer at Harvard in 1869 and 1870, with the support of President Eliot (a suspected traitor to humanism), the Institute refused to countenance him. But for many years it remained one of
the noblest monuments of nineteenth-century humanism, and
many scholars, in the sciences and the humanities, reported how
valuable they found the discipline of presenting their best work
in a form that would be meaningful to an unspecialized but keen-
witted audience.

But beside the great single institutions, there are other features
of Boston life we should glance at. For instance, the role in this
humanism played by the great families, who are often categorized as an oligarchy, rather absurd if not odious. We have
already mentioned the names of Lowells, Eliots, and Adamses in
enough connections to make clear how inadequate such summa-
ries are. But perhaps it is worth tracing one family quickly
through the century. The John Lowell of 1743-1802 had three
wives, and one son by each. Sarah Higginson Lowell was the
mother of John Lowell the Rebel (1769–1840), a remarkably
interesting and impressive figure, who retired from the law in
1803, and devoted the rest of his life to religious, literary, political, agricultural interests. Susan Cabot Lowell was the mother of
Francis Cabot Lowell (1775–1817), the founder of the Lowell
industries and of the greatest part of the Lowell fortune. And

Rebecca Russell Tyng Lowell was the mother of the Reverend Charles Lowell, a fairly important churchman. John Lowell the Rebel wrote for *The Edinburgh Review* and *The Quarterly Review*, and his letters from England were printed as leading articles in *The Monthly Anthology*. He helped found the Hospital, and he was, together with President Kirkland, responsible for those changes at Harvard which made it a national rather than a regional college. He was a great Federalist, and after the death of Fisher Ames, the leader of the Essex Junto; he was also a great Unitarian, and his pamphlets against Calvinism were the first significant work in theology by a layman. His son, John Amory Lowell, the first trustee of the Lowell Institute, and officer of innumerable other institutions, was the father of Augustus Lowell, a great benefactor of M.I.T. and one of those Boston plutocrats who urged their children not to make any more money but to pursue knowledge. He was the father of Percival, the astronomer, Amy, the poet, and Abbott Lawrence, the president of Harvard. Meanwhile, Francis Cabot Lowell was the father of the founder of the Lowell Institute, and the grandfather of Guy Lowell, the architect, and Francis Cabot Lowell, the historian. The Reverend Charles Lowell was the father of James Russell Lowell, and the grandfather of Colonel Charles Lowell, the Beau Sabreur of the Civil War. These are distinguished names, but the really impressive thing is the extraordinarily valuable nature of the inheritance, the vocation they passed down from one to the other. Again and again, as one sees the family influence at work, one is struck by how largely it worked to the public benefit.[15]

This leads us naturally to another of Boston's great sources of self-confidence in the first part of the century, its seeming solution of the social problems of industrialism. Francis Cabot Lowell had come back from England in 1812 with the plans of British cotton-spinning machines committed to memory (the export of actual machines or written plans was forbidden), and together with his brother-in-law, set up the Boston Manufacturing Company, with $400,000 in capital. By 1817, the year he died, it was paying dividends of 20 per cent. But it was successful in more than money. At Lowell and Manchester (Lawrence was built later) there was a system of community housing, which made

respectable accommodation available to all the workers: girls
from New England villages, who were often supporting brothers
in college with their earnings. They began at $1.80 a week, and
averaged (in the thirties and forties) $3.15. In contemporary
England, the Lancashire workers averaged 4s. a week ($1.00).
The girls paid $1.25 for board and lodging, both of which were
of a high standard. Meanwhile, female teachers might get $6.00 a
quarter, plus a less dependably good board, and much less independence. Domestic servants and shoe factory workers got between 75 cents and $2.00 a week. Two sisters in the Lowell mills,
who supported a mother, in ten years built a house costing $600,
bought a church pew for $125, and had $400 saved. In 1845,
Lowell Savings Bank had $100,000 in deposits; many of the girls
were saving to send themselves to normal school, and did in fact
become teachers afterwards. The mills were famous in Europe,
and one need only think of the conditions of life of the industrial
workers there to see why. Dickens wrote an enthusiastic description of the town in his *American Notes; The Lowell Offering*, a
magazine brought out by the girls, was reviewed in the London
Athenaeum and lectured on in Paris. But the arrival of cheap
Irish labour drove the New England girls out of the mills, and
ended the harmony, dignity, and mutual respect of the system.

Boston merchants, and to some extent the bankers and industrialists who succeeded them, had the idea that commerce should
go hand in hand with philanthropy, and even culture; and
should give way to them as soon as the individual had secured
himself an adequate sum. William Tudor founded *The North
American Review* after making a fortune selling ice. Israel
Thorndike bought Ebeling's collection of books for Harvard Library. Samuel and Nathan Appleton endowed a dozen institutions. Like Ticknor's father, Boston merchants often retired
early; Peter Chardon Brooks, one of the richest men in Boston,
retired at thirty-six. His money, through his daughters' marriages, eventually reached the Adamses, the Everetts, and the
Frothinghams. Family connection was one of the main ways in
which the money made in Boston commerce passed into the
hands of Boston scholarship. Samuel Eliot (who also founded the
chair in Greek at Harvard) was the father-in-law of Andrews

Norton and George Ticknor. Nathan Appleton was the father-in-law of Longfellow. Others, like John Murray Forbes and Colonel Higginson, endowed clubs for Boston authors. At the very least, like Augustus Lowell, they urged their sons to pursue knowledge. In Boston, more than in the rest of America, business sincerely acknowledged intellectual as well as social obligations.

The great families represented Boston also in their relations with contemporary England. They had close ties with the liberal intellectual families there; James Russell Lowell was a close friend of Leslie Stephen's, and in fact the godfather of Virginia Woolf; Charles Eliot Norton was brother-in-law to a Darwin. They were in fact very similar to the great chain of those families described by Noel Annan in his essay on 'The Intellectual Aristocracy'.[16] The British evangelical and radical philanthropists acknowledged the same kind of responsibility for their society—the kind described in the quotation in the first chapter from *Education and the University*—and they implemented it by the same blend of intellectual and moral alertness in things like literature. 'They were the first to admire Meredith and Browning and to dethrone Byron for Wordsworth,' says Annan. Like the Bostonians, they formulated an average serious taste for their time. They were humanists in the Bostonian sense. They too wrote for the intelligent public at large, not for a scholarly clique. Their controversial and speculative manner contrasts sharply with that of German scholars. And if they were unspecialized, they were equally unfashionable. They were the professors, tutors, schoolmasters, editors, civil servants, and serious journalists of England. These were the ways the Bostonians served America; civil-service reform, on the English model, was one of the greatest Boston causes of the Gilded Age. But within their own city, the Bostonians were much more completely a ruling class than the English; there was no-one above them; they were *more* responsible for their culture. The English families were a critical opposition to a ruling class, in many ways; in their dowdy and respectable manner, more an intelligentsia. But it is the likeness between the two groups which is striking.

The Bostonians were related to England not only by similarity and by marriage, but by admiration and by imitation. 'Our literary standards, our standards of statesmanship, our modes of thought . . . were as English as the trivial customs of the dinner table and the ballroom,' said Henry Cabot Lodge.[17] And about Lodge, Henry Adams said that he was English to the last fibre of his thought—saturated with English literature, English tradition, English taste—and *therefore*, 'he was Boston incarnate'.[18] At the beginning of the century, New England had refused support to the War of 1812 against England; the war loan that year of $11,000,000 drew only $1,000,000 from New England, and the 1813 loan of $16,000,000, only $75,000.[19] The first article of Federalism, according to John Quincy Adams, was 'Detestation of the French Revolution, and attachment to Great Britain'. At the end of the century, Henry Adams remarked of himself, 'Do what he might, he drew breath only in the atmosphere of English methods and thoughts; he could breathe no other.' [20] He said that though in theory he despised English thought, his theory never affected his practice.

At the same time, the Bostonians remained convinced of American superiority (we shall see evidence of this in both Ticknor and Norton) and got more angry with England from time to time than with any other country (we see this in Adams himself). But they judged England by standards they had learned from her. They still admired 'the real England'. And their admiration for her gave a lead to other elements in American life. Richard Hofstadter points out that the Mugwumps were to be found in New York and Chicago, but predominantly in Boston—'a centre of seasoned wealth and seasoned conscience'. They shared the cultural ideals and traditions of New England, and beyond them of England. 'In this, as in much else, the Mugwumps were the heirs of the Federalists and the Know Nothings.' And the same was true of some of the Progressives. Woodrow Wilson called himself a Federalist, and was a true son of New England by affiliation; and a great admirer of Great Britain.[21]

Boston was then British, culturally and politically; that was the source of many of its strengths and its weaknesses. And what Boston symbolized within America, within the city itself Boston's great families realized, in their political affiliations, their institutional policies, the poetry, history, and social criticism they wrote, their friendships, their marriages, and their manners. But it will not do to dismiss these people or their city as un-American. Even if that charge were true, what they did and were has more prominent features. Given what they accomplished, it would be historically irresponsible not to ponder their experience patiently and sympathetically. And when it is pondered it becomes very illuminating.

Boston cared more about quality than about equality. That surely is at the root of our feeling that it was un-American; but if so, then the remedy must be to revise our theory of America. Equality should not be so exclusively what we mean by American democracy; while it is, we are left with a (very American, admittedly) travesty of that ideal, one which has no power to order or inspire other values—which is in fact destructive of other values. Surely generosity of idealism can also be called the great American and democratic virtue, and by that definition Boston was one of the most American of cities. It was a community that tried to embody and institutionalize an ideal. The attempt finally failed, and even at its best moments there were ugly things, great failures in honesty, in generosity, in sympathy, which look all the uglier to us for their context of solemn moral aspiration. But it wasn't all ugly, or all failure. And perhaps it has suffered in our eyes from its successes as well as its failures. No ideal that can be embodied can seem wholly satisfying. But neither can one that cannot. What Boston attempted on such a large scale—to be a responsible society—is something every community must attempt in some measure if it is to keep the active participation of its thoughtful citizens. We are surely indulging a weakness if we turn away from Boston in favour of places with more picturesque failings—if we call Gold Rush San Francisco more American, more vital, or more interesting.

Chapter Three

BOSTON: THE CITY
OF LITERATURE

BUT WE ARE particularly concerned with the condition, and with the work, of writers in Boston. The laws of relation between those two entities are doubtful and confusing enough; we certainly cannot assume any direct or calculable relation between them together and what we have just been discussing—between the high-cultural conscience of a society and the quality of its particular works of art. We must study the literary world in and for itself. But in so doing—because literature was the most important of the arts in Boston—we shall be led back to the pattern of that high culture as a whole, and shall see what place the creative artist, the critic, the scholar, had in that pattern.

It is a theory common among modern versions of literary history that America in the nineteenth century was a uniquely unfavourable climate for writers. Nobody paid them, nobody read them, nobody respected them, nobody wanted them. It is true of course that many good writers did not get either the recognition or the critical guidance they most needed. But in certain other rewards, and in certain parts of the country, there is material for important objections to the generalization. Above all, such epigrams have an implicit background of contrast with the situation of writers in other ages and places; and as soon as that background is made explicit, this epigram ceases to be convincing. During how many phases of Western literature has a man of literary talent been able to count on earning a handsome living, enjoying high prestige, being taken seriously as an intellectual, being given freedom as an artist? The only honest answer is, Very few. Conditions have varied widely, and some ages have been good times in which to be a writer of the right kind, but those cannot be taken to constitute a norm. Literature must surely give thanks for a period and place in which any two of those conditions held good for a fair number of talented writers who also felt they were satisfying their own standards. Boston in the nineteenth century was such a place in such a period.

There is thus something artificial about the tone of many books of American literary history. Newton Arvin's book on Longfellow, for instance, tells us that the poet's father counselled him against the project (announced when the boy was seventeen) of making his career as a man of letters.[1] Mr Longfellow made his son see 'how little room there was, in society, for the literary career in any practical sense'. Arvin adds that in nineteenth-century America, alas, the counsel had some validity. And later we are told again that the poet had to recognize how 'in the America of his time' a purely literary career was a practical impossibility, and the most dedicated of creative spirits must have some other profession or occupation. 'Bryant and Irving had already proved the truth of this discouraging generalization in their own careers, and Hawthorne and Emerson and Poe were soon to do so.' Now to drag 'the America of his time' into the argument is surely unreasonable; when and where *have* lawyer fathers encouraged seventeen-year-old sons to make their careers purely as poets—indeed, *should* the five writers named have spent more time writing? Moreover, in the next few lines we learn that it was largely because of his literary talents that Longfellow was appointed to be professor of modern languages at Bowdoin (at eighteen) and sent to Europe at the college's expense for three years of free (undirected) study. He was offered the chair at the suggestion of a trustee who had been impressed with his translation of a Horatian ode in the senior examination. He knew nothing except some self-taught French to qualify him for the post. But during the two preceding years (when he was seventeen and eighteen) he had had forty poems published, in newspapers, magazines, gift-books. There was in fact no moment in Longfellow's long career when he was not given every encouragement to write as much and as well as he could. In 1855, when he was forty-eight, he was able to retire from Harvard and devote himself entirely to writing. In 1897, Mrs Fields tells us, twenty-four publishing houses in Europe printed his work, there were three translations of *Evangeline* into German alone, *Hiawatha* had been translated into every modern language and Latin, and the 'Psalm of Life' was to be found in Chinese characters on fans in Peking.[2] He was simply the most popular serious poet in the world. Liszt composed music for his verse; Baudelaire borrowed from him. Mr Longfellow senior could not have been more wrong; the literary career, in a very practical sense, was very rewarding. His mistake, on the other hand, was reasonable as a prediction; what are we to say of the literary historian who repeats it as a retrospect after the events have disproved it?

Of course such a career cannot be taken as typical. But the typical is surely less relevant here than the triumphant.* Such a career was *possible* in nineteenth-century America. To know that must have, for instance, softened incalculably the resistance of average parents to a son's desire to make a career as a poet. New England (after 1840 at least) was one of the places where that career must have seemed *most* promising, and least costly in ordinary human decency and happiness. Moreover, Longfellow's case was far from unique. Prescott made perhaps $100,000 in

* The historians take an opposite view. Merle Curti says, 'In the first quarter of the 19th century conditions did not warrant even the most gifted man of letters in embarking on a professional literary career if he had to earn his livelihood thereby.' But when have conditions warranted that? 'Bryant, our best poet of the 1820s, regarded two dollars as a reasonable compensation for a poem.'[3] But in the next sentence we are told that George Pope Morris could get $50 for any poem he chose to submit, and $3,500 for a play. This, we are told, was an 'exception'. Of course it was an exception; no-one supposes that the highest rates were paid to the largest number; but it was also a fact, and one which must have meant to young writers that people *were* willing to pay handsomely for poems and plays then. Moreover, though Mr Curti does not mention this, Bryant got a contract in 1824 to send the *United States Literary Gazette* a hundred lines of verse a month, and in 1825 was made co-editor of the *New York Review* at $1,000 a year.

royalties on his histories, according to Mr and Mrs Beard. In 1829 Washington Irving got $23,500 from writing. Cooper averaged $6,500 a year during the twenties. As editor of *The Knickerbocker Magazine,* Irving was paid $2,000 a year, and when he was in London as first secretary to the American minister there, Murray offered him £1,000 a year ($5,000) to become editor of a new magazine. And this was not just a matter of money. After London, Irving was sent to Spain as minister because of his literary talents, and when he died in 1859 the flags flew at half mast on the buildings of New York City and on the ships in the harbour. He was a national hero.[4]

Nor was Irving's case exceptional in displaying the patronage of letters by the federal government. At the Court of St James the American minister was more often than not a man of letters, and appointed for being that as well as for his diplomatic training. John Adams was minister from 1785 to 1788, Gouverneur Morris from 1790 to 1792, John Quincy Adams from 1815 to 1817, not to mention those minor secretaries, like Irving in the twenties, and Henry Adams in the sixties. But it is after 1840 that the succession of Bostonians becomes so striking: from 1841 to 1845 Edward Everett, from 1848 to 1849 George Bancroft, from 1849 to 1852 Abbott Lawrence (not a direct tribute to letters, this, but a tribute to Boston and high culture), from 1861 to 1868 Charles Francis Adams, in 1869 Motley, from 1880 to 1885 James Russell Lowell, from 1890 to 1898 John Hay, and from 1912 to 1918 Walter Hines Page. (Hay and Page were Bostonians by affiliation, in the sense Woodrow Wilson was.) It would be difficult to outdo that, in more established countries, as a record of diplomatic patronage of men of letters. When one considers other diplomatic and consular posts, one remembers Hawthorne at Liverpool (where he made $10,000 one year) and Howells at Venice, Motley at Vienna, Lowell at Madrid, Bayard Taylor at Berlin, George Perkins Marsh in Turkey and Italy. Ticknor's friend Hugh Swinton Legaré went to Brussels. Freneau, Barlow, and Paulding got appointments in Washington.[5]

It would be absurd to claim that official appointments for literary talent were the rule in nineteenth-century America. But, at least in this area of diplomatic and consular appointments, they were not the exception either. They formed a recognizable and not unimportant social pattern, exemplified most simply, perhaps, in the writing of campaign biographies of presidential candidates; quite serious authors undertook the job, and were rewarded with appointments that included a chance to travel, a substantial income, and leisure to write. Hawthorne and Howells are the best-known examples.

But let us turn to the conditions of direct payment for literary work. These varied at different periods within the century. Parrington says that it was by 1840 that the profession of letters was established, and Frank Luther Mott also gives this as the date after which contributors to magazines were paid more or less adequately. The two criteria lead to the same choice because it was writing for the magazines—this was generally agreed—which made the authorial life economically feasible. *Graham's Magazine* began the trend; its rates in the forties varied from $4 to $12 a page for prose, and $10 to $50 for a poem. Famous contributors commanded more, and they included serious writers. Lowell was getting $30 a poem by 1845. Longfellow soon rose to $50. Cooper got $1,800 for a novel two hundred and fifty pages long. In 1842 N. P. Willis, writing for four magazines, earned $1,500. (The governor of Connecticut that year earned less than Willis did from three of his magazines—$1,100. (In 1841 Poe was made literary editor of *Graham's,* which meant mostly writing book notices, and was promised that the job would not take up more than two hours a day; for this he got $800 a year. A professor then might get $600 a year.* A (male) teacher in Connecticut got $8 a month and board.[6]

There were, then, rich prizes to be won. And they went, not exclusively, but inclusively, to the serious writers of the time. *Graham's* published Lowell, Poe, Bryant, Cooper, Dana, Longfellow, in its first two years. By 1844 it could claim to be the exclusive magazine publisher of Longfellow, Cooper, Paulding, and Bry-

---

* This is the figure Mr Mott gives. The University of Virginia, at least, paid much more. On the other hand, Lowell got only $1,200 when he went to Harvard as Smith Professor in 1856, which was less than half what he was to get as editor of the Atlantic. It was also exactly the same as what he got from the Lowell Institute.

ant. It had a circulation of 40,000. *Godey's Lady's Book,* which had a circulation of 150,000 by the time of the Civil War, was less serious, but occasionally published Emerson, Longfellow, Poe, Holmes, Hawthorne, and Mrs Stowe. Later in the century, Robert Bonner's *New York Ledger* began paying prices like $3,000 for a poem by Longfellow, and $30,000 for a novel by Henry Ward Beecher. Edward Everett was paid $10,000 by the *Ledger* for a year's supply of weekly columns.*

It is true that *Godey's* and *Graham's* did not pay anything for contributions from totally unknown writers. However, they did print them. It is true that all my striking cases occur in the period after 1840, and that in the period the historians most often cite, 'the first quarter of the century', there are fewer grounds for refuting them. But this was the time of the beginning of the republic; America was a young, small, poor, country; there is every reason for attributing literary hardships then to passing conditions, not national destiny. And conditions were improving consistently and quickly; there is no reason for making those hardships then a paradigm of the literary career throughout the century. It is true that the nineteenth-century writers nearly all supported themselves by editing or teaching or lecturing, something other than looking into their hearts and writing. But do we regret that? Above all, once granted any reasonable background of historical comparison, is it not *more* true, does it not more spring to the eye, that the literary life in America in the nineteenth century offered rich rewards?

What does seem to have made that life difficult (in most of the country) is that corpus of national attitudes which Richard Hofstadter discusses in *Anti-Intellectualism in American Life.* That term, 'anti-intellectualism', is in some ways misleading, since it is not so much intellectualism as intellectual authority which is

---

* I repeat that these are not necessarily typical cases. I offer them as a challenge to the current idea of what the typical earning power of a serious writer then was. What 'typical' can here mean is difficult to determine; should it be what the best writers earned, or the average? the best by nineteenth-century standards or by ours? at the height of their careers or for their best books or when they most needed the money? It is all very puzzling. But surely one *can* say that serious writers in nineteenth-century America could earn handsome sums by their writing.

resisted and resented. One is tempted to say it is any kind of authority, as opposed to power; locating authority therefore in individuals or small groups, power in featureless majorities or in impersonal kinds of physical or intellectual power, in force. Authority would then derive from personal qualities: a differentness, a superiority, in the person as a whole, constituted by the interaction of his different, superior, qualities; it would have much in common with personal distinction. But of course this will not do, when one thinks of Lincoln, who was by any standards distinguished. Perhaps one must say that to the American imagination there seems an incongruousness, an incompatibility, an opposition between personal force and any manners or habits which bear the mark of a privileged minority, whether a social or an intellectual one. The man who displays those manners or habits is suspected of personal feebleness (and often corruption) until he has displayed force, too. Theodore Roosevelt was able to be eccentric and aristocratic even in national politics, because he was also crudely forceful. Lincoln's manners and manner made a point of lacking any minority correctness and polish—and thereby affronted, for instance, New Englanders; his solitariness of judgment and feeling had to express themselves through a manner which promised crowd-conviviality and the breakdown of polite reserves.

In any contest in which the two antagonists can be identified with the two sides of this dichotomy, Americans feel some profound pressures to expect the man of force to win. Most *want* him to win; and few can identify themselves with the other man (however right they may know him to be) without experiencing acute anxiety and guilt. One of the most startling and exciting features of the Army-McCarthy hearings in the nineteen fifties was that people saw this traditional conflict have an untraditional issue; the man of breeding defeated the man of force. He did so by the grace of at least two exceptional circumstances: the man of force lost all control of himself; and the man of breeding was a lawyer, member of a profession which makes available some styles of behaviour that lie athwart this powerful emotional current, this powerful polar discharge, in the national mind. Mr Welch could be witty, could be cold, could be polished, without seeming effete or unpleasant—un-American—largely because he was a lawyer. But those circumstances could not prevent one from feeling the conflict as *the* traditional conflict, for the American intellectual or artist, and from feeling almost bewildered relief at its outcome.

Perhaps I can quote the observation of a non-American here —one able to sympathize with the intellectual and artist's predicament, but not ready to scant the opposite values. D. H. Lawrence discussed this problem often, and at length in *Kangaroo,* but I will refer only to these two paragraphs from *Ft Mawr.*

> Lewis, the groom, staring from between his brush of hair and his beard, watched like an animal from the underbrush. And Rico was still sufficiently a colonial to be uneasily aware of the underbrush, uneasy under the watchfulness of the pale grey eyes, and uneasy in that man-to-man exposure which is characteristic of the democratic colonies and of America. He knew he must ultimately be judged on his merits as a man, alone without a background; an ungarnished colonial.
>
> This lack of background, this defenceless man-to-man business which left him at the mercy of every servant, was bad for his nerves. For he was also an artist. He bore up against it in a kind of desperation, and was easily moved to rancorous resentment.[7]

By saying 'judged on his merits as a man', Lawrence gives full value to the 'democratic' spirit. But let us notice that 'for he was also an artist' is unequivocal; and that in *Kangaroo* Lawrence's own representative (named Somers in the book) suffers from the same problem, and is called a she-man, compared with the he-man, Jack Callcott—though with a vivid reversal of the two phrases' usual values.

Rico's difficulty is Lawrence's own, is the difficulty of every artist in a democratic society. The background Rico lacks, and which 'the Englishman' has, would gain a partial exemption from this rough and ruthless interrogation of Lewis's—rough for the artist and intellectual because it is really a test of strength in an area where he *may* be strong, but is certainly hypersensitive. This area centres in the act of projecting an idea of oneself as simply normal, simply a man, and therefore unquestionable; in the talent for evoking an image of oneself and an image of manhood in the mind of the audience (actual or virtual) and uniting the two; and the artist and intellectual is hypersensitive in this area because he knows he is not simply normal. By assuming what I call minority manners, he deflects attention from this area; the Englishman's 'background' lets him stage his self-assertion, and any competitiveness that may provoke, in areas (of stylishness and eccentricity) where the intellectual's kind of will-power and intelligence move in more freedom.

We can recall here Edward Everett Hale's comment on Clough's American experience.

> Clough came to Cambridge, as I have always supposed, in the real hope of adapting himself to American life, or life in a republic, where 'I am as good as the other fellow, and the other fellow is as good as I'. Alas and alas! how many of us have seen Englishmen who tried this great experiment, who made the great adventure, and then were obliged to go back to the leeks of Egypt.[8]

A moment's thought will remind us how many *American* intellectuals and artists have been obliged to go back to the leeks of Egypt. Hale is only giving us the philistine's version of Lawrence's insight; life in a republic, where 'the other fellow is as good as I', is particularly hard on intellectuals. They find life easier in a more hierarchical society, like England; not because they are snobs; not because of the picturesque and gloomy wrong Hawthorne wanted; not because of the varity of 'things' there James talked about; but because of the minority manners and habits they can assume there. Some artists, perhaps, don't need such protection; their special awareness is merely added on to a quite solid psychological substructure. Some, certainly, have developed their own protection; they can project a hearty manliness on occasion, preserving a separate, individualized self underneath. But many, who pay for their special awareness by a sore insecurity about their 'normality', find minority manners the great mode of self-assertion. That is surely why intelligent Americans will sometimes imitate even an Oxford accent with enthusiasm.

This rough interrogation has been a remarkably constant feature of American life from the beginnings until the present day;

and has been the source of great anxiety and resentment for American intellectuals. Their gifts have won them not admiration and deference, but suspicion and dislike, an extra challenge, an extra hostility. Or let us say that the admiration and deference they have won from women and in the schoolroom has been undercut by the suspicion and dislike from men and in the bar. Hofstadter gives us some vivid examples of the abuse directed at those who sought political reforms in the Gilded Age, and they make it clear how central was the question of manhood: 'namby pambies', 'goody goodies', 'dudes', 'idealists'; 'men who part their hair in the middle', 'men who drink cold tea', 'men with English accents', above all 'men-milliners' and 'eunuchs'. Roscoe Conkling called George William Curtis a man-milliner; and Senator Ingalls of Kansas described reformers as 'effeminate without being either masculine or feminine; unable to beget or to bear; possessing neither fecundity nor virility; endowed with the contempt of men and the derision of women, and doomed to sterility, isolation, and extinction'. [9]

The American writer as much as the American reformer is born into this cruel and exhausting struggle, and surely this is the source of his feeling that the conditions of his life are harder than those of writers elsewhere—the source of many diagnoses of 'America' ostensibly quite unconnected. The struggle is cruel as well as exhausting because all the aggression, all the destructiveness, is on the side of the anti-intellectual. The intellectual is entirely on the defensive. That is why it surely *was* dangerous (self-deceiving to some degree) for an American intellectual, like Cooper, to turn away from New England Federalism, and to a less extent from Whiggery. For the alternative, Jacksonian democracy, was more profoundly identified with the forces of anti-intellectualism.* The intellectual was naturally drawn (though

---

* It is equally dangerous for contemporary writers to ignore or depreciate the history of nineteenth-century New England, or to espouse the Jacksonian cause. Their motives in doing so seem to derive (if not from a merely self-indulgent romanticism) from an insistence on the irremediability of their situation, a determination to make it as hopeless as can be. Imperfect as Boston was, it was there that the attempt was made to build an American culture which included the life of the mind; exciting as other sides of America might be, they did not make that attempt; and therefore the American intellectual's primary loyalty must go to Boston.

there were other considerations, drawing him in other directions)
to those forces in society which would allow him to use the manners and habits of a privileged minority.

And that is why the history of nineteenth-century Boston is of
such great interest; because there, almost alone on the continent,
the cruel struggle was suspended. While assertively American
and democratic, New England offered the means of protection
and privilege. 'In New England,' as Henry Adams points out at
the beginning of his history of the century, 'society was organized
on a system,—a clergy in alliance with a magistracy; universities
supporting each, and supported in turn,—a social hierarchy, in
which respectability, education, property, and religion united to
defeat and crush the unwise and vicious.' That is, authority defeated force; the man of breeding defeated the man of power,
habitually and as a function of the social system. By contrast, in
New York, for instance, aristocrats in politics (the 'natural
leaders of the wise and virtuous') would vote against their class,
quite irresponsibly, in order to further their own careers; Aaron
Burr was a natural result. And in Virginia, though the members
of the ruling class were intelligently and responsibly interested in
politics, they were not interested in education; their common
school system failed; and consequently or causally, the sense of
responsibility they felt for their total culture had severe limitations. But the 25,000 Federalist voters in Massachusetts in 1800
included all the professional and mercantile classes, led by the
church, bar, and magistracy, and all society. 'This union created
what was unknown outside New England,—an organized social
system, capable of acting at command either for offence or defence. . . .' And the defence was quite typically of those minority manners which the intellectual aristocracy of New England
shared with the social aristocracy. This union, Adams says, was
supported by the convictions of the people; and its starting point
was the educational system. Its particular pride and joy, he might
have added, was its literature.[10]

Just how central the position of the writer was (central within
the high culture, and that was central in the culture as a whole)
is made clear by a thousand witnesses. In 1900 William Dean
Howells wrote that 'now' much of American writing was done

outside New England, though he thought it was still character-ized by New England ideals and examples. But in 1860, when he went to Boston first, law, science, theology, and journalism all had a literary colouring. 'I arrived in Boston, however, when all talents had more or less a literary colouring, and when the great-est talents were literary.' [11] These were talents which 'expressed with ripened fullness a civilization conceived in faith and brought forth in good works'. And Edward Everett Hale tells us in *James Russell Lowell and His Friends* that the Boston and Harvard of *his* youth, thirty years before, were peculiarly liter-ary. 'The whole drift of fashion, occupation, and habit among the undergraduates ran in lines suggested by literature.' [12] This was between 1834 and 1839. Not politics or social reform, not athletics or sociology, as 'now'—1898.

> Literature was, as I said, the fashion. The books which the fellows took out of the library, the books which they bought for their own subscription libraries, were not books of science, nor history, nor sociology, nor politics; they were books of literature . . . there was no general interest in science, except so far as it came by way of the pure mathematics.

The word 'fashion' should not mislead us. It was in fact Carlyle whom everyone was reading, and it was the breadth and inten-sity of interests he represents that was meant by 'literature'. It was taken seriously, even in magazine form, by New England readers. When Mrs Stowe published her article on the married life of the Byrons, in 1869, and when Ferris Greenslet published May Sinclair's *The Helpmate* as a serial, many *Atlantic* readers cancelled their subscriptions. They felt it their duty to mark their disapproval, to express their reactions, to take some respon-sibility for what was published. They were not content to be passive consumers.

This, together with other features of Boston life, added up to an environment many writers found ideal. Howells tells us that Turgenev declared Cambridge the ideal community, the perfect place to live and work.* Howells himself says,

---

* The Norwegian novelist Hjalmer Hjorth Boyesen had described the Cambridge way of life to him.

> through the intellectual life there was a complete democracy, and I
> do not believe that since the capitalistic era began there was ever a
> community in which money counted for less . . . a mind cultivated
> in some sort was essential, and after that came civil manners, and the
> willingness and ability to be agreeable and interesting; but the ques-
> tion of riches and poverty did not enter . . . we shall not get a more
> perfect society.

Perfect in the way it treated its writers, notably.

> Elsewhere we literary folk are apt to be such a common lot, with
> tendencies here and there to be a shabby lot; we arrive from all sorts
> of holes and corners of the earth, remote, obscure; and at best we do
> so often come up out of the ground; but at Boston we were of ascer-
> tained and noted origin, and good part of us dropped from the skies.
> Instead of holding horses before the doors of theatres; or capping
> verses at the plough-tail; or tramping over Europe with nothing but
> a flute in the pocket; or walking up to the metropolis with no luggage
> but the manuscript of a tragedy; or sleeping in doorways or under the
> arches of bridges; or serving as apothecaries' 'prentices—we were good
> society from the beginning. I think this was none the worse for us,
> and it was vastly the better for good society.[13]

Some of those alternative fates he lists there may seem to us less
inferior to his own than they seemed to him, but if we remind
ourselves of the 'American' challenges (the cruel and exhausting struggle) he escaped by going to Boston—and he shows us in
The Vacation of the Kelwyns how sharp a sense of those challenges he had—then this paragraph regains its point and its dignity. Thomas Bailey Aldrich makes the same kind of observation
in a letter to Bayard Taylor in 1866.

> There is a finer intellectual atmosphere here than in our city. It is
> true, a poor literary man could not earn his salt, or more than that,
> out of pure literary labor in Boston; but then he couldn't do it in
> New York, unless he turned *journalist.* The people of Boston are
> full-blooded *readers,* appreciative, trained. The humble man of letters
> has a position here which he doesn't have in New York. To be known
> as an able writer is to have the choicest society opened to you. Just
> as an officer in the Navy (providing he is a gentleman) is the social
> equal of everybody—so a knight of the quill here is supposed neces-
> sarily to be a gentleman. In New York—he's a Bohemian! outside of
> his personal friends he has no standing.[14]

To be specific about the ways in which Boston awarded this position to its men of letters, let us list some of the magazines that were based there, and that drew their contributions largely from there. In 1850 New York City was five times as large as either Philadelphia or Boston. But the average annual circulation of periodicals per inhabitant, Frank Luther Mott reports, was 404 in Boston, 157 in New York, 147 in Baltimore, and 125 in Philadelphia. We have already seen how seriously Bostonians took their magazine reading matter, and how much prestige they conferred upon their writers. When we add to that the quantity they read, the amount of time they must have spent in reading, we begin to understand how central a figure in society a writer must have felt himself.

Of the great Boston magazines, the first to be founded was *The North American Review*, begun in 1815 by the members of the Monthly Anthology Club. In its idea of itself it swung for some time between becoming another *Edinburgh Review* and becoming another *Port Folio* (a much lighter Philadelphia magazine); it finally settled in the direction of the first. Its editors were nearly all professors at Harvard; among them were Jared Sparks, Edward Tyrrell Channing, Edward Everett, Francis Bowen, Alexander Everett, Charles Eliot Norton, James Russell Lowell, and Henry Adams. In its first forty-five years, the contributor with the largest number of articles was Edward Everett; not a profound thinker, but a learned one, and an elegant stylist. It also published verse, including Bryant's 'Thanatopsis'. It was thus a house organ of Harvard, and, more loosely, of Boston, but it was also the most important serious periodical in America, until 1878, when it was moved to New York. It is to *The North American Review* one must turn to find the most serious thinking in America, during its Boston lifetime.[15]

Then there was *The Dial*, the Transcendentalist magazine, which produced its quarterly numbers for only four years, between 1840 and 1844, which never reached a circulation of three hundred, and which has yet proved more valuable to literary historians than any other American periodical. This printed a good deal of religious and philosophical speculation, some accounts of modern German literature, discussions of reform issues like 'the woman question', and perhaps most interesting now, some contemporary literary criticism. Margaret Fuller (writing not only for *The Dial*) was capable of the kind of criticism American literature needed. Her remarks on Lowell and Longfellow, for instance, were severe and just, she classed Hawthorne with Washington Irving, and praised Edgar Allan Poe with discrimination. She also defied the excessive prudery of the age, speaking freely of Goethe's love affairs, and of the relationship between Chopin and George Sand, even after meeting them and while that relationship continued. This was a kind of freedom and forthrightness American literature then badly needed, and rarely got.

The Liberator, William Lloyd Garrison's weekly abolitionist paper, ran from 1831 to 1865, despite popular hostility and many kinds of difficulty, and achieved in the end a very susbstantial national circulation. It was the greatest of all the abolitionist papers. When it put an end to its own existence, with the close of the Civil War, some of its functions were taken over by E. L. Godkin's *Nation,* which, although located in New York, was more of a Bostonian magazine, both in its sympathies and in its originators. In *The Dial, The Liberator,* and *The North American Review* Boston possessed three of the greatest organs (of very different kinds) of serious thinking and feeling in early nineteenth-century America.

But the greatest Boston magazine was founded in 1857, and belonged in every way to the second half of the century. The list of editors of *The Atlantic Monthly* reads like a roll-call of Boston's senators of culture: James Russell Lowell, 1857–61, James Fields, 1861–77, William Dean Howells, 1871–81, Thomas Bailey Aldrich, 1881–90, and Horace Scudder, 1890–98. It was, as Barrett Wendell says, mature from the beginning; an instrument of reconciliation and the organ of an establishment, bringing the rebels of *The Dial* and the radicals of *The Liberator* into harmony with the academic respectability of Charles Eliot Norton and Oliver Wendell Holmes. The first issue included contributions by Emerson, Motley, Longfellow, Holmes, Whittier, Mrs Stowe, and Lowell himself. It was a humanist magazine, in a somewhat safe, lax, and bland sense of the word, for Boston was already somewhat on the decline intellectually, and on the defensive socially. On issues like slavery, and freedom of religious speculation, such writers could still speak with energy and courage, but there were more and more issues on which they could only, safely, amuse, console, uplift, and re-assure.

The *Atlantic* set itself to foster, as well as express, this humorous and genial humanism. But for the *Atlantic*, is seems likely, Holmes' series, *The Autocrat of the Breakfast-Table*, would never have been written; nor Lowell's *Biglow Papers, Second Series*. But for James Fields, the magazine's guiding genius, Hawthorne's novels would probably never have been written. The accent was on good fellowship from the beginning; there were a great many dinners and breakfasts for the contributors; it is perhaps symbolic that at the first of these dinners they were five hours at table. However, it also published the serious writing of the time, British and American, and it paid its contributors and editors generously. The usual price for a poem was $50, and for prose $5 to $10 a page, though Emerson got $50 for a brief essay. Most important from our present point of view, it was a major American literary organ, established in Boston.

But the magazines were probably no greater a source of income, prestige, and pride, for Boston authors, than was the lecture-series system. That system had this effect not because the lectures demanded were all about literature (they were about everything), but because the role of lecturer offered literary men in particular the chance to perform in public, to air their opinions, to act as a social force, as well as to earn social rewards. We are all familiar with some of the lectures of Emerson and Thoreau, but these authors were only two out of dozens who gave lectures of, in many ways, comparable seriousness. Lectures were important events. Edward Everett Hale tells us that one habitually went half an hour early to a lecture and talked with friends, and there would be a recess half way through the performance (which might itself last an hour and a half), and at the end one habitually went home to supper with someone else to discuss what had been heard. This was a whole evening's occupation, and of a serious and systematic kind. In the thirties, he tells us, at least five organizations were giving courses almost every evening of the week: the Society for Diffusing Useful Knowledge, the

Boston Lyceum, the Mercantile Library Association, the Mechanics' Association, and the Historical Society. He insists that these lectures were quite different in character from popular lectures in England, to which educated people did not go in any expectation of learning anything themselves. In America, he claims, people expected, and got, something first class.[16]

In the 1837–38 season, we are told, twenty-six such courses were delivered in Boston, not counting those with less than eight lectures. Thirteen thousand people attended, out of a total population of about 80,000. And of course the single lectures were often occasions of importance, too—Emerson and Thoreau again remind us of that. Fees varied between $5 and $50, though someone like Wendell Phillips could name his own price (and time and place) for his 'The Lost Arts'. He calculated he had given that lecture two thousand times, and had earned $150,000 by it; audiences interrupted after every paragraph to applaud. His regular annual income from lecturing was $10,000 to $15,000, and he gave his anti-slavery lectures free.[17]

The great period of lecturing was 1830–50, but it remained important throughout the century. The first lyceum was formed in 1826 in Millbury, Massachusetts. Within two years there were a hundred, and by 1831 delegates from a thousand met to organize the National American Lyceum. The lyceums continued into the seventies. In 1868 James Redpath reorganized them into a lecture bureau, and paid up to five hundred dollars for a single appearance. Though Emerson, Sumner, and Greeley stopped lecturing soon after the war, Holmes, Higginson, Field, and Whipple (not to mention Twain and Artemus Ward) continued throughout the next decade. The lectures became less scholarly, but there was still some demand for seriousness; and the fees increased. Henry Ward Beecher got a thousand dollars for an appearance, and when Stanley came over and gave a hundred-lecture tour, he made a hundred thousand dollars. In the seventies the Chautauqua movement began. Lecturing was one of the main stratagems in a literary career in nineteenth-century America, and a Boston author found it particularly easy to augment his income that way.

A famous later lecturer, and owner of both *The North Ameri-*

can Review and the *Atlantic* at different times, was James T. Fields, the great Boston publisher, and a very important figure in the cultural history of America. Born in 1817 in Portsmouth, New Hampshire, of North Irish stock, he was employed by the Old Corner Bookshop in Boston when he was fourteen, and made himself one of the great directors of taste there until his death in 1881. When he went to Boston the different professions of publisher, printer, and bookseller were very vaguely distinguished one from the other. There were sixteen firms which called themselves publishers, and forty booksellers. But there was no literary publisher in the sense in which Ticknor and Fields later became one; publishers did not look out for, much less risk anything on, serious contemporary writers, and serious American writers least of all. In 1830 1,700 titles were issued in America, of which nearly 50 per cent were reprints of books from abroad; and in the six years before Fields arrived at the Old Corner, the firm had changed hands six times. In these ways too the profession of letters in America still needed establishment.[18] Fields was the man for the job.

He was a handsome and sociable man, a good reader-aloud of poetry, and a great enthusiast for literature as a whole; he collected writers' autographs, rare books, first editions, and the like. He entertained a great deal, even before he was married; Longfellow came to his bachelor literary evenings. He had many friends with literary aspirations, including E. P. Whipple and Thomas R. Gould, and spent a lot of energy pushing and promoting their careers as well as his own. They all three joined the Mercantile Library Association, one of the self-educating institutions of Boston, founded in 1820, which every evening made available to its members its collection of books and periodicals, and frequently sponsored debates, declamations, and competitions in composition. In 1838 it held a celebration, at which Fields was the Poet, and Edward Everett, the governor of the state, was the Orator. (Since Fields was then only twenty-one, and had neither money, family, nor college education, this is an example—his friendship with Longfellow is another—of what Howells meant by the democracy of Boston literary life.) In 1848 Fields appeared at another such celebration, with Daniel Webster, an even greater figure.

With his friends at the Mercantile Library, Fields persuaded William Ticknor, who owned the Old Corner, to introduce some new British authors who were distinctively literary into its publishing venture. In 1840 the firm brought out the Smiths' *Rejected Addresses;* later de Quincey, and then Tennyson, to whom Fields gave the handsome sum of $150. It was a part of his reputation that he was generous with his authors. He was in fact 'a literary man himself'. These ventures all succeeded, and in 1843 Fields was made a junior partner in the firm, which then became the great organ of the New England Renaissance, and a major instrument of New England's cultural ascendancy.

Fields was the publisher of such American authors as Whittier, Hawthorne, Longfellow, Lowell, Holmes, Mrs Stowe, Emerson, and Thoreau; among British authors, he was the publisher of Dickens and Thackeray, Tennyson and Browning, Arnold, all the big names. He was moreover the friend, the dinner-host and guest of all these people. He gave the whole literary world the aspect of a genial dinner-party. He tried to censor the manuscripts of writers unfriendly to his authors. He refused to publish Poe because of Poe's attacks on Longfellow. When the Boston *Traveler* criticised *Hiawatha,* Fields declared it had betrayed his trust, and should have no more of his advertising (thus indiscreetly baring the ethics of contemporary book-reviewing, and provoking a scandal). He personally promoted his authors' careers. He got the British firm of Chapman and Hall to give Hawthorne $1,000 for *The Blithedale Romance.* Hawthorne's whole existence as a novelist owes much to Fields, who first had to tear the story-length manuscript of *The Scarlet Letter* from the reluctant author's hands, and then persuade him to rewrite it at novel-length. When that was a success, Fields drove his lethargic author to produce seven new books in the next three years, plus two new editions; and three of those books were novels, a form with which Hawthorne had never felt easy. William Charvat defines a cultural centre as a place where writers and readers influence each other through the medium of a publisher; by that definition it was Fields more than anyone else who made Boston a cultural centre.

When Dickens came to America in 1867, Fields was his principal host, and was agent and manager for his readings in Boston. Dickens took over $1,000,000 on the tour, and Fields' 5 per cent of the Boston takings amounted to $10,000. More important, he managed Dickens' glittering social life, offering the deserving and the friendly some appropriate measure of intimacy with the greatest literary lion of the age. He made Boston the centre of a continuous literary-social life, and established the mode of that life. With his second wife, Annie, he gave an extraordinary profusion of breakfasts, dinners, evenings, and picnics, which were largely responsible for the impression that so excited Howells and Aldrich (and indeed Twain and others), that in Boston all you needed was literary tastes to be welcomed into the most exhilarating community life. Above all, he made the literary and the social life very much the same thing.

But the social life available to an author in Boston, like the opportunities for publication there, the money he could earn, and the intercourse with other writers, were only signs of something more important, the seriousness with which the literary profession was taken there. A larger sign of that was the place assigned by agitators and statesmen like Wendell Phillips and Charles Sumner to, for instance, political poems by Lowell—a Boston author supplying Boston orators with crusading texts. (One of Lowell's poems was the text for that speech of Sumner's in the Senate which led to the savage attack on him by Preston Brooks.) Another such sign was the character of, for instance, Emerson's work. 'Days' was published in the *Atlantic;* literature in Boston, even when published in a periodical, aspired to the character of eternal truth. The writer was both the favourite son and the spokesman of the city of culture. Boston protected him from the American interrogation, and respectfully asked him for pronouncements on every kind of moral, social, and political issue. To become a writer there was to take up a very large career. And if Emerson reminds us of the heights to which it could rise, George Ticknor may be the representative of its breadth.

Chapter Four

GEORGE TICKNOR:
THE ARISTOCRAT
IN A DEMOCRACY

THE MAN we have chosen to represent literary
Boston in the first part of the nineteenth century was not an important writer, or a typical
one. He is not representative because of what he
wrote, or what he was paid for it, financially or
socially. He is representative because of the fullness and firmness with which he realized certain
ideals in that society's theory of the literary life
—ideals which reveal the breadth and scope of
that theory. He was the moralist, the humanist,
the democrat, and the statesman of cultural responsibility, in remarkably many phases of his
career and personality; and his style in all these
things was Bostonian in one of the best senses of
that word.

Although Ticknor is now only a name or less
to most people, during much of his lifetime he
was so much the social-intellectual centre of
Boston that it was said the city should be re-
named 'Ticknorville.' Of course, if we allow the
term 'Boston' to include Cambridge and Concord (as we do on the whole in this book) then
the remark loses some of its   (anyway hyper-
bolic point. But if we distinguish the city
sharply from its immediate neighbours (which
means allegorically to isolate the worldly-wise

and worldly-powerful elements in the New England character-complex), then Ticknor becomes the man to emblemize it, not merely by historical precedent, but also by poetic justice. The period from 1820 to 1865 in Boston is sometimes called its Periclean Age, and if Ticknor is more Roman than Greek, there is something genuinely classical about him.

It will perhaps be best first simply to describe him and his career. He was born in Boston in 1791 of typical New England parents. Both had taught school, but the father had become a grocer, and had quickly accumulated a modest fortune—enough to retire on early, and enough to let his son choose a literary career. George was, however, trained for the law, after his first degree at Dartmouth. He and Edward Tyrell Channing were admitted to the bar together in 1813. Both of them subsequently abandoned legal for literary studies, which was something of a pattern of the times: Prescott, Longfellow, Cogswell, Edward Everett, Alexander Everett, all followed it. The idea of the literary life was establishing itself even then in Boston, as a socially responsible career, a way to serve both the nation and one's own soul. We can see it in the 1809 Phi Beta Kappa address of Ticknor's older friend Dr Buckminster, entitled 'The Dangers and Duties of Men of Letters'.[1] This is an interesting and quite impressive expression of the mood of intellectual Boston at the beginning of our period, full of anxious idealism about the future of the infant nation, and about the role of literature in that future. America will undoubtedly become a nation great in size, he says, and within a very few decades. But would anyone now choose to have been a citizen of great Assyria? Would not everyone now choose to have been a citizen of tiny Athens? America will certainly be 'an empire unparalleled in extent', but will it be also 'a nation of men of letters'? Dr Buckminster, a pioneer Unitarian, in places foreshadows Emerson in his enthusiasm for literature. But the literature he foresees being written would not be Transcendental or Romantic in any sense. This is a Johnsonian, not an Emersonian, idea of the man of letters; and this was Ticknor's idea.

He grew up in a Federalist and Unitarian Boston, still full of pride in its role in the War of Independence, and eager to assimilate itself to classical Greek democracy. Ticknor said the town meetings during the War of 1812 were more like city meetings in Athens than anything else the world had seen. Everything was brought to the bar of public speech and public judgment; everyone was trained in oratory and the criticism of oratory. Edward Everett Hale tells us that during his boyhood, in the next generation, every Boston boy had to be ready to declaim at any family or school occasion.[2]

In 1814 the merchant Samuel Eliot gave Harvard $20,000 to found a chair in Greek. Harvard awarded the chair to Edward Everett, who was then twenty-one, and just graduating, with permission to spend two years in Europe on full salary, preparing himself. (It is gestures of this kind, like the similar appointment of Longfellow, that give us an idea of that fresh, clear atmosphere of hope and possibility.) Everett decided to go to Göttingen, and Ticknor, his friend, decided to go with him. Two sons of John Quincy Adams sailed with them, and Joseph Cogswell (later librarian at Harvard) followed them to Göttingen, as did the historian George Bancroft, in 1818. This was the very beginning of the period of influence of the German universities (before he sailed, Ticknor had great difficulty in finding the simplest German textbooks anywhere in New England), and it is interesting to see him anticipate the new century in some ways, while remaining importantly of the old.[3]

At Göttingen he maintained a severe scholarly schedule. He rose at five, studied Greek until seven thirty on three days of the week, and until eight thirty on the other three. At eight on the first three days, he did an hour's German with a teacher. At nine every day there was a lecture on the Gospels. Then a fifteen-minute walk home, and German until twelve. After dinner he took a half-hour nap, and then a cup of coffee, and at one thirty began to read Blumenbach's *Manual*, in preparation for that professor's three o'clock lecture. Then he took a walk with Everett, and at five read Greek with a teacher. From six to seven he fenced, to take care of his health. And in the evening he read German until ten and went to bed.

There was no room in that schedule for any social life, and he made no exception to it except that on Sunday evenings he went to a professor's house. This was 'the student's life' in a very different sense from the modern; a student there would get a visit from one friend once a week, Ticknor says. And this was a real deprivation to Ticknor, who possessed remarkable social gifts. (According to Maria Edgeworth, he was one of the best conversationalists in Europe. His talk was like his writing—exact, balanced, interesting, full of information, full of intellectual vigour.) In London, on his way to Germany, he had made the acquaintance of, won the friendship of, Sir Humphrey Davy and Byron, two brilliant social figures, neither of whom suffered bores kindly. It was also a real deprivation to him to be in Germany at all. He counted his years in Europe, for all their triumphs, a sacrifice.

From paintings and verbal descriptions he emerges as an agile, dark, imperious little man, with thick, curly black hair and a rich, swarthy complexion; his eyes, 'large, and so dark that they might almost be called black, were very bright and expressive'. He had, one gathers, a certain fierceness of nature, which ensured him quick, warm sympathies and antipathies, and very strong attachments to friends, family, and country. Several of his friendships were life-long. They were also, notably often, with men famous and important in their line. He had that kind of stateliness and formality which makes the constrained uneasy, but which the assured welcome as the medium of the best kind of freedom. But he had a great range of 'manners'; he travelled from Seville to Lisbon in the charge of a band of smugglers, and established his place among them. They came to accept him as a kind of leader, and he made conversation with as much profit as usual to his store of observation:

> . . . two of them were evidently men of much natural talent, and from them I gathered a pretty definite account of the principles and feelings of the fraternity, and of their political and religious principles, which were strongly marked and well accommodated to their situation.

There was also, one gathers from his enemies, a haughtiness of nature, and sharp limitations of intellectual sympathy. He never had any patience with Transcendentalism, or with abolitionism, for instance.

Theodore Parker called him 'the arch devil of the aristocracy', and clearly his was the Tory temperament in many ways. This made him seem very limited to his younger contemporaries, and to later Boston. But we are likely to disagree with their judgment, and to find his way of belonging to a democracy a particularly interesting one. In politics, for instance, he was not merely or dismissably Tory; he took the keenest interest in all the major questions, and though on slavery he tended to restrict himself to the argument that the evil was too profound to be cured by legislation, he did not get to that position by mental inertia, or allow mental inertia to proceed from it. His prophecies about the war, from twenty years before, were remarkably prescient, especially about European reaction to it.

Equally clearly, he was neither a genius nor a brilliantly intelligent man. But he was a remarkably vivid and solid human type, who took up, as of right, a lot of space wherever he lived, and who afforded shelter to a great many cleverer people under his branches; who gave body to the aspirations of his society with a personal distinction which dignified those aspirations as much as any artistic or speculative expression of them could. In 1816, still at Göttingen, Ticknor was offered the Smith Professorship of Modern Languages at Harvard (subsequently held by Longfellow and Lowell). This meant, if he took it, more years in Europe, in preparation, since Spanish was 'a new subject of study proposed to me'. So he sent his father (he was then twenty-five) two alternative replies to Harvard, one accepting and one declining the appointment, and submitted the decision to him. His father accepted for him. In 1817 he left Göttingen and went to Paris, where he became a friend of Mme de Staël and her daughter, Mme de Broglie; and of von Humboldt. From there he went to Rome, where his principal friends were the Bonapartes; there is something richly stimulating to the imagination in the thought of this very Bostonian young man in the salons of Madame Mère, Cardinal Fesch, Lucien, Prince of Canino, Louis, formerly King of Holland, and Pauline Borghese. And these were no single visits; with Lucien's family, at least, he became quite intimate. From Italy he went to Spain, from there to England and France again, and in 1819 he arrived back in Boston.

There his closest friendships were with Daniel Webster, Washington Allston, William Ellery Channing, Nathaniel Bowditch, the Everett brothers, and the Prescotts, father and son. These are rather formidable lists of celebrities, and there can be no doubt that Ticknor liked to know men of note; on the other hand, it seems clear that he liked to know them for what made them notable as much as for the fame itself, and that he managed really to like those he knew. One of the keys to his personality is a combination of the private and the public, a fusion rather than a confusion, which shows itself in, for instance, his epistolary style. His letters are not to be compared with those of Keats. On the other hand, they compare favourably with those of Shelley, because though, like the poet's, they verge on the essay form, they never affront one's sense of the simplicity due a letter. Short quotation does not do him justice, but perhaps this last point at least can be made clear by this paragraph from a letter written to Sir Edmund Head in 1861.

> But there are other things to talk about now. The heather is on fire. I never before knew what a popular excitement can be. Holiday enthusiasm I have seen often enough, and anxious crowds I remember during the war of 1812–15, but never anything like this. Indeed, here at the North, at least, there never was anything like it; for if the feeling were as deep and stern in 1775, it was by no means so intelligent or unanimous; and then the masses to be moved were as a handful compared to our dense population now.[4]

This is naturally more animated than his usual manner, but it still has his beautiful order and control, and it demonstrates the ease with which he could vary his style. It demonstrates too how he could respond to the popular mood even on an issue in which he had so long opposed it.

From his *Journal* we can take this description of the Roman Campagna.

> The heavens are of such an undisturbed and transparent blue, the sun shines with so pure and white a light, the wind blows with such soft and exhilarating freshness, and the vegetation is so rich, so wantonly luxuriant, that it seems as if nature were wooing man to

cultivation . . . But when you recollect that this serene sky and brilliant sun . . . serve only to develop the noxious qualities of the soil,
and that this air which breathes so gently is as fatal as it is balmy,
and when you look more narrowly at the luxuriant vegetation and
find it composed only of gross and lazy weeds, such as may be fitly
nourished by vapors like these,—when your eye wanders over this
strange solitude, and meets only an occasional ruin, . . . or at most,
a few miserable shepherds, hardly more civilized than Tartars, de-
crepit in youth, pale, haggard, livid, . . . it is then you feel all the
horror of the situation.[5]

This is, I think, a fair example of Ticknor's talent. It is clearly
an exercise in a well-known and slightly old-fashioned genre (it
was written in 1817)—the literary equivalent of Richard Wilson's landscape paintings. Presumably these are notes towards a
description; I reproduce the continuous text as given in the
Journal, and I presume the omissions represent erasures or trail-
ings away in the manuscript. In that case, it is an admirable
exercise in that genre; copious and precise in diction, fresh with
some genuine feeling for both the actual scene and the style of
painting; language in the act of ennobling experience.

Perhaps the best example of his fusion of the private and the
public would be one of his anecdote-portraits, like this one, written when he was twenty-four, forty-six years before the letter to
Sir Edmund Head.

But what was more to me than his table or his fortune, John Ran-
dolph is his guest for some weeks. The instant I entered the room my
eyes rested on his lean and sallow physiognomy. He was sitting, and
seemed hardly larger or taller than a boy of fifteen. He rose to receive
me as I was presented, and towered half a foot above my own height.
This disproportion arises from the singularity of his person. His head
is small, and until you approach him near enough to observe the
premature and unhealthy wrinkles that have furrowed his face, you
would say that it was boyish. But as your eye turns towards his
extremities, everything seems to be unnaturally stretched out and
protracted. To his short and meagre body are attached long legs
which, instead of diminishing, grow larger as they approach the floor,
until they end in a pair of feet, broad and large, giving his whole person the appearance of a sort of pyramid. His arms are the counterpart
of his legs; they rise from small shoulders, which seem hardly equal
to the burden, are drawn out to a disproportionate length above the

elbow, and to a still greater length below, and are at last terminated
by a hand heavy enough to have given the supernatural blow to
William of Deloraine, and by fingers which might have served as
models for those of the goblin page.

In his physiognomy there is little to please or satisfy, except an eye
which glances on all and rests on none. You observe, however, a mix-
ture of the white man and the Indian, marks of both being apparent.
His long straight hair is parted on the top, and a portion hangs down
on each side, while the rest is carelessly tied up behind and flows
down his back.

His voice is shrill and effeminate, and occasionally broken by those
tones which you sometimes hear from dwarfs or deformed people. He
spoke to me of the hospitality which he had found in Philadelphia,
and of the prospect of returning to a comfortless home, with a feeling
that brought me nearer to him for the moment; and of the illness of
his nephew Tudor, and the hopes that it had blasted, with a tender-
ness and melancholy which made me think better of his heart than I
hand before. At table he talked little, but ate and smoked a great
deal.[6]

This is skilful prose of its kind and time—the half-century
lapse between it and the first extract is nicely reflected in the
difference of rhythms and phrasing. It is also a letter equally
adapted to be read either by the recipient alone and to himself,
or aloud to a circle of interested acquaintance—as a newsletter.
This kind of integrity, admitting no radical split between public
and private experience or manner, seems to have held throughout Ticknor's personality. It is a quality we scarcely ever meet
today, and therefore never look for or aspire to. Since Romanticism, or more exactly, Romanticism-and-the-Industrial-Revolu-
tion, it has seemed that to achieve any intensity of thought in
either the public or the private sphere means at least acknowl-
edging a deep split between the two in one's approach, a schizo-
phrenia of attitude. Ticknor was in this respect an eighteenth-
century man, perhaps. But this quality was not merely quaint in
him, nor he unique in it. It was one of the manifestations of that
Boston humanism which we can learn from.

Ticknor became Smith Professor of Modern Languages at Harvard on the same day in 1819 as Andrews Norton ('the Pope of
Unitarianism') became Dexter Lecturer (later Professor) in Sacred Literature; and two years later they married Anna and

Catherine Eliot, the two daughters of that Samuel Eliot who gave the money for the chair in Greek occupied by Edward Everett. The two brothers-in-law may be taken to symbolize that part of Boston and Cambridge which set its face against Transcendentalism. This marriage brought Ticknor money enough to collect his famous library, and to entertain freely and splendidly. He and his wife bought a house on Park Street, across from the State House and overlooking the Common, and Mrs Ticknor became a social queen of Boston.

At the university, however, Ticknor met a series of severe disappointments. In the first place, after he had drawn up a fairly elaborate scheme of lectures as Professor of Modern Languages, President Kirkland told him that a good deal of the subject-matter he proposed to cover was already the prerogative of this or that other professor. And when he suggested a reorganization of the teaching (one that would have put Harvard a generation ahead of the other American colleges, and that was put into effect fifty years later) he met opposition, delays, and finally defeat. After his experience at Göttingen, he knew that Harvard was not even a bad university; what he aimed at with his reforms was making it a 'respectable high school, to which young men may be safely sent to be prepared for the study of a profession'. These proposals and criticisms are all admirably substantiated, detailed, and moderate in tone, and at least in those of his papers published, there is no embitterment at their defeat. His own lectures, though he was not in any degree an original critic, were generally admitted to be admirable teaching.

In 1835 he resigned from Harvard, and partly because of Mrs. Ticknor's health, went to Europe again. He returned in 1838, and from then on his life was divided between two major projects: the *History of Spanish Literature,* which appeared, in England and America, in 1849, and the Boston Public Library, which opened in 1854; both of these, against the practice and the advice of colleagues, he made accessible to the general reader, as well as to the specialist. Ticknor was in matters of this kind an active democrat as well as a humanist. Both these projects occupied him long after the dates mentioned, the first because of his continual revisions—a fourth edition appeared shortly after his

death—and the second because of his continual book-buying—
part of both 1856 and 1857, for instance, he spent in Europe
again at his own expense, buying in quantity. He had, too,
of course, many minor interests and duties of the Bostonian
kind. He was active in all the charities mentioned in Chapter
Two, and in advancing the Massachusetts public-school system.
He participated in the Boston tradition of giving financial help
to young men of talent (recipients ranged from Jared Sparks at
the beginning of the century to Bernard Berenson at the end); he
helped send Horatio Greenough to Italy. He was trustee and vice-
president of the Athenaeum and trustee of Agassiz's Zoological
Museum (and in both capacities he made important policy proposals). He interested himself in civil-service reform and became
a cultural elder statesman of New England; after the Prince of
Wales' visit to Boston in 1860, Ticknor's letter to Sir Edmund
Head about its results for Anglo-American relations was read to
the Queen.[7]

He died in 1871, after a singularly happy and successful life.
This is what his biographers say, and despite his disappointments
in personal and national affairs (for American development
seemed as wrong to him as to most Bostonians) the summary
carries conviction. He had the gift of good fortune and the gift of
success. He believed in the society he belonged to, as the best in
the world, with all its faults, and the duties he performed for it
were also acts of personal imagination and modes of self-
assertion. Though some of the incidents of his life would have
been, for other men, the marks and the source of misfortune, for
a man of his integrity, his blend of enthusiasm and moralism, of
forcefulness and self-discipline, of civic dutifulness and self-
assertion, they could only be the raw materials of more self, more
personality, more richness.

In the introduction to the 1909 edition of Ticknor's *Life, Letters, and Journal*, Ferris Greenslet observes that he fulfilled a
number of indestructible ideals of the literary character. In developing this point we cannot do better than follow Mr Greenslet's outline.

First of all, he says, Ticknor was America's first cosmopolitan
author:

The first to acquire in the universities of Germany the scientific method of humane learning; the first to open to American readers the books of the great cosmopolitan poets and prose-writers—Dante, Montaigne, Goethe, Cervantes, and Molière; the first to prove to the countrymen of these that a stranger from the wild lands over the sea might be a gentleman and a scholar, the peer of their ripest and best.

We must remember that the raw materials of scholarly research were in those days very hard for an American scholar to lay his hands on—a disadvantage in addition to the lack of training, co-operation from others, and a general atmosphere of understanding. Consequently, such scholarship as America had was, before Ticknor, Prescott, and a few others, literally unworthy of comparison with the scholarship of Germany. But Ticknor knew the great texts, and their backgrounds, with a thoroughness that defied every test; and his range was not limited to French and Spanish literature. In the study of Dante, for example, one of the great features of high-cultural life in nineteenth-century America, Ticknor played a key role. From 1800 to 1830, Angelina La Piana tells us, Dante studies in America were the work of cultured amateurs in Boston, Philadelphia, and New York, but between 1830 and 1900 they were a New England specialty, and of a much more scholarly nature. Ticknor contributed largely to this development. He was the first of the great Boston enthusiasts for Italy; he taught a special class in Dante at Harvard; his protégé Pietro Bachi taught Italian there and greatly helped Longfellow. One of Ticknor's best friends was Prince, later King, John of Saxony, whose Academia Dantesca was a model for the Cambridge Dante Circle.[8]

Next, he was an originator of the university idea in American education. That is, he brought back the German ideal he had found exemplified at Göttingen, saw how far short of it the American college fell, and worked out a series of proposals that would have advanced Harvard towards that ideal. Had those proposals been accepted, Samuel Eliot Morison says, Harvard would have been put a generation ahead of every other American college. They would not have made it a university completely on the German plan. Most of Ticknor's reforms, except for some purely disciplinary measures against dissipation, were intended to improve teaching and learning methods. He wanted

classes to be divided up into groups according to ability (the
whole Harvard class was then taught as a unit), the hearing of
recitations to be replaced by formal teaching, and a final examination to test what had been learned. He wanted departments of
studies, organized as a whole, and a graduate school; he wanted
the possibility of special studies for no degree, and free movement for students from school to school. He wanted vacations to
be in the summer instead of in the winter. He wanted a much
larger library. (He bought for it after he ceased to teach there.)

The resident teachers and the president worked against his
proposals, however, and such reforms as were accepted were put
into effect only in his own subjects, where they worked very well.
It is worth noting, because he has so often been categorized as
'conservative', what enthusiasm and energy he deployed in the
cause of innovation and reform. Though he was discreet, he
could also be frank about his opinions: he declared the university examinations 'a miserable farce'. Though he accepted defeat
when it came, he had fought hard, with committees and with
individuals—for instance, Andrews Norton, Edward Everett,
Jared Sparks (John Lowell the Rebel supported him)—to bring
them over to the reforms. One need only compare Ticknor with
Everett to recognize the man of integrity and energy, the truly
distinguished personality.[9]

In the third of his great achievements, the founding of the
Boston Public Library, Ticknor's work was again that of a radical innovator and democrat. On two occasions (1826 and 1853)
he tried to persuade the Athenaeum to pool all its books with
those of the smaller city libraries, to make one large collection
which would be available to all Boston. He conducted a powerful campaign to that end in 1853, but was defeated by indiscreet
triumph in the City Council and resentful Conservatism in the
Athenaeum. He had to build a new library from scratch. In 1851
Everett had given the city a thousand volumes of public documents, and Ticknor, who had long tried to organize a city library, proposed to him that they should join forces, and draw up
a report on the project that would convince the mayor of its
practicability.

Ticknor insisted that such a library should include 'new and
popular' works, available in such numbers that anyone could

borrow them, and that the great majority of the books should be freely circulated. Borrowers were to be given cards on which to suggest new books to be bought. The library was to be— otherwise he refused to work on it—dedicated to serving the less favoured classes of the community, not the scholars, the men of science, and the like. These were all new ideas. Everett did not like the idea of *any* books being freely circulated, much less most, nor the idea of 'new and popular works'.* He was still thinking in terms of public documents. But Ticknor's force of will (he was ready to do most of the work) carried the points against both Everett and the mayor. He wanted the Library to be, among other things, the crowning glory of the state school system; pupils who won Franklin medal prizes (and later pupils with good-conduct prizes) were to be allowed immediate access. Education, he felt, 'can be carried deeper in our society than in any other in the world, because we are better fitted for it'. The library was also for the glory of Boston in particular; John Jacob Astor had endowed a great library in New York, on his death in 1848, and it was feared that 'the scientific and literary culture of this part of the country would follow trade and capital to the metropolis, which was thus taking the lead'. The report (drawn up mostly by Ticknor) persuaded Joshua Bates to endow the library with $50,000, and later a lot more. Thanks to Ticknor's untiring efforts (in organization as well as book-buying) the library was a great success. By the turn of the century it was the largest free circulating library in the world, and the second largest public library in America. Ticknor gave it his own important collection of Spanish literature. It became another of the great Boston institutions which made high standards of culture available to the majority.**

* What Ticknor meant by that may be indicated by the fifty copies of Florence Nightingale's *Notes on Nursing*, twenty of Everett's *Life of Washington*, and twenty of Smiles' *Self-Help*, which he gave the library in 1860.

** Perhaps the best way to make a first acquaintance with Ticknor is to read *City Document 37—Report of the Trustees of the Public Library of the City of Boston, July 1852*. Ticknor's contribution to this is reproduced in Walter Muir Whitehill's *History of the Boston Public Library* (Cambridge, Mass., 1956), where one can also find some of Joshua Bates' letters reproduced. Bates too was a remarkable man, and the co-operation of the two is an example of Boston at its noblest.

Fourthly, he was the author of a great scholarly magnum opus, the *History of Spanish Literature*. This seems to be, as far as critical insight and intellectual approach go, a quite ordinary nineteenth-century history of literature; it sees literature as an expression of 'national character', something which blazes up or dies down in response to the country's moral vicissitudes. But it is exceptional in the thoroughness of its execution and the combined vigour and elegance of its style. It was universally praised when it was published, in all the European journals. It was soon translated into French and German and Spanish itself. At the end of the century Edward Everett Hale reported that it was still the working book of reference in the Royal Library in Madrid.[10] This is an exceptional success for a thoroughly academic piece of work, and it was due in part to the skill with which Ticknor had combined the new scientific scholarship with the old broad humanism, and made a book which the general reader, comparatively speaking, could enjoy. Coming from a Boston scholar, it gave Harvard—though Ticknor was no longer teaching there —one of its first glimpses of full status in the international academic world.

Lastly, says Mr Greenslet, Ticknor was an 'American gentleman whose whole life gave to the profession of letters a dignity which it had not hitherto attained in this country'. That dignity took too many forms to enumerate, but one of them was the level of political seriousness on which he communicated with, for instance, Sir Edmund Head, the governor general of Caradax, with his statesman friends Daniel Webster and Hugh Swinton Legaré, and with his former pupil Charles Sumner. Ticknor's professionalism in literary studies was of a kind—since he regarded them as a field for the exercise of general intellectual and moral judgment—which enabled him to move to and fro between them and his political and social interests with ever-increasing insight.

Another form of that dignity was his international friendships. That an American man of letters should be on terms of equal, and sometimes intimate, friendship with European kings, ministers, novelists, scientists, poets, scholars, and aristocrats of every kind made the literary profession important, independently of money and direct power. In England he knew Whewell and

Sedgwick at Cambridge, and in London was most often in the liberal intellectual circles of Lord and Lady Holland, Monckton Milnes, Macaulay, Sydney Smith, Grote, Jowett, Milman. In France, he was a friend not only of the de Staëls and the de Broglies, but of the Comte de Circout, an encyclopaedic scholar. In Spain, he became great friends with the French ambassador— the Duc de Laval Montmorency, the Premier Baron Chrétien— and with Cesar de Balbo, the son of the Sardinian ambassador. Montmorency was reputed to be the finest conversationalist in all Paris; and conversation then was a highly discriminated and appreciated form of literary performance, engaging considerable stores of information and powers of logic and eloquence, as well as the more limitedly social qualities of personality and manners we associate with the word. These three friends took daily rides together, engaging in the freest argument, and in their letters to Ticknor one reads real affection and respect. These are friends, as opposed to friendly acquaintances like Talleyrand, Metternich, and Guizot, with all of whom he had frank and very interesting conversations. Since he was much more fixed in his religious and moral views, much less agnostic, than, say, Barrett Wendell or Henry Adams, it is striking that it should be Ticknor who was the friend of Byron and Pauline Borghese. At the least, it constitutes a criticism of the form later Boston humanism took. More than that, it shows the freedom proper to a 'Puritan'—that is, a moralist—as much as to any man of firm beliefs, and rebukes the whining against their New England heritage of those later writers.

To these points of Mr Greenslet's one would add only that Ticknor actively embodied the literary tradition in New England by shaping the careers and personalities of his colleagues, either for others after their deaths or for themselves during their lives. His activities in this kind pale beside those of Charles Eliot Norton, but in any other contrast shine brightly. We have already mentioned his directing hand in Horatio Greenough's career. When he was only twenty-one he had the care of Dr Buckminster's papers committed to him; he was Webster's literary executor; and in the case of William H. Prescott, Ticknor not only wrote the official biography, he was responsible for beginning that whole career as historian of Spain, for procuring books and reading drafts, and for arranging the reviews of the first volumes in *The Edinburgh Review* and *The Quarterly Review*. His ideas of what was and was not worth doing by a man of letters, reached out directly into dozens of lives, and indirectly into hundreds.

Ticknor was in many ways an eighteenth-century man. Greenslet tells us that to the end of his life his salutation was, 'Your servant, sir', and there are phrases in his writing all the time which carry us back to that past. 'Mr Jefferson seems to enjoy life highly, and very rationally. . . . His house was one of the most agreeable in Philadelphia, for Mrs Hopkinson was a lady of much cultivation and knowledge of the world. . . . I walked up and down with Palfrey, but as for dancing, I could not undertake it.' These remind us that Edward Everett Hale claims to have known Jane Austen by heart as a young man, and that Josiah Quincy's daughters had obtained and treasured manuscripts of hers, having learned the taste from Chief Justice Marshall. This is eighteenth-century and Federalist Boston. Ticknor described himself as a Federalist to the end of his life, and though he became a Unitarian, he had no sympathy with any further liberalization of Christianity; nor with any hasty demands for a clash between the states over slavery. His sympathies were markedly with Webster, and on the side of preserving the political structure of union.

On the other hand, the straightforward strenuous moralism of his schedule as a student, his highly emotional patriotism, his sensibility to scenery, his Romantic enthusiasm for Webster, his energetic eagerness to reform existing institutions quite radically; these, though compatible enough with features of the eighteenth century, let us see him also as a typical son of his own age.

Later, Boston apologized for Ticknor in ways that seem to us curious and excessive. Ferris Greenslet says, 'It must be confessed that Ticknor's observation does not always penetrate to the heart, whether of men or of affairs, but when he writes of a poet or a statesman he gives us the *social* man better than almost anyone else.' What is this heart Ticknor does not reach? Some sentimental aphorism Mr Greenslet was hoping for? Something, we are bound to guess, which we no longer regard as so separate from, or so superior to, the social man. Ticknor's comment on Talleyrand, after meeting him in 1818, is psychologically acute enough.

> His recollection of all he had seen and of all the persons he had known in America seemed as distinct as if he had left the country only a few days since; and he spoke of them with a fresh and living interest that continually surprised me. I remarked, however, that if I spoke, in reply to him, of anything that had happened since to those persons, or of any change in the circumstances that were still so familiar to his thoughts, it made not the slightest impression upon him. It was only his own recollections that interested him, and the persons he had known then occupied him only as a part of himself, so that it was indifferent to him whether they were now dead or alive.[11]

One imagines Mr Greenslet liked that; but what he does not seem to have sufficiently appreciated is the clear and controlled thoughtfulness which gives such an insight its exactly calculated shape and weight and place, and which is always there even when the point is not so typically Victorian—so George Eliot-like.

The Quarterly Review, after Ticknor's death, said that his social success was due to his being 'the personification of earnestness', with no wit, humour, or vivacity. Here surely one can only disbelieve; the man who wrote that prose and maintained those friendships cannot have been lacking in wit, humour, or vivacity; though it suits one's sense of him that he should have had that 'American' manner which often deceives and irritates an Englishman by its seemingly unmodulated seriousness and explicitness, its copious flow of information, its gravity of attentiveness, its careful courtesy, its single-minded openness of expression. And when Henry Adams speaks of the blinders of the moralist in Ticknor, the literalness of the earnest scholar, and the dogmas of the conservative republican, and declares that the range of his experience and perception were sharply limited by the way he defined his role, one can only say again that what happened to the New England mind between the two avatars was a deteriora-

tion. Adams was the more intelligent man of the two, but 'the
way he defined his role'? Surely all the advantages lay with Ticknor there. What about the blinders of the immoralist? [12]

Consider Ticknor's comments on Pauline Borghese in 1818.
She was then forty-two, 'an uncommonly beautiful form and a
face still striking if not beautiful', and one of Europe's most
notorious women, notoriously luxurious in her household,
promiscuous in her relationships, immodest in her dress and conversation. Here is one of Ticknor's comments:

> On another evening she showed her jewels to four young men of us
> who happened to call on her, and I am sure I shall never forget the
> tricks and manoeuvres she played off. It is, after all, but coquetry,
> and it is possible to have but one opinion of her character; but it is
> not a vulgar coquetry, and it is the talent and skill about it which
> redeem it from ridicule, and make her a curiosity,—like Napoleon
> himself,—not respectable, to be sure, but perfect in its kind.[13]

It is not easy to imagine Henry Adams handling a comparable
experience without some terrible longueurs about the unpre-
paredness of 'the young man from Boston', and the strides his
moral education made in those few minutes, and the extent to
which his contemporaries would have been confounded had they
known. Or remember Hawthorne, morally baffled by statues in
the nude, and blaming Boston's provincialism on the nearness of
the Puritan heritage; that heritage was nearer for Ticknor, both
in date and in theology, but he found it no problem. Mme de
Tatistcheff, wife of the Russian ambassador in Madrid, did 'attitudes', like Lady Hamilton: Guercino's Penitent Magdalen,
Raphael's St Cecilia, Domenichino's Sybil; an entertainment,
one imagines, as far from the Bostonian norm as could well be
devised. Ticknor described her performance as 'among the most
striking pleasures I have enjoyed in Europe'. For him there was
no crucial opposition between Europe and America to inhibit
such pleasures, and if later Americans found there was, it was not
something they were bound to 'inherit'.

In Chapter 13 of *Home as Found*, Cooper has this paragraph.

> Eve actually fancied that the position of an American gentleman
> might really become, nay, that it *ought* to be the highest of all human

stations short of that of sovereigns. Such a man had no superior, with
the exception of those who actually ruled, in her eyes, and this fact,
she conceived, rendered him more than noble, as nobility is usually
graduated. She had been accustomed to seeing her father and John
Effingham moving in the best circles of Europe, respected for their
information and independence, undistinguished by their manners,
admired for their personal appearance, manly, courteous, and of noble
bearing and principle, if not set apart from the rest of mankind by an
arbitrary rule connected with rank. Rich, and possessing all the habits
that properly mark refinement, of gentle extraction, of liberal attain-
ments, walking abroad in the dignity of manhood, and with none
between them and the Deity, Eve had learned to regard the gentlemen of her race as the equals in station of any of their European
associates, and as the superiors of most, in everything that is necessary
to true distinction.

That paragraph is enough to remind us of all the ways in which
Cooper himself was, in his behaviour, in his career, in his books,
and in his beliefs, the American gentleman he describes there.
And we agree with Marius Bewley when he tells us, after quoting
that paragraph, how important such an idea is to any American
who believes in both democracy and personal distinction.[14] It
was a bitter usurpation that made not Cooper but Washington
Irving ('dear and good Washington Irving,' as Thackeray said,
'gentle, generous, affectionate, self-denying . . .') the type of the
American gentleman.* Cooper certainly takes precedence over
Irving; and is, as we look for our patrons and predecessors in the
democratic dilemma, an attractive candidate from several points
of view; but there is a certain ineffectuality about him, too. His
enthusiasm for Jackson, 'the old Roman, the old hero, old hick-
ory', who will save the old Republic from the Bank, surely strikes
us as being just as Romantic in politics as his endless furious
lawsuits were in social life, or, in the world of fiction, his picture
of Effingham marrying Effingham. Surely Ticknor (just as much
the American gentleman personally) was doing more to work out
that idea in practical detail and for the future and in relation to
some conceivable American society? The course of American his-

* 'A delightful example of complete gentlemanhood', even though—as
Thackeray artlessly rehminds us—'born in no very high sphere'. And 'the
first Ambassador from the New World of Letters to the Old', another role
Ticknor played much better.[15]

tory cheated Ticknor, as it cheated Boston, of the practical effects his efforts deserved, but there is no need for us to compound the injustice by denying them the power over our imaginations they still deserve. The preference for Cooper is surely as Romantic as Cooper's own politics. Ticknor simply, soberly, sensibly, *was* the American gentleman.

Cooper's quoted description fits him very well, and we have seen how exactly that phrase, 'American gentleman', came to Ferris Greenslet's mind when he tried to explain Ticknor's achievement. Ticknor's own ideas of this kind were radically American. Here is part of his report of a conversation with the grand duke of Tuscany in 1836:

> He asked me where I thought it the greatest fortune for a man to be born. I told him in America. He asked why. And when I replied, that the mass of the community there, by being occupied about the affairs of the state, instead of being confined, as they are elsewhere, to the mere drudgery of earning their own subsistence, are more truly men, and that it is more agreeable and elevating to live among them, he blushed a little, but made no answer.[16]

And in the next year we find him writing similarly to R. H. Dana, a really Europeanized Bostonian. Dana had asked if Ticknor could give him some news of Europe to comfort an old Tory. 'I cannot,' replied Ticknor.

> In the United States we have the opposite defects; but I greatly prefer them. We have the great basis of purity in our domestic life and relations, which is broadly wanting here. We have men in the less favored portions of society, who have so much more intellect, will, and knowledge, that, compared with similar classes here, those I am among seem of an inferior order in creation. Indeed, taken as a general remark, a man is much more truly a *man* with us than he is elsewhere; and notwithstanding the faults that freedom brings out in him, it is much more gratifying and satisfying to the mind, the affections, the soul, to live in our state of society, than in any I know of on this side of the Atlantic.[17]

This belief remained vigorous in him throughout his life, and the idea of the American gentleman and the American man of letters which he realized was the result of integrating that belief with his enthusiasm for personal distinction. That idea was not unlike Cooper's; both men seem eighteenth-century to us, because in the nineteenth century no voice dared call so clearly for aristocracy of personality. But surely Ticknor did more for that idea, relating it to the conditions of nineteenth-century life and letters, by his work at Harvard, in the Boston Public Library, on the *History of Spanish Literature,* and by his personal influence, than Cooper did by his lawsuits, his Effingham romances, and his pamphlets for Jackson?

And surely Ticknor was able to do more just because he was a Bostonian, because of the corpus of institutions and associations that made up that city, and did not make up the New York of Cooper, or the Charleston of Ticknor's friend Hugh Swinton Legaré. Because in Boston there could occur such bequests as that of Samuel Eliot, in 1820, to John Lowell the Rebel, another of Ticknor's friends.[18]

> I give to my dear friend John Lowell Esquire of Roxbury Eight thousand dollars, in case of his decease before me, which God forbid, I give the same sum to his son John Amory Lowell. With Mr Lowell I have had a long Friendship and I thank God for the great Blessing. This gentleman has been the eminent friend of his country and of every good man. Witness his labours for the public as evinced by several able Judicious and luminous Pamphlets and many other Publick Writings. Consider him in the Corporation of Harvard University, in the Agricultural Society, in the Establishment of the General Hospital, and that excellent institution the Savings Bank, and in one word wherever good is to be performed there you will Constantly find Mr Lowell exerting his strong mind and not sparing the most Laborious Services.*

Men like this and like Joshua Bates, meeting each other in these activities, treating each other in this liberal style, formed the natural, necessary setting for George Ticknor, and he is the natural, necessary emblem of this attempt at a responsible society. That attempt did not succeed, and even during its best years there were gross failures in social justice, personal morality, intel-

* It is fitting that this will, disposing of a million dollars in twenty closely written pages, was a model of its kind, and after it was probated members of the bar requested copies to use as patterns.

lectual vigor. Ticknor himself was not, by international standards, a great man, even among men of letters. But it was an
attempt—and that it failed can seem the point about it only to a
perverse sensibility—to establish a decent society in which a man
of letters could feel himself fully a citizen—both as democrat and
as aristocrat. For Ticknor's aristocracy was no merely external or
merely personal attribute; it derived just from his literariness, in
a society which so looked up to its men of letters, and gave them
so many kinds of responsibility. The Gilded Age brought a sharp
decline in the standards of that society, a cruel contraction in its
idealism, and if we identify the city of culture only with Fields
and the Saturday Club, we shall be tempted to dismiss that culture as at best genteel. But there was another, better Boston
behind that, to be identified with Ticknor and the great institutions—the moralist, humanist, democrat, *responsible* Boston—
and if we look for that even in the Gilded Age, we shall find it
there.

Chapter Five

THE GILDED AGE
IN BOSTON

THE HIGH-CULTURAL climate of Boston after the
Civil War has been described in a number of
epithets, as the New England Indian Summer,
and the Golden Age of Harvard Yard, as well as
the Gilded Age and the Silver Age. Put these together, and, what they have in common is a sense
of serenity and autumnal splendour, of richness
and dangerous ripeness, of decay gaudily plated
over. Where they differ is in their evaluation of
the precious metals employed.

Strictly speaking, perhaps, the Gilded Age
never happened in our Boston. The grosser scan-
dals of Washington and New York were not re-
duplicated there, that is, and such as there were,
were not the responsibility of Yankees. All city
politics had been taken out of the hands of the
old Bostonians by the Irish pretty completely.
The humiliations imposed on Henry Adams' eld-
est brother, John Quincy Adams II, are sufficient
proof of that. The Boston we have been discussing had been squeezed out of all direct political
power; and corrupt use of political power is
surely essential to the idea of 'the Gilded Age'.
Thus when Lincoln Steffens muck-raked Boston,
as he reports in his autobiography, it was Irish
bosses and ward-heelers he had to see, not Yankees. The power of the West, crushing that of
New England in the nation's scale of importance,

and the power of the immigrants, squeezing the Yankees out from within, had killed the old Boston politically, and thus maimed it culturally.

The immigrants were not only Irish, of course, but as elsewhere in America, they delivered their votes to Irish-dominated party machines. In 1900, 35 per cent of the city's inhabitants were foreign-born, and over 70 per cent were of foreign parentage.[1] But there is no point in using the term 'Boston' to include all the communities that then lived in the city; from our point of view, they never made one community, because they never made one culture. The Yankee cultural institutions struggled on, opening their doors to all Bostonians in theory, but it became clear that very few of the 35 per cent (Bernard Berenson was one of the exceptions), few even of the 70 per cent, could or would accept their invitation.

The Yankees were more than ever benefiting financially, and deteriorating culturally, from the new prosperity of the nation as a whole, and from the over-brimming labour market in Boston in particular. The contrast between rich and poor, the conflict between Anglo-Protestant and Irish Catholic, became much sharper than before. The Yankees found themselves taking up a stance more and more simply over-privileged, reactionary, on the defensive, withdrawn.

And there were some distinctively Gilded Age developments. The city did not remain, materially, a patchwork of the old Boston and the new slums. As a result of the draining of the Back Bay, 1856–86, and even more as a result of the great fire of 1872, Boston was extended and rebuilt on a grander, more metropolitan, more plutocratic scale. The classical Bulfinch State House was dwarfed by new and unclassical buildings. With plutocracy came vulgarity, in Boston as elsewhere. In 1869 the National Peace Jubilee was held in a temporary coliseum in what was to be Copley Square. The Anvil Chorus from *Il Trovatore* was performed by ten thousand singers, a thousand musicians, a hundred firemen beating anvils with sledge hammers, climaxed by cannon that were fired by electric control from the platform. John S. Dwight, Boston's Yankee music critic, left town for the occasion. That is the symbol, and the setting, of Boston culture in the Gilded Age, 'culture' meaning the whole way of life of the community.

However, in the narrower sense of the word (the art, entertainment, and learning of the community, seen in its generally educational aspect) the Yankees did not merely retreat before the conditions of the Gilded Age. They fought a vigorous rear-guard action; they even advanced and won ground.

Richard Hofstadter says, describing all American society at this time,

> What was left was a gentlemanly class with considerable wealth, leisure, and culture, but with relatively little power or influence. This class was the public and patron of serious writing and of cultural institutions. . . . It developed its own gentle tradition of social protest. . . . But if one thinks of this class as having inherited the austere traditions of the older republican order, the traditions crystallized by the Founding Fathers, one sees immediately the relative weakness of a type that kept the manners and aspirations and prejudices of an aristocratic class without being able to retain its authority. . . . [It] inherited from the Puritans a certain solemnity and high intent, but was unable to sustain their passion. From the Founding Fathers . . . a set of intellectual commitments and civic concerns. In the mugwump ambience, however, the intellectual virtues of the 18th century type dwindled and dried up, very largely because mugwump thinkers were too commonly deprived of the occasion to bring these virtues into any intimate or organic relation with experience.[2]

Let us repeat that this is largely our own argument, though it seems worth making one or two suggestions in qualification. The extent to which the Yankee found himself excluded from politics is vividly illustrated by an anecdote given earlier in the same book. In 1868 R. H. Dana (the friend of Ticknor, Sumner, Charles Francis Adams) ran for political office against Benjamin F. Butler, already 'a symbol of cynicism in politics'. (While military governor of New Orleans during the War, he was said to have made $80,000 for himself out of one bank alone.) To people thinking in terms of moral responsibility in politics, the election was a classic 'contest between the intelligent, sober-minded, reflective men of the district, and the unthinking, reckless, boisterous, don't-care-a-damnative portion of the community'. This was the judgment of *The New York Times,* and within Yankee Boston of course that feeling was stronger. But Dana got under 10 per cent of the votes; and Butler owed his success to the forces he was running against. He was able to present himself as the defier of Harvard and the Yankees; he was able to move audiences on to his side by the sneer that Dana wore white gloves.[3]

However, one of the qualifications to make is that in Boston at least the traditions of political responsibility did not entirely die. In *Cheerful Yesterdays* T. W. Higginson says it was a myth that all the scholarly men in New England withdrew from public service. Looking back (in 1900) over fifty years, he declares that he cannot find five years when he was not working for either state or city: and he did not feel unique. Popular hostility to educated men on the hustings only became significant, he thinks, when it was evoked by a rival candidate, usually a renegade gentleman himself.

Also, it was possible for the Yankee political tradition to be followed in an anti-plutocratic, indeed an anti-conservative direction. Parrington says one can find all of Marx in Wendell Phillips' speeches during his labour-reform period of the sixties and seventies; but Phillips was appealing very insistently to a New England tradition.

> What we need is an equalization of property. . . . My ideal of a civilization is a very high one; but the approach to it is a New England town of some two thousand inhabitants, with no rich man and no poor man in it, all mingling in the same society, every child at the same school, no poorhouse, no beggar, opportunities equal, nobody too proud to stand aloof, nobody too humble to be shut out [*sic*]. That's New England as it was fifty years ago.[4]

Phillips was hardly a full member of Yankee society by then, but Edward Everett Hale too came to denounce laissez-faire in favour of a kind of communism.

More importantly, the largest section of the Progressive leadership across the nation, as Hofstadter himself points out in *The Age of Reform*, were Mugwump types, socially and intellectually. And the Mugwumps were Bostonian, by ideal and sympathy when they weren't by race. 'Their conception of statecraft was set by the high example of the Founding Fathers, or by the great debating statesmen of the Silver Age, Webster, Sumner, Everett, Clay, and Calhoun.' If there had been no Boston, there could have been no Mugwumps. And but for that saving remnant of the nation in the Gilded Age—whose president was Cleveland, whose election cry was tariff reform, whose spokesman was Godkin in *The Nation*—an essential element in the American political tradition would have been lost.[5]

Godkin, himself British, and sponsored by New England, preached consistently throughout the period the Boston doctrine that the educated classes should take part in the government of the country. His magazine was founded in 1865 (due largely to the efforts of Charles Eliot Norton) with specific ambitions to promote the reconstruction of the South—it inherited the mantle of Garrison's *Liberator*. Most of the New England intelligentsia wrote for it: Norton, Lowell, Curtis, William James, Henry James Sr, Henry James Jr; and liberal Englishmen like Stephen, Dicey, and Bryce. The voice of the Boston tradition—its 'set of intellectual commitments and civic concerns'—was not lost; it was transferred to New York.

And but for the Mugwumps, there would have been no Progressive movement, as we know it. The greatest of the Progressive leaders drew heavily on the Boston tradition. Theodore Roosevelt through his friends, like Henry Cabot Lodge; Woodrow Wilson through his theory of American politics, which assimilated them to the British. This is more than 'its own gentle tradition of social protest'. Where would the whole reform movement in American politics have been without it? Boston's civic concerns had not wholly 'dried up'; displaced from the power-centres of their city they had partly redirected themselves to federal matters.

Another of the qualifications it seems worth making relates to the 'purely cultural activities'. To be the 'public and patron of serious writing and of cultural institutions' meant more in Boston than elsewhere, and more than the phrase by itself suggests. It was not a matter of renewing one's ticket for Symphony. Symphony had to be created first. Harvard and the General Hospital had to grow and change enormously, to become as important as they did. A great deal more than 'relatively little power or influence', was exerted and expended in making such things happen. The organization of high-cultural life in Boston had always tended to overshadow politics on the one hand, and literature itself as an art on the other; and in the period after the war this became even more true. This was the mark of the Gilded Age in Boston, the organization and engineering of a high culture whose major forms or achievements belonged to the past, the mediation and socialization of the arts in forms guaranteed to adorn without endangering. The older, Periclean Boston, had not dealt in anti-social literature, but in the new Boston literature had to be pro-social. There had never been any danger that it would subvert the reader's mind; now it was guaranteed not to absorb it, not to rival common-sense interests and activities.

It may seem a paradox that this was also the period of the Boston aesthetes; but both these facts are in parallel relation to the dominant fact of plutocracy. A society which loses faith in its power to realize values in itself—to *be* valuable—tends to create an antithesis for its members between the arts, where values reside, and reality, where they do not. It forces its members to choose either one or the other. If the first, then it must accept the fact that all political and social reality will seem to them a bit dirty, unsatisfying, profoundly alien; they will become to some degree aesthetes. If the second, it must accept the fact that all ambitious art will seem to them too highbrow, socially exclusive, and morally dangerous; they will become to some degree philistines. The only kinds of art they feel comfortable with will be easy, safe, tame kinds.*

But in Boston, because of the powerful old tradition of 'culture', this alternative seemed less obligatory than it did in the rest of America. It seemed possible to have things both ways. While what now struck the taste of educated Bostonians as beautiful and valuable had changed like the equivalent for other people—it was now more obscure, learned, expensive art, out of ordinary reach, and out of relation to moral or social reality—

* This analysis is of course highly schematic. The form the alternative will take in a particular society will depend on quite other factors, too; in this case, for instance, the enormous increase in personal fortunes, and in reckless speculation, and in exploited immigration—the enormous gap between the rich and poor.

they still insisted on offering that to the whole community as educationally valuable, in the way they had offered Wordsworth, Carlyle, and Emerson. Indeed, this work of organization and engineering engaged very powerful energies and even passionate commitments; the idea of culture swelled as it grew emptier, acquiring even more charisma as a symbol while its content as an experience lost the old firmness and fullness. People were even more determined than before to be cultured; even while contemporary European literature was getting beyond them, as was contemporary science. One might say that instead of having it both ways, they had it neither—aesthetes and philistines were reduced to a common poverty of response to the liveliest manifestations of the contemporary mind. But the less intellectual and less morally risky areas of high culture, above all the more colourful and aesthetic, were cultivated with great enthusiasm. In a vaguer sense of 'culture' this was a period of remarkable achievements in Boston.

For instance, there was Henry Lee Higginson's creation, the Boston Symphony Orchestra. There had been music societies in Boston before; one commissioned an oratorio from Beethoven in 1823, though it never got written. But there had never been a full-scale orchestra permanently based there, with musicians who were employed full time—who belonged to the orchestra. Higginson's immediate predecessor and master was John Sullivan Dwight, a Brook Farmer and writer for *The Dial* in its day, whose Harvard Music Association gave concerts between 1866 and 1883, and whose *Journal of Music* published Boston's best criticism between 1852 and 1881.[6]

Higginson himself was born in 1834 and died in 1919. He belonged to one of the old Yankee families, was a friend of the others, and was very conscious of his role as a defender of old values. During his youth he hoped to become a composer or a pianist, which was not a typical Boston ambition. But in his remarkably interesting letters to his father, one can see the typical Boston form that ambition took in his mind.

> As everyone has some particular object of supreme interest to himself, so I have music. It is almost my inner world; without it, I miss much, and with it I am happier and better. . . .

You will ask, 'What is to come of it all if successful?' I do not know. But this is clear. I have then improved my own powers, which is every man's duty. I have a resource to which I can always turn with delight, however the world may go with me. I am so much the stronger, the wider, the wiser, the better for my duties in life. I can then go with satisfaction to my business, knowing my resource at the end of the day. It is already made, and has only to be used and it will grow. Finally it is my province in education, and having cultivated myself in it, I am fully prepared to teach others in it. *Education* is the object of man, and it seems to me the duty of all of us to help in it, each according to his means and in his sphere. . . . But I entirely disavow any such intention or aim in my present endeavour—and this I wish to be most clearly expressed and understood, should anyone ask about me. *I am studying for my own good and pleasure.* . . . I am only carrying out your own darling idea of making an imperishable capital in education. . . .

What is money good for, if not to spend for one's friends and to help them? You've done so all your life—let me do so while I can, for it is in me (I have always known it) to be a close man, a miser. I know about this.

He wrote that in 1857, when twenty-three, while studying in Vienna for a second time, after a period in a Boston counting-house. He suffered from the headaches and other aches so common among the Yankees, and on one occasion, having had eight ounces of blood drawn from his arm to cure a headache, he continued his schedule of practicing too rigorously, and lamed himself. He had to give up his hopes of becoming a pianist.

In Higginson we have that figure rarely met, though often referred to, the true Boston Puritan; the figure which so interested, for instance, Santayana. The idea of education expressed in his letter ('education is the object of man') is a central tenet of the Bostonian philosophy, and its nearest approach to Puritanism in any valid sense. But detached as it is from any theological or metaphysical creed, this is more a matter of temperament than of philosophy in any sense. Boston offered its citizens (among other things) a tradition of personality-style in which powerful forces of will and intellect were harnessed to firmly moral purposes. This is as far as one can go towards assimilating the city to 'the Puritan community' or 'Puritanism', and such a tradition is surely a more normal development of man's social potentialities than such terms suggest. History is full of similar traditions, and, even more strikingly, the historian's mind most naturally expects them—though it expects other things, too, of course. It is mere perversity to talk as if such traditions were unnatural and barely comprehensible oddities, and the rest of history offered us only the various combinations of epicurean amoralism and strenuous immorality.

Higginson came home in 1860, having given up music, rose to be a major in the Civil War, tried cotton planting with freedmen in the South, came to the Boston banking firm of Lee, Higginson, and Company, and by 1881 was worth $750,000. In that year he made his plan for an orchestra, to consist of sixty members, all of whose working time he would command. He allowed for a salary of $1,500 for each of them, $3,000 for the conductor, and $7,000 more for concert-masters, soloists, and so on; $100,000 a year as a whole. He counted on $50,000 a year in receipts (tickets at night to be 50 cents each, in the afternoon, 25 cents) and undertook to make up the other $50,000 a year himself, for as long as the orchestra should exist. It was a god-like act; he not only created but sustained in being this world of music, for the aesthetic delight and moral improvement of his city. The two effects would be one: the high art would uplift ethically too; he would ensure it. 'But of course anything *unworthy* is to be shut out' of the programmes.

The note of that 'unworthy' is significantly different from that of, for instance, the charming comments ascribed to the Transcendentalists fifty years before on Fanny Elssler's dancing: 'Waldo, this is poetry'; 'Margaret, it is religion'. Though Emerson worried about the ballet's effect on college students, he decided, characteristically, that such problems were for the individual to decide. Ethically anxious, sometimes a bit absurd, often a bit provincial, they were still not cultural policemen in the sense that Major Higginson was—and that even Charles Eliot Norton was. In that sad story of the MacMonnies 'Bacchante', Norton, the professional aesthete, played a quite ignominious role. This conventional fountain sculpture, given by Charles McKim to the Boston Public Library in 1896, was judged 'inappropriate for public exhibition' by a committee on which Norton served. The gift was in effect rejected, and Norton was one of the members most firmly against it. Yankee responsibility had by this date somehow joined forces with the Irish philistinism of the Boston papers, which were bitter against the sculpture. Even Henry Adams—emancipated from more prejudices than any other two men were ever enchained to—was similarly prudish about contemporary personalities like Sarah Bernhardt and Oscar Wilde and Lily Langtry; more prudish, in effect, than Margaret Fuller and George Ticknor.

The symphony orchestra was a great success. The deficit never rose above $52,000. This Higginson was always able to meet, though he was close to bankruptcy on more than one occasion; including his eightieth year, when his brother took over the deficit. The risks that were run, the efforts that were made (one thinks of Mrs Gardner living on porridge) should not be forgotten behind the imperturbable façade of the institutions thus created.

Major Higginson was a notable figure in other sides of Boston life. He gave Harvard Soldiers Field, in memory of the war dead, and the Students' Union, in order to restore some democracy to college life. He prevented the election of Theodore Roosevelt as president of the university in 1909. He gave free advice to the federal government. His stiff-backed autocracy and social frigidity seemed the epitome of the old Boston manner. But he considered himself to have much in common with as dissimilar a figure as Mrs Gardner; and his orchestra with her Fenway Court. In 1908 he wrote to her,

Jack, you, and I have held the same view of life and its duties, and in doing so may have forgotten *the* painful subject—one's self. It was the natural result. You have conceived nobly and have lived beyond your conception—of beauty and duty. Clearly it was your dream, and Jack helped you as he could. To our country full of life and enterprise what dream could have accomplished more?

Fenway Court had been opened to the public in 1903, at a fee of a dollar per person. All Boston society had already been led through that extraordinary collection of *objets d'art* and curiosities, that extraordinary blend of art collector's and interior decorator's taste. It was of course more than that. Fenway Court had its concerts, with great soloists, small operas and ballets, dancers like Ruth St Denis, star pianists; Sargent had a studio there; many young men in the arts were patronized. Above all, it was, as it seemed to Boston, a cultural, indeed a moral, achievement. In 1909 Henry Lee Higginson presented Mrs Gardner with a book put together for her by her admirers, thanking her.

> You have conceived and built a beautiful house and have filled it with treasures of art. To this end you have worked with untiring energy and love of your task, a task involving ungrudging self-denial.[7]

Mrs Gardner was not someone we can take as seriously as, say, Ticknor, or even Higginson, because of the large admixture of coquetry, vanity, and sheer frivolity, which we see in her motives. But those motives belonged substantially also to the great Bostonian traditions, and her contemporaries always spoke of her achievement in that vocabulary. Their tributes ring a little false in our ears; they seem to have been exacted from them by her queenliness, and that vocabulary has sometimes the humiliated air of being a convention of praise, but once that is granted, something else remains solid.

We have already quoted Barrett Wendell's letter to Mrs Gardner, in Chapter One. William James wrote, after his first view of the house,

> It was a very extraordinary and wonderful moral influence—expected by nobody, not designed, I am sure, by you, but felt, I am confident, by everyone today.

And Henry Adams,

> As long as such work can be done, I will not despair of our age, though I do not think anyone else could have done it. You stand quite alone. Only I must admit that no-one else has ever done it before you, though many have tried. If I were obliged to treat it like the scientific gentlemen of our world who preach evolution, I should have to say that your work must be classed as *tour-de-force*—no Evolution at all—but pure Special Creation in an adverse environment. You are a creator, and stand alone.

Mrs Gardner's achievement was like Major Higginson's, and unlike the institutions of earlier Boston, in bearing the marks of plutocracy, and a plutocratic culture. Both were the work of millionaires and of autocrats; both were single enormous foundations, with no quality of co-operation, much less of a whole community being involved in their development. There was a corresponding difference in the kind of art they served, which cost a great deal of money, and could only exist in great halls; could not be taken, like a book, into each man's home. Mrs Gardner's pictures and Major Higginson's soloists cost thousands of dollars. That was a large fact about them. And this was the period also of the foundation of the Boston Opera (1908) and of the Museum of Fine Arts (1870). This was luxury art, and it was also interpretive and executant art, rather than the art of composition. It was the composers, above all the writers, earlier Boston had been interested in. Their work is much more easily assimilated to acts of moral and spiritual education. Now the focus was on actors, dancers, violinists, art-critics, collectors. This made much more prominent all the sub-feverish excitements of virtuosi and connoisseurship in the arts. This was an art for which one had to dress up. But it was still also an art cultivated and recommended for the sake of the social-moral effects it would have, however vague the theory of those effects had become. Boston was still the city of culture.

Of course literature was still being written in New England during the Gilded Age. It was the period of nearly all the big names, when the thought of Boston literary society really frightened a Westerner like Mark Twain. Literature was in fact the most revered of all the arts, and the work of the New England poets was still theoretically accorded cultural primacy, but one feels less conviction in the reverence as the period progresses. Reading poems (in English at least) could not become as exotic as the appreciation of operas, or the comparison of cathedrals, in which the aesthetes now delighted. It became instead the prime example of the easy, safe, tame art with which the philistines felt comfortable.

The literary limits of the period we might identify with those of Eliot's presidency of Harvard, 1869–1909. There is no point, with our focus of interest, in quarrelling over the later limit, the point at which the Gilded Age in literature turned into the equivalent of the Age of Reform. If that equivalent was realism, its effect on Boston was minor, and not worth tracing. In literature the really new era began in 1917, and in some sense it never reached Boston. That is, Boston as a coherent cultural entity, a significant autonomous centre of culture, had disintegrated before the new movement could reach it.

Or perhaps a better unit would be forty-eight years of *The Atlantic Monthly,* between 1861, when Fields became editor, and 1909, when Ellery Sedgwick came from New York and bought it. Here both the limits may seem artificial, since the magazine was not so different, either before, under Lowell, the first editor, or after, under Sedgwick, who was himself a New Englander and a nephew of Professor Child's. But the magazine under Fields stood closer than Harvard did to what got written and read, and its tone more and more imposed itself on books not intended for publication in it.

We have already discussed some of the ways the *Atlantic* treated its writers, and therefore, some of the crucial conditions of Boston literary life in the Gilded Age, in Chapter Three, 'Boston: The City of Literature'. A representative portion of the serious writing of the time is to be found in the magazine, but what was published there was more representative and more serious in the early years. There was much Emerson, prose and verse, then, and Lowell, Longfellow, Whittier, Motley, and Holmes; in those days, moreover, Emerson was still thought a heretic, and Holmes was severely attacked in the religious press. During the war, there was more of Edward Everett Hale ('The Man Without a Country') and Julia Ward Howe ('The Battle Hymn of the Republic') than of Emerson. In 1870 Bret Harte was given $10,000 for whatever he wrote during the next twelve months, and in 1875 Twain's *Old Times on the Mississippi* was serialized. In the eighties James' and Howells' stories and serialized novels may be taken to represent something more Bostonian; but in 1891 Sarah Orne Jewett's 'Country of the Pointed Firs' shows symbolically how far the *Atlantic* was from realism as other parts of America understood it. The muck-raking articles were mostly written for New York magazines, and the realism of Howells' and John W. de Forest's serials has some air of being a compromise with that rawer, rougher literary movement centred round Chicago and New York. Vitality the *Atlantic* preferred to get from Westerners like Twain and Harte, or Britishers like Kipling and Stevenson.[8]

One chooses the *Atlantic* under Fields as an emblem, because his 'gentle spirit' and 'delightful humour', his 'fun and chaff and story', came to set the note for so much of Boston literature. Fields directed not merely his magazine, but the literary life of its contributors, who constituted literary Boston, and unfortunately he was inadequate to that position. That is, he directed the social manifestations of that life, and these came to be more and more important, to make their influence more and more felt on the essays, poems, and stories that got written afterwards in the locked and solitary studies.

The literary work of Boston in this period is notable for a manner which engages the reader in a chatty discussion of the story or scene or character, comparing it to parallel things in previous books, and hinting (often explicitly stating) that this is no more real than they were. This manner is also to be found outside Boston literature—in Thackeray, for example—but it specially characterizes these writers. Literary subjects are thereby reduced to the status of legends, neither true nor untrue, and the work of the poet or novelist is assimilated to that of the antiquarian scholar. Indeed, legends in the more ordinary sense are the material of most typical Saturday Club novels, from *The Scarlet Letter* to *Elsie Venner,* and poems, from *The Vision of Sir Launfal* to *Christus.* It is therefore typical of this work that the supernatural is always being evoked and then evaded. Hawthorne and Lowell are perhaps the worst offenders in this way, but the case of Dr Holmes is the more striking because the habit contrasts so sharply with his positivist temperament. It is more clearly something he acquired from the group he belonged to, not evolved from inside himself. In such work the course of the narrative and the consistency of the illusion are always being interrupted by, sacrificed to, minor anecdotes, moralizing reflections, humorous passages, references to other books, which the writer can discuss with the reader as fellow club-members, can handle with more ease than he can the main subject. Longfellow's two pieces of fiction, *Hyperion* and *Kavanagh,* may stand as examples of all this. These habits, which between them ruin so much of the work of these authors, derive from their desire to remain on dinner-table terms with their readers. They dare not jeopardize their geniality by asking their readers to take them on any other terms—as artists, for example. Their literary aspirations are brow-beaten by their social consciences, which ever quiver in response to the decorum of Saturday Club dinners.

The literary society Twain found when he came to Boston (so important to him, to Howells, to everyone) was much more the work of Fields than of Ticknor, or of any mythical Puritans. As for Emerson, he was absorbed into Fields' ambience. But as poet, essayist, critic, *intelligence,* Fields was insignificant.* As a literary figure, therefore, he was in the important sense a fraud. And yet it was to his level that the company of fireside poets assimilated themselves. Whereas Phillips (the publisher who first projected the *Atlantic*) had written home to his family in great exultation of the dinner at which *he* had sat down with Emerson and Lowell, Fields had them constantly round his table.

He was perfectly amiable; he was indeed what they said, an energetically 'good fellow'; and since each of them suspected himself of not being one, and beat his secret breast in grief at the thought, they submitted to him as to a leader. Hence all those dinners at which these sage and saintly men capped each other's puns, and laughed till their sides ached, and pretended afterwards to have got drunk. It is worth noting that Ticknor had nothing to do with all this, during the fourteen years of his life after the magazine began. He neither wrote for the *Atlantic* nor sat joking with the others at the festive board. He preferred to stay home and write letters to Sir Edmund Head; and one must say one sees his point. (Ticknor never belonged to a club in his life until he was nearly seventy; and he made only one after-dinner speech, when he was forced to. But it was he, not Emer-

---

* To put the record of Fields' activities and acquaintances in Europe beside Ticknor's is to demonstrate the validity of this way of judging a man; the first-rate quality stands away from the third-rate unmistakably.

son, who was good at social life.)

Fields' principal friends were Hawthorne and Longfellow. In 1862 Hawthorne proposed him as a member of the Saturday Club, saying, 'There is no better fellow'. Among so many intellectuals, he added, 'there should be interposed a genial and kindly nature'. One has not read many volumes by Saturday Club authors, however, before one is longing for something (something intellectual would be fine) to interpose between so many genialities. Fields' Old Corner Bookshop, and the offices of the *Atlantic,* and later his Charles Street home, were the scenes of innumerable social gatherings; there were endless dinners, breakfasts, evenings, and above all clubs, at which light verse, after-dinner speeches, humorous anecdotes, dialect poems, epigrams, puns, and above all, jokes filled the air for hours at a time. It was as good fellows, members of a goodly literary fellowship, that these men most wanted to be remembered; and they counted that evening lost from which they did not return with the tears of laughter streaming down their beards.

How this worked as a system of literary training one can see clearly enough in Howells' *Literary Friends and Acquaintances,* where he describes his first visit to Boston, his breathless excitement at the literary life he saw there, and his initiatory dinner with Holmes, Lowell, and Fields. He quite openly offered himself as an apprentice—to this whole life—and they quite openly looked him over. He let them know his ardent desire to write, and to write in Boston, and to learn everything they had to teach him.

Holmes said, with a laughing look at me,
   'Well, James, this is something like the apostolic succession; this is the laying on of hands.' [9]

Which of course it was; Howells did in fact receive that tradition humbly and preserve it as best he could, and would have transmitted it had there been anyone to receive *his* laying on of hands.

How it worked to lower standards in the simplest sense is made clear in his anecdote about Whittier.

There is great inequality in his work, and I felt this so strongly that when I came to have full charge of the magazine, I ventured once to distinguish. He sent me a poem, and I had the temerity to return it, and beg him for something else. He magnanimously refrained from all show of offence, and after a while, when he had printed the poem elsewhere, he gave me another. By this time, I perceived that I had been wrong, not as to the poem returned, but as to my function regarding him and such as he. I had made my reflections, and never again did I venture to pass upon what contributors of his quality sent me. I took it and printed it, and praised the gods; and even now I think that with such men it was not my duty to play the censor in the periodical which they had made what it was. They had set it in authority over American literature, and it was not for me to set myself in authority over them. Their fame was in their own keeping, and it was not my part to guard it against them.[10]

The dignity of the magazine, and of the contributors, worked to their own disadvantage. Worse than that, it bruised the self-esteem and the honesty of the inheritor; the laying on of hands was too heavy. Howells, in his oddly feminine way, chooses language which conveys more than he admits to meaning. This anxious currying of favour with the audience, this self-reproving wallow in humiliation, is the most effective criticism of his apostolic succession.

Literature, then, did not bear the marks of serving a plutocratic society and an uneasy community as simply as did the other arts. But it bore them. It continued the modes of an earlier and happier age in inflated form, and betrayed the inauspicious passing of time by an enfeeblement, a hollowing out of the substance beneath the puffy surface. Writers were anxious to be found genial, human, even boyish; and their more serious moods were described as serene and pure, or grand. These are unreal, placatory, other-directed terms; these writers were anxious to measure up to the demands society made of them, at whatever cost to that sense of psychological-moral sincerity which is the writer's conscience. They made literature an easy, safe, tame art, with which the philistine might feel comfortable.

Thus, when one examines the literary life in Boston, all the qualifications one might make to Hofstadter's general judgment cannot add up to a serious quarrel with it. Despite the massive

The Gilded Age in Boston   119

achievements in organizing culture, and despite the continuation
of the political tradition in national affairs, there *had* been a
failure of nerve in that society; that is indeed the main point of
the contrast between the first and second half of the century.
When Ellery Sedgwick, newly editor of the *Atlantic,* took his first
dinner at a Boston dining-club, he had Brooks Adams and Barrett Wendell as his neighbours. Fresh from New York, he was
startled by the genial, habitual, matter-of-fact pessimism and cynicism of their talk. Their view of the world and its progress
derived from the idea of entropy, material and moral—in culture
as a whole. Sedgwick says of this world view, 'Its high priest was
of course Henry Adams, to whom Poincaré and other mathema-
ticians had pointed the way; among Boston intellectuals it was
received as gospel.' There was a famous story of Barrett Wendell's demanding of an acquaintance, 'Did you ever hear me
admit of an improvement in the world?' Surely not. 'Did you
ever hear me imply that progress did not lead downhill?' No,
certainly. 'Thank God.'[11]

There is a good deal of clubman epigrammaticism in this, but
when you come to examine the less self-conscious, ad hoc judgments of these people and their contemporaries, you find how
deep, if urbane, their despair was. Wendell and Woodberry
thought that American literature had died with Lowell; More
and Babbitt spoke of it as a minor and moribund branch of
English literature. And in Wendell's *Literary History of America,* of 1900, one finds the most marked sense of being irremedi-
ably cut off from the Boston of fifty years before, of being culturally, morally, so much older, wearier, worse. He insists on the
national inexperience of Americans before his own time; an inexperience of which the opposite would obviously be largely bitterness and disillusionment. People in those days, he is always
saying, believed human nature to be fundamentally good. They
were so much in earnest. Having described the anti-slavery feeling in New England, he quotes a pro-slavery poem from the
South, and comments:

It is hardly extreme to say, however, that this opinion is more
consonant with New England temper today that it was seventy years

ago. Modern ethnology seems to recognize a pretty marked distinction between human beings in the Stone Age and human beings as developed into the civilization of the 19th century; and though native Africans are not literally neolithic, they certainly linger far behind the social stage that has been reached by modern Europe or America.[12]

What Wendell retains of the older Boston tradition are its weaker elements, made weaker yet by a kind of inflation. For instance, the refusal to discuss 'personal' matters; he says of Poe, 'The unedifying question of his personal habits need not seriously concern us.' Poe had been dead well over a generation; and Wendell was no New Critic, to concentrate his criticism on pure form. For him to refuse to discuss Poe as a man meant to refuse half his subject-matter. A second instance, the odd, unreal, sexual primness and complacency; he speaks of 'the stainless pages of New England literature' and of 'that purity of life which has been characteristic of the American upper classes everywhere'. When one thinks of Wendell's general cynicism, and general dissatisfaction with American morality, one would prefer to think him insincere in that statement. But it is more likely to have been the result of sheer muddle in his mind.

And last, the connection between America and England. 'Our common language' and 'our common legal tradition' are always on his lips, and with a trumpeting sound. But in him this has turned into imperialism, quite openly.

> There is a sense . . . [in which] what we call imperialism seems a blundering awakening to the consciousness that if our language and our law are to survive, they must survive by unwelcome force of conquest. . . . Shall our language, with its ideals of law and of conduct, dominate; or shall it recede and yield to others? [13]

Here we see how completely, even in that realm of literature which had been the ark of the Boston covenant, the conditions of plutocracy had undermined the ideals of democracy; 'unwelcome force of conquest' had replaced the authority of truth. None of these elements of the Boston tradition were ever so crude in Ticknor as they are in the more 'sophisticated' Wendell.

The Gilded Age then saw the inflation and corruption of the

Boston tradition. But that is not the whole story. This is the time when New England's domination of American high culture reached its peak. Throughout the period, Frank Luther Mott tells us, it was New England authors who received the highest critical praise in magazines across America. Whenever serious subjects were to be discussed, New England lecturers were in demand. And this was not merely a legacy of past virtue. The memory, the idea, even the inspiration, of the responsible society continued in Boston. For one thing, the political reforming tradition of the Yankees never really died, though it was checked and redirected. For another, this was a period of great achievements in cultural organization, at the University, the Hospital, the Orchestra, and so on. Above all, some men, and men with power, were still worthy to be compared with Ticknor, as moralists, as humanists, as democrats, as statesmen of cultural responsibility. The culture which supported, and was supported by, Charles Eliot Norton, cannot be dismissed as merely corrupt.

Chapter Six

CHARLES ELIOT NORTON:
THE ARISTOCRAT
IN A PLUTOCRACY

ONE IS TEMPTED to make James Fields the emblem
of all of Boston's literary life in the Gilded Age;
but that would make the point about its deterioration too easily, too angrily, and in the long run,
unconvincingly. One could avoid the anger by
nominating Edward Everett Hale, a respectable
and likable figure enough, and prominent in
most spheres of Boston life. But to make the
other point, about that life's continued vitality,
to be fair in the comparison with Ticknor, even,
ultimately, to make the most of the contrast,
there can be no other choice than his kinsman.
Charles Eliot Norton.

Norton was born in 1827, the son of Andrews
Norton, the professor of sacred literature, and of
Catherine Eliot Norton, the sister of Mrs Ticknor. He was thus born into the crimson of Harvard, and his ancestors in New England went
back to the earliest times. When there was talk
of Lowell resigning the Smith Professorship in
1873, the president of Harvard (Charles W. Eliot,
Norton's first cousin) promised it to him. If this
had happened, the chair would have passed from
Ticknor to Longfellow, to Lowell, to Norton,
which would have been symmetrical and symbolic. But we need wish him no more qualifica-

tions for his emblematic position than he has—it must have seemed to him often that he was overburdened with them. He appeared in the first issue of the *Atlantic* and again—a sole survivor—in the fiftieth-anniversary issue. He was the first professor of the history of art at Harvard, 1874–1899, and professor emeritus until his death in 1908. He was the man behind the Cambridge Dante Circle, and (with Olmsted) the man behind *The Nation*. He was teacher, editor, emender, critic, guide, philosopher, and friend, to the whole complex of New England literary life, including its protégés in the rest of America, and its sympathizers in Britain, for half a century and more. Despite all their differences, he and his uncle stand together, the masters of ceremonies of their city's cultural life, issuing the invitations, effecting the introductions, determining the decorum, decreeing the activities.[1]

The resemblance has been seen before. Ferris Greenslet's introduction to Ticknor's *Life, Letters, and Journal* in the 1909 edition includes this paragraph:

> The men of this generation who have felt in their own lives the gracious influence of the personality of Charles Eliot Norton, can best gauge perhaps the part played in an earlier day by his kinsman George Ticknor. Norton's subtle magnetic sympathy with generous ideals, whether in life or in art, his exquisitely light social touch, his wistful humour, were not perhaps within the scope of Ticknor, but kinsmen they were nevertheless in intellect as in race. We find in both an urbanity, dignity, and high seriousness that admirably fulfil certain indestructible ideals of the literary character, and a sober judgment of events, springing from a richly nourished imagination, a wide personal intimacy with the first minds of their respective periods, that makes too many of the little judgments of our time seem both provincial and jejune. And if at times they looked by preference backward, rather than forward, who shall say that they came not as near to seeing life steadily and whole as those of us who fix what we are pleased to call our attention upon the noisy present or a misty future.[2]

A paragraph like this, incidentally, is the best guarantee of the interest of this inquiry. It is an intelligent prose, expressing a firm, clear understanding of some complex problems; for instance, the whole idea of the literary character. But this is an intelligence originating in the community, the culture, rather than in the brilliant individual. The two cannot be taken as mutually exclusive alternatives, of course—the individual must be intelligent to grasp and manipulate any complex meanings his culture offers him. But we all in practice distinguish between men who happily grasp and apply what others have with difficulty thought through, and men who must with difficulty think for themselves. That Mr Greenslet belongs to the first group is clear in his use of 'high seriousness' and 'see life steadily and whole', phrases from that tradition of culture criticism all New England and England shared. It is clear too in the contrast between this prose and that of Mr Greenslet's autobiography, which is less handsome.

This is prose of its period—the best prose of its period, if one allows that phrase its broadly categorizing, not just its narrowly evaluating, function. A culture which makes available to its intelligent citizens the best prose of its period is a good culture, from more than the literary point of view. And it is because Boston so strikingly did that in some ways, and so strikingly failed to do it in others, that we are interested in it. (It is because Ticknor and Norton so transparently reveal in their prose—and other things—the best quality of intelligence of their culture that we have chosen them as emblems of it.)

To return to the substance of that paragraph, we see that it is the words 'subtle', 'exquisite', and 'wistful' which are used to differentiate Norton, and as soon as we look at his portraits or busts we see why. A small, narrow-shouldered, narrow-faced man, stooping forward in later years, and with a wide, drooping moustache, he had large, heavily lidded eyes and high semi-circular brows, a domed forehead, a long, perpendicular nose, and a wide, melancholy mouth, set in one of those elegantly finished faces, with no roughnesses or irregularities, all harmony of line and texture. His manner, by all accounts, had a similar effect, and seems to have demanded description in the vocabulary of, say, George Eliot analyzing Cardinal Mazarin.

At the same time, he was clearly a man of considerable force. This becomes deductively clear as one considers all he accomplished, but it is not accounted for in what people said about

him. Boston decorum (by Norton's decree, largely) was so discreet that biographers and reminiscers omitted a great deal; in
the case of Ticknor, the references to his harshness of manner
which we come across in odd corners when people are discussing
something else are quite unconnected with the considered descriptions, and we have to use our imaginations. In Norton's day
the decorum was even stricter, but people were becoming indiscreet, as we see in Mrs Gardner's career; and John Jay Chapman
(who had spent a lot of time in New York) blurts out that
Norton was 'mulish'.[3] And when one looks again at that calm,
elegant, wistful face, that quality is there too. More than almost
anyone else, Norton stood on his principles (including his prejudices) and the rest of the world had to come round to him. It was
in a protective and tutelary relation that he stood to many of his
friends, including someone as unlikely as Ruskin (who in fact
called him 'my tutor' and 'Papa', though Norton was the younger
of the two.) Chapman insists on the resemblance between Norton
and his cousin, President Eliot, despite their radical disagreement over what the university should be. The resemblance was
in their both being men of imperious nature and formidable
force. Norton had, he says, 'the power of the rooted aristocrat';
and though he was also, in his way, a democrat, the first word
defines him even more sharply than it does Ticknor.

Chapman 'did not more than half like him', but he acknowl-
edges him as the most important man at Harvard while he,
Chapman, was an undergraduate. His dislike was aroused by the
preciosity of Norton's personality, his highly developed manner
of weary disillusionment. Norton, he says, assumed that the
things of the mind were all playthings, and that he knew all the
rules, all the difficulties, and all the possible outcomes of the
game before it was begun. In other words, he was an aesthete, in
one, common, use of the term. In Chapman's disgust with this
pose, his reaction away from it towards some simpler faith,
through social rebelliousness and activism, he was typical of his
generation. (And this can symbolize the end of Boston's power to
command the livelier young minds.) And in this pose itself, this
quizzical, gentle weariness, this preoccupation with the aesthetic
qualities in moral experience as well as with aesthetic experience

proper (so unlike Ticknor's Boston), Norton was typical of *his* generation. We remember phrases of Santayana's: 'disappointed, shabby-genteel, picturesque old Yankees, with a little bitter humour breaking through their constitutional fatigue'.[4] And Wendell's first impression of Lowell (Norton's great friend): '. . . he seemed to me the most *quizzical* man I had ever met.'[5] And Henry Adams' comments on Harvard students:

> negative to a degree that became positive and triumphant . . . as a body the most formidable critics one would care to meet . . . intimately and terribly intelligent . . . the love of line, form, quality; the horror of ennui; the passion for companionship and the antipathy to society—all these are well-known qualities of New England character.[6]

The Bostonian personality had changed since Ticknor's day,* and in parallel with the change Hofstadter describes in the political tradition in New England. At the same time, it would be a mistake to suppose either that the vitality had been simply replaced by mere feebleness, or that the preciosity had simply dislodged the moral earnestness about society. At the end of his life, Norton was engaged in a series of school-children's readers, the Hearts-of-Oak series, six volumes of which he compiled in 1894–95; just as Mrs Gardner instituted her prizes for tenement-house gardens even later. As late as 1903, at nearly eighty, Norton was corresponding with W. L. Mackenzie King, then the Canadian deputy minister for labour, about labour disputes and union legislation.

One of the ways in which Norton, and perhaps no-one but he, can challenge comparison with Ticknor, is in the number of his distinguished friends, and in what he made out of his friendships. He was the kind of man to whom words like 'subtle' and 'complex' are applied; which means, no doubt, that he was less complex and more complicated than Ticknor, that the different

---

* Figures like William James and Charles Willian Eliot still represented, in different ways, the earlier character. The optimism of the one, the rectitude of the other, were aspects of what one might call a 'simplicity', to contrast with the 'complexity' of the later people. Attractive, forceful, effective, as these men were personally, it is clear that this simplicity has seemed to most writers, of their time and ours, to belong categorically to the past.

parts of his personality were further disjoined from each other, and held more threats of disharmony, which it required more will and policy to avert—that we cannot attribute to him so noble and pastoral a union of the public and private functions of his personality. Norton was nearer to being a snob, nearer to flattering his superiors and patronizing his inferiors and manipulating both, nearer to fastening on Ruskin's weaker side, further from that princely disengagement and equality of Ticknor's. But these potentialities remained remarkably unrealized. The main design of his personality, his interests, and his relationships, was so large and steady, and his different talents, energies, feelings of responsibility, and powers of self-discipline all worked into that design so well, that he achieved something commensurate in dignity with Ticknor's achievement.

Norton stood between America and England (and to a slighter extent between America and Europe, and between New England and the rest of America) explaining and evaluating each to each, in a way that we are bound to find superior to, say, Lowell's performances in that role. Lowell had an equal number of English friends, was much better known in England, had in fact been American minister in London. There are volumes of his letters, too, and warm tributes to him. But Lowell's talents and energies, in this as in other spheres of his life, did not serve any large design, his feelings of responsibility and powers of self-discipline did not build up any comparable achievement.

Within America, or at least within New England, one may as well say that Norton knew everyone in the cultural world, from Mrs Gardner and Mrs Wharton to Ticknor and Emerson, and was something more than an acquaintance to each of them. He was a life-long friend of Professor Child, the ballad collector, and Professor Wright, the mathematician and philosopher; and was even closer to Lowell and George William Curtis, the editor, publicist, reformer. Longfellow, Holmes, and Howells he of course knew and guided; all the Adamses and Jameses of Henry Adams' generation; Godkin and Olmsted, outside New England; and his pupils and epigones, Babbitt, Woodberry, Santayana, Berenson. It is among British men of letters that his range is most remarkable, and that the richness of his various relationships commands most respect. At twenty-three, for instance, he developed friendships with Mrs Gaskell and the Brownings, in Rome; friendships he maintained the rest of their lives. Two years later he became intimate with Clough when the latter was in America. He was a close friend of Leslie Stephen's, and somewhat less close to Arnold and Dickens, Forster and Mill. His most eminent friendships were with Carlyle, and even more with Ruskin, whose literary executor he became. Both these difficult men trusted and respected him, and allowed him in some degree an ascendancy over them. Late in his life, Kipling, Dicey, and Ker joined the band.

For example, picked more or less at random, of the energy and quality of mind at work in these relationships, here is the beginning of a letter to Chauncy Wright, from the first volume of his *Letters*:

> Villa Spannocchi, Siena
> September 13, 1870.

> . . . Once a week comes the best of all possible journals, 'The Nation', and I find it at once the support and the disappointment of my Americanism. I am American only so far as our political and social systems are, to use your favourite phrase, in accordance with the principles of utilitarianism, and there are plainly many efforts to be made and many disappointments and failures to be achieved before the accordance becomes in any good degree complete. I don't know whether I have expressed the thought to you in any one of my former letters or not, but even if I have done so it will bear repetition, that in spite of all the tremendous disadvantages under which England is labouring she is essentially in advance of us in regard to the ultimate settlement of the main social problems, on account of the more solid training and the more serious temper of her best men, as compared with those of our best men. 'Best' men are indeed few in either country, but their influence is very strong on great numbers, and frames a temper which by degrees becomes national. No best man with us has done more to influence the nation than Emerson,—but the country has in a sense outgrown him. He was the friend and helper of its youth; but for the difficulties and struggles of its manhood we need the wisdom of the reflective and rational understanding, not that of the intuitions. Emerson (like most original men of the intuitive order) is in some sort the contemporary of his youth. He belongs to the pure and innocent age of the Presidency of Monroe or John Quincy Adams—to the time when Plancus was Consul,—to

the day of Cacciaguida; he is as remote almost from us as Plato himself. But we have nobody to take his place in supplying us with the thought itself on which the spiritual growth in good of the nation mainly depends. Really the 'Nation' and the 'North American' are almost the evidences of thought in America, and they drag out a difficult existence in the midst of the barbaric wealth of the richest millions of people in the world!

Now in England there is abundance of contemporary thought; abundance of solid reasoning faculty applied to the difficulties of the time; abundance of the strong convictions and firm principles that result from the possession and exercise of trained and disciplined reason. And instead of there being a decline in seriousness and thoughtfulness, and in respect for devotion to intellectual pursuits, there is a marked revival of (mainly under the stimulus of Mill) and interest in the higher branches of speculation, in philosophy as applied to life, in a word, in the pursuit of wisdom for her own sake, and for utilitarian ends, using the epithet in its best and largest significance. The 'Fortnightly Review' affords good indication of the range and vigour of English thinking,—and of the rapid increase in England of a class of men with settled principles and solid acquisition, but with open candid minds. Frederic Harrison's recent articles have seemed to me remarkable in many respects, while Mill has hardly supported himself at his usual level. . . .

We see there how firm but easy was Norton's grasp of the idea of culture—how he moved from the individual to the institution to the social atmosphere to history—from Emerson to *The Fortnightly Review* to Cacciaguida—and we also see how serious a meaning he gave that idea. We cannot but regret that he (and the other American culture-critics) did not push further, in their writings, this sort of analysis; did not invest more emotion and more thought in it, and achieve something comparable with, say, Ruskin's or Arnold's essays, instead of the dull and prim plaintiveness of most of Norton's own. That they did not is a clear case of the problem of Boston, to which we shall return. I want to point out further in that letter that since Norton was essentially a man who acted on such insights—who founded and edited such magazines, for instance—his comments are more vigorous and significant than they first seem, than other people's in the same genre. The vigilance of his scrutiny of both nations, and its marriage of detachment with involvement, give him at such moments a largeness of style comparable with Ticknor's. And Ticknor's stateliness could hardly have encompassed the tone of this next letter, or presumably the relationship out of which it sprang.

> My Dear Ruskin,
>   Your last note gave me great pleasure,—and so have your lectures done. And yet what you write never seems to me to do full justice to yourself. I am ready sometimes to quarrel with it on that account. You are in truth so different from the image which men form of you from your books that I wish always that your writings were completer mirrors of yourself. When you become an historical character you may perhaps be better understood; but for the time being you have no right to expect better treatment than that which commonly awaits the prophets; not exactly, perhaps, material stones or actual rotten eggs, but other things, symbolic, as bad if not worse. You are, there can be no doubt, terribly provoking, so absolute, and so aggravatingly right, and at the same time so wrong-headed. You hit even your friends such blows! . . .
>   I am pretty well,—busy as usual with every day work,—with my two little children,—with writing more or less, mainly on political affairs,—with reading just now Grote's Plato, and Munro's Lucretius. . . .
>
> Ever Affectionately Yours,
> Charles Eliot Norton.

A letter like that shows how right Ruskin was to trust Norton as a friend who could admire (without completely understanding) and yet was neither overborne by enthusiasm into mere discipleship, nor undermined by irritation into mere resentment; someone who could sustain the difficult kind of relationship that was alone possible with a man of his genius and his temperament. Norton could work off his personal exasperations, as here, without endangering either his personal warmth or the equally valuable impersonal deference ('when you become an historical character') with which he discreetly reassured Ruskin.

I have included the last paragraph for the sake of the books mentioned; one of the impressive things about the letters is the reading recorded, and even more the facility with which he refers to and quotes from a real range of erudition. Marcus Aurelius, Horace Walpole, Dante, Milton, St Francis, Gray, are quoted with an exactness, a fullness, an apparent ease, that dazzles. I only regret that in these excerpts there is no example of his gaiety, which, though Norton was not a brilliant writer, is often nicely handled.

The events of Norton's life are quickly told. He graduated from Harvard in 1846, at nineteen, and spent five years in the firm of the East India Merchants, Bullard and Lee. He went to India in 1849, and came back through Rome, Paris, London. In 1853 his father died, and his first book was published: *Considerations of Some Recent Social Theories,* Federalist-style disapproval of radical theorists like Cabet and Saint-Simon.

The years 1855 to 1857 he spent in Europe again with his mother and sisters; there he established his friendship with Ruskin, and developed his interest in Dante. He began to translate the *Vita Nuova.* During the Civil War he worked for the New England Loyal Publications Society, as editor. He solicited articles helpful to the Northern cause, and looked for others already published, to reprint them all once or twice a week in broadsides which were sent (one or two thousand of them) to the editors of loyal papers across the country. Some articles were thus read by a million readers. This work is neatly symbolic of Norton's function in American high culture through the rest of his life.

During the war he also married, guided Lowell in the composition of the second series of *Biglow Papers,* collaborated with him as editor of *The North American Review,* and gave his lectures on the twelfth century in Europe, which he repeated often enough (alternately with his Dante lectures) for Berenson to hear them as a young man. In 1865 he helped in the foundation of *The Nation,* collecting donations in the Boston area. And in 1867 he, Lowell, and Longfellow (later Howells joined them) began to meet on Wednesdays to discuss Longfellow's *Divine Comedy* translation, and on Saturdays to discuss Norton's version of the *Vita Nuova.*

Between 1868 and 1873 he was again in Europe, where, in 1872, Mrs Norton died. He stayed with Dickens at Gads Hill, and saw much of Carlyle, who promised him to leave a collection of his books to Harvard. In 1874, back in Cambridge, he began teaching the history of art at the university. It was on this return that everything in America struck him unfavourably; everything he valued was being uprooted and replaced by kinds of Ameri-

canism he could have no truck with. He had travelled back with
Emerson, and found him hopelessly naive—in some sort to blame
for America's thoughtless materialism and moral ignorance.*
The *Atlantic* and its galaxy of local celebrities seemed to him
hopelessly provincial; Howells, he said, 'bids fair to be a popular
American author'. He had written for the magazine himself, and
dutifully recommended and promoted it as a healthful force in
American culture, but he was largely bored by it. This was typical of him. But what he wished the magazine were—and this too
is typical—would not strike us as much of an improvement. He
wanted all the contributions to be of the level of Lowell's and
Longfellow's. The truth was that his taste turned more eagerly
and responded more finely to medieval cathedrals and Japanese
paintings than it did to contemporary literature.

Norton had written a famous pamphlet, 'The Soldier of the
Good Cause,' in 1861, on behalf of the American Unitarian Association, but his religious faith soon ceased to be robust. His
conversations with Chauncy Wright confirmed him in a 'gentle,
discreet scepticism'. Here again he represents his age, like his
uncle. Ticknor moved from Calvinism to Unitarianism; Norton,
from that to agnosticism. By the end of his life he was becoming
interested in the Roman Catholic Church.

In 1879 he began his Ashfield Academy dinners, of which more
will be said later, and worked with Olmsted in the movement
which preserved the Niagara Falls area from exploitation. In the
same year also was founded the Cambridge Dante Society, whose
early presidents were Longfellow, Lowell, and, in 1891, Norton.
In the latter year his prose version of the *Divine Comedy* appeared. But by this time he was more and more occupied in
editing and introducing to the public the works of his friends. In
1894, for instance, he edited Lowell's *Letters,* Curtis's *Orations,*
Longfellow's *Poems,* and wrote an introduction to *The Stones of
Venice.* In 1898 he retired, and he died in 1908.

He had become profoundly pessimistic and melancholy in later
years—about America, about Western civilization, about life as a
whole. Thus at Longfellow's death he found that he had no wish

* See Appendix A.

the poet was still alive, and in fact regretted that Emerson and Ruskin still lived. When Mrs Lowell died, he wished Lowell had died with her. He had in fact a profound longing for death which, while painfully personal, was also cultural, both in its expression and in its source. Edmund Wilson has discussed Justice Holmes' preoccupation with killing and death, a preoccupation which shows itself in seemingly unconnected areas of his thought.[7] Mr Wilson attributes it to Holmes' experience of battle in the Civil War, but Norton shows something very similar. New England then was living through the experience of death.

What were the achievements of this life? Certainly not his writings. Neither Ticknor nor Norton were men of first-class literary talent, but whereas the *History of Spanish Literature* was a really respectable and useful piece of scholarship, unduplicated in its day, Norton's translations of Dante were only a part of the general interest in the subject.

Another answer to that question is this quotation from Sainte-Beuve, used as an epigraph in Norton's *Letters.*

> Les écrivains illustres, les grands poètes, n'existent guère sans qu'il y ait autour d'eux de ces hommes plutôt encore essentiels que secondaires, grands dans leur incomplet, les égaux au dedans par la pensée de ceux qu'ils aiment, qu'ils servent, and qui sont rois par l'art.

This has its relevance to men like Ticknor and Norton, but it obviously has more to do with Sainte-Beuve himself and his *roi par l'art,* Hugo. One could hardly call Lowell or Prescott *un roi par l'art;* the kings, in these cases, were rather Ticknor and Norton themselves. They disposed of a personal force comparable to Hugo's, in their letters and conversation, their editings and advisings, and though it was not in art that they were royal, they ruled in the world of literature too.

A better answer is suggested by what George Eliot wrote to Mrs Norton in 1869:

> I imagine Mr Norton is brooding over some work that he will give us all by and by. Not that men need write if they have influence in other ways. I think the lastingness of results from a social position adequately filled, is grievously underestimated; and the very abun-

dance of print serves to be continually reducing its efficacy compared with the fine rarities of speech and action.[8]

Here, with her usual tact and insight, the English novelist found the perfect thing to say to and about Norton. He had influence in other ways; he had a social position adequately filled. All that one wants to add is that 'social position' is not quite adequate to what Norton made of his role. He was not merely the Squire of Shady Hill; he was the Arbiter Elegantiarum of American high culture—*that* was his social position. More than that, he was the last great organizer and engineer of the arts as general education, the last great statesman of cultural responsibility.

Early in his life, he engaged in the kind of social work we met in Ticknor's Boston. Between 1846 and 1849 he ran a night school for the poor in Cambridge, two evenings a week. The future Professor Child and two other young men assisted him. In the same line is his article on 'Dwellings and Schools for the Poor', published in *The North American Review* in 1852, which displays a more simply passionate feeling and thought than we find in him later, and a confident appeal to his audience (he quotes contemporary poetry to them freely) which became impossible in later New England. The article gave an account of the Model Lodging Houses in England, with woodcuts. In 1853 he drew up a plan to build something similar in Boston (because of the flood of Irish immigrants) and collected $40,000 for the purpose. In 1854 two such houses were built, in brick, each holding twenty families. They were a great success; by 1860, the investment was bringing in 6 per cent interest, and private builders were copying the design, which was what had been hoped for. Abbott Lawrence left $50,000 to be spent on more such lodging houses.

In the last quarter of the century his Ashfield Academy dinners were a continuation of similar efforts in the later manner. He had begun spending his summers in this Massachusetts township, and his friends had followed his example. In 1879 Norton became engaged in the project of collecting money to restore its ruined academy. He organized an annual dinner with a speaker whom people would pay a dollar to come and hear. The dinner became a centre of Mugwump oratory, with Curtis, Lowell, Howells, Booker T. Washington, speaking on civil-service reform, tariff reform, Negro education, anti-imperialism. The dinners continued for twenty-five years.

Perhaps more typical of his later interests and activities were the Archeological Institute of America and the Dante Society. He issued the circular proposing the former in 1879. The Archeological School in Athens was founded almost immediately afterwards. The Dante Society was founded in 1882 by Norton and Longfellow. It published individual works of scholarship, and two concordances; and a Dante collection was assembled in Harvard Library. Norton seems to have been its effectual head from the beginning. Lowell was not the Dante scholar Norton was, according to the report of the Society for 1909, and Longfellow was mostly a figurehead. Dante was one of Norton's major interests; he brought out his last edition of his version of the *Divine Comedy* in 1901. Here again he continued Ticknor's tradition, but was also in tune with his own times. A Dante society was established in 1878 at Oxford, in 1881 in London, and in 1882 in Cambridge, Massachusetts. And it was through the work of that Dante Society that Santayana and T. S. Eliot acquired their interest in Dante.

But larger than any of these was his work at Harvard, though he was not, from the more pedestrian points of view, a good teacher. His courses in the history of art were large and popular, but that was apparently because they were easy to pass. Nor does it seem that they can have been very energetically directed at strictly aesthetic problems. The students' notebooks preserved in the Harvard archives report that the course in Florentine art begun in October, 1885, reached the following January before any particular painting was mentioned. Norton's interest was architectural, and indeed historical and moral. His son suggested that the course should be called 'Lectures on Modern Morals as Illustrated by the Art of the Ancients'. His inspiration was of course Ruskin's work, and it is one of his accomplishments that he brought that stream of new ideas to work on the imagination of American students. But in Norton's version those ideas became more conventionally humanist, less socially conscious, and much less socialist. 'For many years he has been at Cambridge the Oracle of the Humanities,' said a colleague. 'His power to humanize knowledge . . . the applicability to yourself of whatever art or history or nature presents to you . . .'—these are the phrases used, and they can only indicate a safe and comfortable experience.

However, these courses were also a significant experience, to a large number of students, as John J. Chapman admits. 'He taught two hundred at a time that there were such things as the fine arts.' As Chapman says, everyone *knew* him, and had to come to terms with him. And for the few, he was very important. The testimony of an anonymous contributor in the introduction to the *Letters* carries conviction. Norton was

> *the* great influence in my life. All that I have been and am was and is affected by his teaching and his character. He was the only *real* 'master' I ever had. . . . He gave me a desire to think clearly and speak accurately, and an admiration of elegant scholarship; he implanted in me the seeds of a loathing of affectation and vulgarity; and he conveyed to me a minute part of his own exquisite scrupulousness of taste which, while it has caused me to suffer many things acutely, has on the other hand been the source of my greatest joys.[9]

But it was perhaps as editor even more than as teacher that he exerted his control over American culture. He did most of the work when he and Lowell together edited *The North American Review;* he published Henry Adams' and Henry James' first work there. *The Nation,* of which he was an unofficial recruiting editor at the beginning, was described by Ferris Greenslet as being, at the beginning of his career, the only market in America for the reviewer who wanted to quote Latin when he felt like it. As for books, besides those we mentioned in the year 1894, here are a few others; 1877, Chauncy Wright's *Philosophical Discourses,* with a biographical sketch of the author; 1833, *The Correspondence of Thomas Carlyle and Ralph Waldo Emerson 1834–72;* 1894, *The Letters of James Russell Lowell;* 1904, *The Letters of John Ruskin to Charles Eliot Norton;* 1907, *Henry Wadsworth Longfellow; A Sketch of His Life.* Let us note that this is editing of the kind that establishes the image of its subject-author with the public, and the image of literary decorum. The editor decides which letters to include, and which incidents in the poet's life to mention, and to have mentioned. Norton took duties of this kind very seriously; his rule was, whenever in doubt, to omit and not to mention. This was cultural editing.

But we come back to George Eliot's word, 'influence', which, vague as it may seem, alone describes Norton's achievement fully. He launched and guided half the writers of New England on their literary careers. In his twenties, he went over Parkman's history with him, and Clough's poems with him. He read the manuscripts of the unpublished, wrote letters of encouragement to the newly published, and was the first reader of new things by the already famous. In a multitude of ways he helped. When Henry James went to London in 1869, Norton found him rooms, and introduced him to Dickens, to Ruskin, to Stephen, to Morris. When James went on to Rome, he sent back literary letters to Norton, which the latter read out loud to Ruskin. There is practically no career in letters in the later period in which we do not find Norton's hand at work at some fairly significant moment. He corrected Longfellow's Dante before publication, and defended it afterwards. He arranged for Ruskin's publication in America, and found him special printers in Switzerland. He guided Lowell's *Biglow Papers,* and emended the Agassiz ode. For Lowell, Norton did everything; he is practically co-responsible for the poetry; he suggested subjects, deprecated others, urged publication, arranged publication, read proofs, praised, blamed, altered, circulated copies, organized support, told him to work on this now and that later. Nothing was too much trouble for Norton, providing he believed in the other man. He endlessly put off his own career to promote the careers of others.

His personality and his career seem to have been the supreme form of an inspiration—to put high-cultural values above all others—which many people acknowledged. Gardiner Martin Lane, for example, is cited as an example of Norton's influence.*

* By Charles Francis Adams and M. A. de Wolfe Howe, in a pamphlet of the Massachusetts Historical Society in 1914, called 'Charles Eliot Norton'.

Born in 1859, Lane went into banking with Lee, Higginson, and Company, in 1892, but in 1907 gave that up to become president of the Boston Museum of Fine Arts. The best part of his time had always been given to high culture. In a rather different style—more plutocratic, more exotic, more foreign—were James Loeb, the wealthy founder of the Loeb Classical Library, and Paul J. Sachs, the associate director of the Fogg Museum. Loeb, after graduating from Harvard in 1888, served his time in the family firm, and then retired to more congenial pursuits. He was quite personally devoted to Norton till the latter's death, and to Norton's values till his own. He founded the Charles Eliot Norton Fellowship in Greek Studies in 1901; he identified himself with the Archeological Institute of America; he made many gifts and loans to the Fogg Museum. Sachs, graduating in 1900, also served his time in his family banking firm in New York, and then returned to Harvard in 1915, where he became professor of fine arts. He too made many gifts to the Fogg Museum; even more strikingly, he bought Norton's house, Shady Hill, lived in it, and eventually gave it to Harvard.

What we seem to see Norton counting for in these careers is not simply the aesthetes' split between culture and reality (with the preference going to the former) but the combination of that with some supervening sense of broader responsibilities, so that the two halves of reality, now so instinctively in recoil from each other, are yet yoked together again by a personal and aristocratic effort of will-power—and by the power of example of Charles Eliot Norton.

Teacher as well as inspirer, Norton taught Mrs Gardner and Mrs Wharton what to look for in Italian art; he taught Ruskin what to look for in Japanese art; he taught Ferris Greenslet— while the latter was writing his life of Lowell—how to make a biography. Every Wednesday morning Greenslet called at Shady Hill for a chat about his book and about literature in general: 'It was like a symposium with Plato.' And George Edward Woodberry, at Columbia, and Irving Babbitt, at Harvard, made their careers out of teaching Norton's values applied to literature.

As a disciple, Babbitt is an impressive addition to the evidence of Norton power. (Woodberry too, but he illustrates the less fortunate aspect of Norton's influence.) If one sees Babbitt in the context of Ph.D. academicism in the humanities, or of Paterian dilettantism and aestheticism, both of which were real dangers at the time, there is much to be said for his muscular moralism. His comments on contemporary literature, which one tends to re- member first, express much his worst side. He stood for some largely healthful things ('standing for' was his strength as well as his weakness) and in so doing he spelled out, so he believed, Norton's message. Norton's picture hung in his study, and his name (conjoined with Matthew Arnold's

> . . . his hope of escape from these evils lay not in framing a correct dialectic, but rather in the fact that Charles Eliot Norton was actually living a life of strenuous moderation and sensitive decorum. It was the living presence of Norton that made the great sages of the past— the Buddha, Aristotle, Confucius, Pascal—come once more alive to be our example and our succor.[10]

By such standards, however, Norton's influence and power must be judged in many ways destructive. He was so completely and so hopelessly on the losing side in the battle for American culture that his larger professions of faith became rhetorical and empty, lost authority beside his smaller private gestures of de- spair. His attitude to America, after the war, the landscape as well as the human scene, betrays in unpremeditated phrases an accumulating distaste. 'Nature certainly did not show half so much poetic imagination in the construction of America as she did in Europe,' he declared in 1873; and in 1887 to Woodberry (who always brought out the worst in him), 'Nature to be really beautiful to us must be associated with the thoughts and feelings of men. An Italian sunset is better than a Californian for this reason; a daisy of more worth than a mayflower.' [11] He looks back with overwhelming nostalgia both to Europe and to earlier times in America. Thus he describes Lowell's youth:

> There were no railroads, with their tremendous revolutionary forces; no great manufacturing cities; no flood of immigrants; no modern democracy. . . . The days before the advent of General Jackson are pleasant to look back upon.[12]

But such looking back made the present bitter to return to; and that was a good deal Norton's effect on his hearers, to make the present seem bitter, and the passage of time a decay.

But his idealism, if it lacked contagious vitality, did not lack tenacity or nobility. After the deaths of Lowell and Curtis (the first in 1891, the second in 1892) Norton wrote an article about them, describing them as the two men who in their time had done the most for the civilization of America. (It was in these Bostonian terms that he measured his friends, and it is one way of summing up his career to remember that the two men he describes like this were 'Uncle James' and 'Uncle George' to his children.) In this article, for *Harper's* in 1893, he said they were the two men most truly representative in their generation of

> the ideals of American culture and citizenship. I say *American* culture and citizenship because . . . [they exemplified] New England principles and New England practice. They were gentlemen as gracious, as refined, as well-bred as any of the line of gentlemen, from Sidney down to Sidney's peers, in the Old World today, but with this difference, that the sentiment which inspired them was not the lingering exclusive spirit of chivalric superiority, but the larger, more generous, modern spirit of democratic society . . . ; and this spirit . . . shows itself in character which seems to me to be, on the whole, of fairer and more promising quality than any which the world has hitherto known. The virtues of such men as these . . . become exemplary; they give reason for faith in the progress of man.[13]

We see there how much more of the old Ticknor and Cooper faith there was in Norton than in Barrett Wendell or Brooks Adams; if he deplored 'modern democracy', he still believed in 'democratic society', and even in 'American' ideals, though he must have found it difficult to identify any manifestations of the latter he could delight in. That faith and his 'mulish' streak both achieved their finest gesture in 1898, when he told his students that the Spanish-American War was dishonorable, and that he hoped none of them would fight in it. He was attacked as unpatriotic by the newspapers, abused by Senator Hoar in public speeches, threatened by Boston-Irish politicians and in private and anonymous correspondence. But his long self-training (as aristocrat in a plutocracy) enabled him to endure it all without any retractions—without feeling any regret for what he had done.

What we see most clearly in Norton is perhaps the power of the Boston tradition as a vocation: the quantity of energy and dedication it could evoke in the right temperament, even in its decadence. What he stood for we cannot be enthusiastic about, but that he did stand for something is splendidly manifest, and the massiveness with which he did so compels admiration. Ticknor's was the happier fate; he *was* what he believed in, he moved among people and institutions which to some significant degree realized his ideals. Norton only stood for what he believed in; the people and institutions around him were visibly losing vigour and needing protection. He had *standards;* and with them, like a nobler Mrs Partington, he and his disciples brushed back an ocean in which they fully expected to drown.

But if we cannot be enthusiastic about what he stood for, when we spell out his proposals in detail, and recite to ourselves the poems and essays he played some part in getting written, still we can—once we recall the context of the Gilded Age, we *must* —respect what he stood for. When we recall what alternatives were then available to writers, teachers, critics, readers, we see that those Norton chose to endorse added up to a large idea of intellectual and moral discrimination; an idea, lacking perhaps in energy, but not in nobility; an idea which gave the arts an important link with other forms of thought, an important place in the total culture. If literature under Norton's influence lost its vitality, and became an art with which the philistines could feel comfortable, at least it kept its dignity, and never reduced itself to being merely entertainment. The theory of the responsible society survived, at least as a discipline. And indeed, under the less intended aspect of Norton's influence, literature regained some vitality. If Norton failed to respond to the possibilities of American realism, he was in sufficient sympathy with the great American aesthetes to in effect launch their careers. Under his guidance Boston high culture remained the flagship of the American fleet, and even sent up, as it finally sank, the most brilliant displays of imagination and wit it had ever achieved.

Chapter Seven

THE BOSTON AESTHETES

WE SAID BEFORE that the Gilded Age in literature
had no successor in Boston; that the Indian summer of the mind Santayana described stood in
some parallel (and remotely effectual) relation to
the Gilded Age in politics, but that by the time
the Age of Reform and its literary equivalents
took effect—by the time of the Progressive Era—
Boston as a cultural centre had ceased to exist.
(That is why the nineteenth century is such a
usable unit in the city's history.)

There is a partial exception to this in the four
significant Boston writers whose work follows on
that of Norton; follows on chronologically in no
very neat or satisfactory pattern, but follows on
indisputably in the sense of taking off from it
and developing into something dialectically related.

First, Henry Adams, who was born in 1838,
only eleven years later than Norton himself, and
some of whose major work, notably his massive
History of the United States, appeared as early as
1889 and belongs in every sense to that earlier
period. The history and aesthetic of his autobiography and his book on Chartres do not; they
start with, but end far from, those of Norton's
lectures on the twelfth century or on Italian
church-building; and further yet from those of
the earlier Boston historians, Prescott and Parkman, Bancroft and Motley. Adams' later work
clearly marks the beginning of, or an attempt at,

a new mode. It differs from all their work much more than any one of them differs from any other.

Then Henry James, born in 1843, and a great friend of Lowell's; that figurehead of the old Boston. Some of his mature work also appeared in the eighties, while Norton was still at the height of his powers. And like Adams' *History,* these early mature works of James's were not markedly 'aesthetic'; they had not developed away from the Bostonian norm categorically. But his later novels differ from, say, Hawthorne's in the same ways as Henry Adams' later work differs from that of his Boston predecessors. This was partly due to James's cosmopolitan awareness of Flaubert, Turgenev, Balzac, replacing Hawthorne's provincialism; the novel for him was an international form, art an international language. But the difference was also a matter of the enormous elaboration and aesthetic ambition of James and Adams. Howells, after all, also read Ibsen, Tolstoy, Zola, with enthusiasm; in his way he followed them; he too had moved on from Hawthorne (and from Lowell and Norton) in that way. But his novels do not mark the transition to a new phase that James's do, because of their modesty of form and manner.

Then Santayana, born twenty years later than James, and dying only in 1952. He may seem to be of another generation than the first two, but he lived in the same worlds, socially and intellectually. His work in formal philosophy (much of it on aesthetics) and even more his informal comments on New England culture—in *Character and Opinion in the United States,* for instance—mark the end of the old Boston tradition. He was fully able to appreciate Emerson, for instance, and to point out his qualities; but he came at him from enormous cultural distances, placed him in enormous perspectives of world history and world religions, within which Emerson, and all Boston, looked on the whole quaint. He ended that tradition rather in the way he says Henry James ended and transcended it. In *The Genteel Tradition* he says James escaped the limitations of that tradition by turning it—'as he turns everything else'—into a subject-matter for analysis. William James, on the other hand, he says, transcended it by accepting it so enthusiastically, and by continuing it—with all the force of his masculine vitality—into something logically its opposite. This last he calls the romantic method of transcendence; the other the classical; and it is one way to characterize the achievement of these four writers to say that they all transcended the genteel Boston tradition by the classical method. One must then add that they can also be called romantic by the same definitions; for they also continued that tradition without interruption into something logically its opposite; and perhaps the word 'baroque' will do better than either 'classic' or 'romantic' to describe their method.

Lastly, Bernard Berenson, born in 1865, and remaining alive until 1959. He was young enough to be Norton's student at Harvard, and indeed William James's and Barrett Wendell's. He was, at least in the world of literature and general thought, a less intelligent man than the other three, but he is interesting for his career, especially when it is seen in relation to their work. He emblemizes, in simple and vivid fashion, their shift to predominantly aesthetic values.

What is meant by 'aesthetic values' must vary widely between crudity and subtlety, according to cases, and even as a pure idea the phrase must mean more than one thing. At its most comprehensive, moreover, it cannot claim to fully take account of these writers' achievements. But it does indicate a very significant aspect of their work, and an even more significant aspect of their relationship to each other and to what went before.

One of the simplest meanings can be exemplified from Berenson, for whom *Marius the Epicurean* was a seminal book. During the Second World War he was reading it for the eighth time, sixty years after his first reading. Norton balked at Peter—he told Berenson *Marius* was a book you could read 'only in your bathroom'—and held by Arnold. This marks the sense in which he was not a full aesthete; and we have seen how Babbitt and his disciples followed Norton. Here we see one way the new men diverged from—and thus developed—the old Boston tradition.

Berenson protested to Mary Costelloe, when she sent him Fabian pamphlets before they were married, 'I am afraid you will end by making me feel it is my duty to give up everything that I have cherished hitherto.' [1] His whole inspiration from boyhood, he explained, had been to regard 'culture' (he meant high culture) as a religion; it would be a cruel thing for him to have to give that up for 'socialism', which he took to be its irreconcilable enemy. Of course he never did, and his idea of culture became so purely aesthetic as to lose all sense of social or institutional reality.

> I dream of a society composed of individuals, each realizing himself entirely and the by-products of these realizations combining to make a civilization and a culture. There would be no prestige connected with one occupation rather than another. There would be no re-wards. There would be thus no ambition to attain power and place.[2]

And again, 'The world consists of one's personal friends, one's thoughts and one's dreams, and one can manage to live anywhere with these three.' [3] We are a long way from Ticknor here, a long way from Norton, some way (and downhill) from Oscar Wilde. Civilization is to have no institutions. Culture has become crudely an alternative to, a refuge from, reality.

For another meaning of aestheticism, and in subtler forms, we can perhaps turn to Santayana's portraits of the Harvard philos-ophers, or his appreciations of national types in *Character and Opinion in the United States*.

> The luckless American who is born a conservative, or who is drawn to poetic subtlety, pious retreats, or gay passions, nevertheless has the categorical excellence of work, growth, enterprise, reform, and pros-perity dinned into his ears; every door is open in this direction and shut in the other; so that he either folds up his heart and withers in a corner—in remote places you sometimes find such a solitary gaunt idealist—or else he flies to Oxford, or Florence, or Montmartre to save his soul—or perhaps not to save it.[4]

Here one is conscious, as in Berenson, of a purposeful exclusion of all moralizing possibilities from the vocabulary—'pious re-treats or gay passions'—but the thinking has that fullness, firm-ness, and sobriety, which is so often lacking in aesthetic writers. A little further along he points out, with an acuteness and breadth of sympathy worthy of George Eliot, how Americans 'are extreme idealists in the region of hope, but not at all, as poets and artists are, in the region of perception and memory. In the atmosphere of civilized life they miss all the refraction and all the fragrance.' [5] The point of view could not be more aesthetic, but to share it involves no mortification of one's more moral interests. (These quotations also remind us how often, and how exactly, Santayana delineates some of Henry James's major themes.)

But by aestheticism I mean also the hypertrophy of form in the work of Henry James and Henry Adams; the devouring interest in art of all kinds; the interest in the 'show business' of art, the virtuoso and the connoisseur, the dilettante and the immoral artist, rather than in the plain living and high thinking of a Wordsworth; the aesthetic attitude to history; the investigation of past periods in terms of their art; the creation of houses that both contained and were works of art; the approach to the world as a place of line, colour, and form, rather than of right and wrong; the avoidance of a simply moral vocabulary; the hatred of provinciality and philistinism; and a great many other things. All of these were present in Norton's Boston, and to some degree in Norton himself. They owed their popularity, in part, to the unsavouriness of so many non-aesthetic cultural interests; for example, politics. 'The image of a society organized in terms of value' was shattered; art seemed the only world left in which values reigned. That is why these new writers, though they rebelled very sharply against Boston, and did their writing far off, in England, France, Italy, Spain, yet deserve to be called thoroughly Bostonian.

It is worth noting that none of these writers (except Berenson sometimes) sank to a merely nineties aestheticism; the intentions as well as the dimensions of their work were more massive than those of someone like Lionel Johnson or Oscar Wilde. They each had a remarkable personal vitality, but it surely is not fanciful to see in that massiveness (perhaps even in that vitality) something cultural. They belonged to a powerful tradition; they were continuing it as well as inverting it; between them, they created their own. The great nineteenth-century imperatives were more real to them, between them they 'dealt with' them more, by incorporation and rejection, than Wilde did (in anything but his best essays). Was it that they were more intelligent as individuals? I doubt if Berenson at least was; it was rather that he

belonged to a more intelligent community, had a better idea of
his historical role: he could guide himself by Henry James and
Henry Adams, Mrs Wharton and Mrs Gardner, as well as by
Peter. I Tatti was another Fenway Court, but with Mrs Gardner's idea carried to extremes—an Italian palace transported to
Boston and, this time, back again to Italy. It was left to Harvard
as a serious cultural monument, a serious testimony to and inspiration in, the art of living. Wilde had no guides of comparable weight. He was wholly dependent on Pater.

What the aesthetes achieved was a kind of apotheosis or
Transfiguration and Assumption of the Boston tradition, in
which it left the earth where it had dwelt so long and for which
it had been designed, and mounted aloft, to Rome, Settignano,
London, Paris. In so doing it became of course etherialized, lost
contact with all its more mundane functions, like social service;
in some respects—to use Santayana's phrase—it was continued
into something logically its opposite (amoralism and world-
weariness). But it achieved thereby as it departed a glorious
effulgence it had never had before, and one on which many eyes
are still fixed, though it bedazzles and dissatisfies.

Let us offer what reasons we can in justification of our claim
that the four were significantly similar, significantly a group. We
have already pointed out how exactly Santayana's sense of the
American and his problems followed Henry James's. This resemblance was exact enough for his sensibility to reproduce key per-
ceptions and tones of voice, symbolic moments of memory. In
Persons and Places, for instance, there are passages about his
family's Boston house, and its view of the Charles, which are
made to express a general point about the Bostonian temperament. This is strikingly like James's descriptions in *The Bostonians,* written long before.

> They took us into the diningroom to show us the 'beautiful view'
> from the back of the house—a great expanse of water, with a low line
> of nondescript sheds and wooden houses marking the opposite bank.
> It was Bostonian to show us the view first.[6]

We notice the powerfully ironical resonances, concentrated in
the word 'Bostonian'; none of the aesthetes could use that word
without a quiver of agitation. James describes how Basil Ran-

som, at dinner with Olive Chancellor, gets 'another view, through a window where the curtain remained undrawn by her direction (she called his attention to this—it was for his benefit) of the dusky, empty river, spotted with points of light'. And later Ransom tells Mrs Luna of this dinner.

> 'That's what they call in Boston being very "thoughtful",' Mrs Luna said, 'giving you the Back Bay (don't you hate the name?) to look at, and then taking credit for it.' [7]

Santayana in his book describes the view from this window thus,

> This view of water reflecting the sky was unmistakably impressive, especially when the summer sunset lit up the scene, and darkness added to distance made the shabby bank opposite inoffensive. Gorgeous these sunsets often were; more gorgeous, good Bostonians often believed, than any sunsets anywhere else in the world; and my limited experience does not belie them.

We note again the habitual, self-baffling irony. We are told this was a characteristic note of Norton and Lowell in conversation, and in written work surely Adams, James, and Santayana are the supreme ironists of all time—in quantity, at least. James, in Chapter 19 of his novel, describes the same view quite brilliantly, but also stressing its shabbiness and sordidness; then he comments,

> Verena thought such a view lovely, and she was by no means without excuse when, as the afternoon closed, the ugly picture was tinted with a clear, cold rosiness.

The two writers are identical in their mode of unwilling subjection to, ironic participation in, various too-simple imperatives, imperatives which the name of Boston evokes perhaps better than anything else.

Santayana's chapter on 'The Church of the Immaculate Conception', in the same book, bring out all he had learned from Henry Adams. 'Yet it may be well to mention those two points here, in order that the skein of my meditations at the Immaculate Conception may be seen unravelled.' Both form and sub-

stance are very like those of Adams' chapters on French churches
in Chartres. These were the two great legislators of aestheticism,
the two great (highly moralizing) enemies of moralism. Almost
everywhere in the *Education* and in Santayana's autobiography
you find key passages of that creed and that psychology, however
obliquely expressed.

Here is Santayana:

> These travels of the intellect helped me in boyhood to overcome the
> hatred I then felt for my times and my surroundings; and later they
> have helped me to overcome the rash impulse to claim an absolute
> rightness for the things I might have preferred. . . . I could forgive
> the world anything except the ignorance and arrogance of thinking
> its condition alone possible or alone right.[8]

The non-forgiveness of the world there expressed almost openly
is an important clue to our understanding of all these men; and
the search for intellectual tactics that enable one to outma-
noeuvre emotional difficulties is another. Henry James often
criticised people for 'taking life too hard'. He applied the phrase
to his brother William—it is a key to that crucial relationship *
—and to several Bostonian characters in his novels. What seems
to us like James's evasiveness seemed to him like 'not taking life
too hard'.

Here is a passage from Adams' *Education:*

> The boy Henry wanted to go to Europe; he seemed well-behaved,
> when anyone was looking at him; he observed conventions, when he
> could not escape them; he was never quarrelsome, towards a superior;
> his morals were apparently good, and his moral principles, if he had
> any, were not known to be bad. Above all, he was timid and showed
> a certain sense of self-respect, when in public view. What he was at

* Henry Adams' relationship to his elder brother, Charles Francis, was
strikingly similar. The elder brothers represented to the younger, indeed
pressed on them, certain traditional challenges—to take part in 'the life of
action', typically; challenges which the younger brothers evasively but deci-
sively declined. Because all intellectual Boston was then turning away from
such challenges, the younger brothers were able to express in their work a
full, rich, many-sided movement of the spirit, personal and cultural. It is
thus they count for more today than their brothers—and than most other
people.

heart, no-one could say; least of all himself; but he was probably human, and no worse than some others.[9]

It is a curious mingling of self-dislike and self-love one feels in Adams, neither resolved, and issuing in an oblique but strenuous self-assertion; an intellectual equivalent to the condition Lawrence portrays in the figure of Sir Clifford Chatterley.*

> The habit of doubt; of distrusting his own judgment and of totally rejecting the judgment of the world; the tendency to regard every question as open; the hesitation to act except as a choice of evils; the shirking of responsibility; the love of line, form, quality; the horror of ennui; the passion for companionship and the antipathy to society —all these are well-known qualities of New England character.[10]

There is a very oblique attack on all crucial problems, avoiding the obvious measures ('the shirking of responsibility'), which is interwoven with aestheticism in a simpler sense ('the love of line, form, quality; the horror of ennui').

The aesthetic temperament was, as we said, an exaggeration of certain elements in the contemporary Boston temperament. It began with a passionate interest in 'the picturesque', that category of objects, effects, history, thought, life-style, which was to be found above all in Italy. James's friend Constance Fenimore Woolson, when she reached Italy, wrote,

> here I have attained that old-world feeling I used to dream about, a sort of enthusiasm made up of history, mythology, old churches, pictures, statues, vineyards, the Italian sky, dark-eyed peasants, opera-music, Raphael and old Michael, and ever so many more ingredients, —the whole having, I think, taken me pretty well off my feet.[11]

We need not call Miss Woolson an aesthete. She was a cultured and intelligent lady, fully belonging to her place and time and social position—not wanting to escape from those in any intellectually passionate way. But if Henry Adams used more sophisticated terms to discuss such themes, the ultimate source of his

---

* It is an equivalent also to James's character Ralph Touchett, in *Portrait of a Lady*. James and Lawrence give their characters very similar traits, but interpret them very dissimilarly. Adams belongs with James—indeed Ralph Touchett is James's 'Henry Adams'.

fascination with them surely remained the same as hers—the antithesis between all such things and contemporary America. The difference between them was that Adams took such feelings much further. Much of the aesthetes' outrageousness was only an extension of what was quite conventional. The picturesque was an ordinary minor theme in the thinking of most cultured people then; in the aesthetes' writing it became major and extraordinary —because of their remarkable skills, but also because of the act of intellectual courage which enabled them to follow up and follow out what they found themselves thinking. Rome was the supreme city for Norton, too, and because it was supremely picturesque. But it was the aesthetes, for instance James, who almost flatly regretted those modernizations of the city that made it healthier to live in, because they also made it less picturesque. For many people (for Norton much of the time) values like public health, formerly held in tension with the aesthetic in the idea of culture, had lost their old vitality. The aesthetes, discreetly, obliquely, relinquished them. And this idea of 'the picturesque' was allied to that of 'the aristocratic', and several others. Santayana was very interested in 'the aristocratic', as we shall see. And the hero of James's story 'The Passionate Pilgrim' says, 'I came into the world an aristocratic. I was born with a soul for the picturesque.' The combination (also to be found in Norton, in typically muted form) could seem a paradox, in other contexts. Such ideas were allied for the aesthetes only because they were all the great enemies of 'work, growth, enterprise, reform', the syndrome which Santayana says every cultured American felt demanded from him. They renounced responsibility for social and political reality—resigned it to the philistines—and in so doing they only carried to completion a tendency incipient in all cultured Bostonians then.

There were of course other Boston writers who carried the tendency far enough to be called aesthetes. I concentrate on these four on the assumption that they count for something today in a sense the poets—say, George Cabot Lodge and Joseph Stickney —do not. These four made something sizable and durable out of an experience (and a resolution of that experience) which many others shared. Of course they did so by making use of quite generally available and current ideas. There was an international 'aesthetic movement' then, and from one point of view they only participated in that. In the same way of course the fate Boston was then undergoing was shared by many other American cities, and from *that* point of view these four gave expression to a generally American, not a specifically Bostonian, experience. But there is also *this* point of view—that the Bostonian experience made them aesthetes. And that view surely derives some plausibility, some dignity, some vividness, from the special strength of the Boston tradition, including its transformation in the aesthetes' lifetime, and from the special poignancy of the contrast between what that tradition had been and what it became. Mrs Gardner, because she was a Bostonian, is a more interesting figure than Mrs Potter Palmer—perhaps than Mabel Dodge Luhan—because she was closer to the crucial *cultural* choice of her time. The aestheticism of Adams, James, Santayana, and Berenson constituted a living link—involuntary, indirect, recoiling from both termini—between the old Bostonianism and the twentieth-century imagination.

So probably the best sign under which to group all their values is still the old Boston word 'culture' (in my vocabulary, 'high culture'), but given a newly aggressive character, as largely an alternative to social and political reality. That is what Berenson thought he believed in. James's interest was more dialectical—he had a loyalty to simpler, plainer values, too—but what he can affirm with any force is cultural in that sense. And what Adams and Santayana finally have to offer is the value, the richness, of life and thought taken not simply on their own terms but for their 'educational' effect as a spectacle. Of course words like 'education' have lost half their old Bostonian meaning; 'culture' itself has become aestheticized. But one feels the new men deserve the word, deserve to inherit it, because of the continuity of their work with that of the past, and because of its similar relation to the Boston of their day. (This point will be argued more fully later.) Even the most crudely aesthetic of them, Berenson, thought of himself as a humanist, and is so described by his disciples. Iris Origo, in her article on him in 1960, said that the photographs of him reproduced there represented a farewell to a whole world—perhaps to the last steady light of humanism in Europe.[12] By our definition, a humanist is exactly what he was not. A conspectus of contemporary knowledge and thought was exactly what Berenson, with his rejection of the sciences and the social sciences, never attempted.* But he thought of himself as a humanist, as a man of general culture.

The four men were not very intimate friends—James and Adams maintained the closest relationship—but they moved in the same circles and according to the same life-style. They were all aesthetes, they were all exiles; they had in common a certain framework to all their experience. There were castles to be visited, cathedrals to be appreciated, paintings (of fabulous price) to be autheenticated; there were lavish entertainments to be attended, other people's lives to be observed, rich women to be flattered; all the gaudy, expensive, stagy life of a foreign salon —the kitchens they knew were all in America. The most famous, and in some ways the most characteristic, relationship they shared was with Norton's former students, Mrs Gardner and Mrs Wharton. (Their relationship with Norton himself was the most significant one they shared intellectually, perhaps.) These formidably wealthy and wilful ladies, energetic and unhusbanded,** were always in the act of making some imperial progress across Europe, or of setting up some new home to be filled with art

---

* *Aesthetics and History* is sometimes cited as an exception to such generalizations, but I must confess I cannot see why. Berenson's theory is not wholly self-consistent, and includes some bows in the direction of the responsible society, but the general tendency is clear enough, and crude enough. The artist 'indulges in the free play of his gifts, and has nothing else in his head; certainly no idea of teaching or preaching' (p. 18 in the New York edition of 1948). Like Santayana, Berenson has transformed the ethical idealism so characteristic of earlier Boston into an aesthetic idealism with a marked—and quite religiose—quietism. 'The aesthetic moment is a moment of mystic vision,' he says on p. 85. This is an aestheticism with a marked recoil from the rest of life. 'Ideated sensations are life-enhancing only when they remain intransitive, stimulating no appetite. They belong to a realm apart—beyond actuality, where the ideal is the only reality, a realm of contemplation, where nothing can happen except to the soul of the spectator. Possibly this is where our first parents lived before the itch for action took hold of them. Conceivably it may anticipate a Heaven in which . . . we shall ideate the ideal Athens, the City of Man' (p. 70).

**This was not strictly true of Mrs Gardner, but she seems to have given that impression.

treasures in the finest taste, and in either case commanding the services of their talented friends. The men under discussion all had a feminine streak in their natures, and in addition something of a mystique of Woman—both not unconnected with aestheticism, perhaps. At any rate, they were not very sure of themselves with such powerful female natures, and shared a rueful state of subjection to their queenly and telegraphic commands.

But there was, beyond these two, a whole world of aesthetes and exiles—American and otherwise—scattered across Europe. Iris Origo, Berenson's disciple, is the daughter of Lady Sybil Cutting, who by a second marriage became the wife of Geoffrey Scott, the author of *The Architecture of Humanism* and *The Portrait of Zélide,* and by a third marriage became the wife of Percy Lubbock, the author of *The Craft of Fiction.* Mr Scott was secretary to Berenson. Mr Lubbock was a close friend of Henry James. He was also a close friend of Howard Sturgis, the author of *Belchamber,* and a cousin of Santayana. All three, James, Lubbock, and Sturgis, were intimates of Mrs Wharton, who in her turn became a close friend of Nicky Mariano, the companion of Berenson's later years. This is one corner of the network of relationships and activities which constituted the social context, the home country, of the exiled aesthetes.

Those are our reasons for calling these four a group, both in their lives and in their work. How are we to evaluate the change that work constituted in the Boston tradition? Let us first assert that by its size and power that work made itself the main current in that tradition; if it turned at an angle from the old river-bed, and if some water continued to flow in the old direction, we still call this the main stream. We say the river turned at this point. Babbitt may have followed Norton more literally than Berenson did (and more in accordance with one's own taste), but it was at a time when the truest fidelity demanded a disagreement.

What that disagreement amounted to was that the new men disbelieved in the responsible society. They did not believe that Boston made a high quality of life (as they understood that phrase) available to its citizens, and they did not believe that any similar enterprise could. To attempt such a thing, deliberately and institutionally and righteously, was to defeat one's own aims.

A rich culture was for them not one which excluded lawlessness, disease, or vice, or one which earnestly offered to raise all its members to a common high level, but one which included enclaves where a few chosen spirits could make their own civilization; where they could enrich their own and each other's experience by sampling, appreciating, and criticising the contrasts of a brilliantly and unequally developed society. From this fundamental disagreement derived a thousand minor differences: of attitude, towards democracy, religion, America; of style and structure and subject matter in what they wrote; of preference and enthusiasm and taste among works of art; all the differences between what we have called a responsible culture and what we have called aestheticism. They disagreed then very importantly with Ticknor, and even with Norton and his more orthodox disciples.

But because Norton's responsible culture was not a fully alive or healthy thing, that disagreement and rupture were radical in only some ways. The continuities were equally striking. We have noted Norton's interest in Catholicism at the end of his life, and we could have said as much of Mrs Gardner and Mrs Wharton. Of the aesthetes proper, Berenson was the only one who entered the church, but Santayana and Adams were for a long time fascinated with the idea, and some of James's stories imply the same about him. They were none of them fascinated with any of the Protestant sects; it was the picturesque they were seeking in religion, and so were their Boston contemporaries.

Another instance is that late Boston scepticism. Justice Holmes, for instance, praised Santayana's *Winds of Doctrine* to him. Santayana comments,

It is or was usual, especially in America, to regard the polity of which you happened to approve as sure to be presently established everywhere and to prevail forever after. To have escaped this moralistic obsession, at least for a moment, evidently was a great pleasure to Judge Holmes.[13]

It was a characteristic pleasure, and not only to Judge Holmes; this was the kind of insight the Bostonians' experience was driving them all towards. Their polity was not going to prevail; it was crumbling under their eyes. That experience profoundly conditioned a temperament like that of Barrett Wendell, the great Harvard teacher and Boston character, with his conviction that New England was exhausted. To be born a Boston American was to be born old—Indiana had vitality, but it was a new kind, which he could not share. Wendell in his neurotic, epigrammatic pessimism was very much in tune with the aesthetes.

Another instance of a continuity is that late-Boston Anglophilia. Merle Curti says that the horrors of the Gilded Age revived the colonial-deferential feeling towards Europe in Boston. This feeling was more than colonial and backward-looking, however; it was also the feeling Norton expressed in his letter to Wright, that the things New Englanders so much wanted to see *develop* in America, were instead developing in England; Leslie and Fitzjames Stephen are always being quoted by people like Holmes and William James, as *leaders* of thought. It was also, for instance, the feeling that British fiction-writers were offering the Boston reader—the American reader—more of what he wanted. Kipling and Stevenson owed their popularity to what they wrote, not to where they came from. But no doubt it was dissatisfaction with his own position in America that turned many a cultured Bostonian's eyes yearningly towards England. And consequently, within the British literary tradition it was Thackeray who became the great master. Brownell held him the greatest master of English prose ever, and Santayana, reminiscing over his days with the *Lampoon,* talks of the enthusiasm of everyone at Harvard for Thackeray and *Punch.* This marks a change of meaning for 'the British literary tradition'. In the earlier Boston it was Dickens we heard of, but now it is Thackeray whom men like Wendell and Holmes admire and respond to.

What is more surprising is that the aesthetes, too, for all their sophistication, allowed Thackeray and 'England' the same sway over their imaginations. Berenson, choosing 'timeless' books to be read to him in his extreme old age, chose *Vanity Fair* to be the last of all. Henry Adams in his autobiography identifies himself with Pendennis often, and it could be in part from Thackeray's attitude to his personae that Adams learned his curious handling of 'Henry Adams'. Which leads one to remember that Thackeray had his sophistication too, and to realize that what the aesthetes meant by the term was not so different from what Thackeray meant. Thackeray was one of the sponsors of their cult of Woman—'the tutelary power of a woman of thirty' is Henry Adams' phrase. Thackeray could 'draw a gentleman', and Dickens never could, and Bostonians after the war were all condemned to be gentlemen, condemned to feel Thackeray's uneasy blend of dissatisfaction and satisfaction in the status. The aristocratic and aesthetic poses of the new men were, in one way, variations on that theme. In Adams' correspondence, even Disraeli, that least Bostonian of authors, plays an important part. He semi-seriously modelled himself on Tancred at times.

Indeed, the more one reads Berenson and Santayana, the more one sees them as basically Bostonian minds, and their exotic heritages as causing only minor variations in that pattern. Their anti-Bostonianism was no more radical than that of Adams and James, or indeed that of Barrett Wendell; it was itself a Bostonian trait. And then, despite the cosmopolitan scepticism, and in many ways the boldness, of their imaginations, the aesthetes remained markedly discreet in their personal behaviour, and even somewhat Puritanical in their personal tastes. This is a very Bostonian life-style, and they carried it no further than Norton himself. Nor was their life-style any less relevant to the pattern of their thoughts and feelings than other people's. This shows itself best, as patterns usually do, in the limitations of their taste. Their preferences in fiction—we shall give examples later—were markedly unsophisticated. This had to do with their determination to see reality in picturesque terms; contemporary reality (so important in contemporary fiction) suffers more distortion than the past from such an attempt. The aesthetes' vision of Europe, of England, was in some ways as simply drawn and brightly coloured as that of much naiver travellers. Berenson and Santayana were both devoted to Oxford, the place and the students, as a kind of dream come true. 'Something so crude and vulgar and stupid about many if not most Harvard men,' noted Berenson, comparing them. They were not interested in the England out of which, say, D. H. Lawrence came. When Santayana met Henry James in England, he immediately felt more at home with him than he ever had with William (whose pupil and colleague he had been). For Henry James shared Santayana's 'attitude to living in England', an attitude which seemed, to people like William, to have too much the character of self-indulgent fantasy. Santayana and James were, in these ways, typical Bostonians abroad, and their marvellous talents were at the service of some fairly ordinary prejudices.

For these reasons, it seems right to call the aesthetes' work truly Bostonian, truly a continuation, as well as a development. But to estimate that development in any sense, we need to measure it by evaluative standards too. Not that we could attempt any full evaluation here; * we will take it for granted that each of the four men was in his own field a brilliant and major figure; we will try to estimate only a few characteristics they all have in common as aesthetes, and their significance for later American culture.

If the main current of New England literature—which was itself a major current in American literature—turned with and followed the aesthetes, this is not to say that even the serious American writers of their time, or since, have generally admired or imitated them. The 'writers of their time' included men like Hamlin Garland, Theodore Dreiser, and Sinclair Lewis. Nor did they command—what they emphatically disclaimed—general moral authority. People like Jane Addams in Chicago and Vida Dutton Scudder in Boston were brought up in the tradition of aesthetic appreciation, but abandoned it to work in settlement houses and in other kinds of social reclamation. Like John J. Chapman rebelling against Norton, they turned to a more simply moral tradition, like that which in the old Boston had been united with aesthetic and intellectual appreciation. Historically —at least as seen in a short perspective—that main-stream ran away into sand and disappeared.

And it is undeniable that the aesthetes did sacrifice a great deal of intelligence and dignity to their habit of irony, their tone of disillusionment, their air of sophistication. Santayana, perhaps the most intelligent of them all, says of his 'aristocratic people' that they

* James's work I have discussed in some detail in *Re-Appraisals*. On the others I am not competent to comment.

are indifferent to the disputes of critics and pedants, and perhaps to
the maxims of preachers; such things are imposing only to those who
are inwardly wondering what they ought to do and how they ought
to feel. A truly enlightened mind is all the simpler for being enlightened and thinks, not without a modest sort of irony, that art and
life exist to be enjoyed and not to be estimated.[14]

That last sentence, especially the alternative it offers us, is surely
the work of a (temporarily) inferior mind. We are not surprised
to hear him proceed to cite first the Greek lawgivers and then the
Fascists (this is 1931) as an example of 'those who are most intelligent and determined'; they are proud of their special customs,
like schoolboys, without claiming any absolute rightness for
them. This is another example of those blinders of the immoralist we noted before on Henry Adams. The perfect aristocrat

> smiles at his own ways as he might at the ways of the natives any-
> where. He seems to himself only an odd native of an odd world; but
> perhaps the chief advantage which his good breeding bestows on him
> is that he can afford to regard the other odd natives without hatred
> or envy.[15]

The aesthetes all affected a languor which is on occasion profoundly irritating. *Ça vous amuse, la vie?*, the phrase John Hay
often used to Henry Adams as a comment on distressing experi-
ences, may stand as their collective epitaph. Henry Adams tells us
that Kipling (a ship-mate on a voyage to America) was a very
vivacious companion; over 'Henry Adams' he dashed 'his exu-
berant fountain of gaiety and wit,—as though playing a garden
hose on a thirsty and faded begonia'. Senator Howe had first
compared Adams to a begonia, but Adams' own 'ironical' use of
that comparison was much the more damaging to him. It is in
Adams' *Education* that this begonia quality is most protracted
and unpleasant. This sentence, describing his loss of money in
the financial panic of 1893, should be a sufficient reminder.

> For several years a sufferer from insomnia, his first thought was of
> beggary of nerves, and he made ready to face a sleepless night, but
> although his mind tried to wrestle with the problem of how any man
> could be ruined who had, months before, paid off every dollar of
> debt he knew himself to owe, he gave up that insoluble riddle in

order to fall back on the larger principle that beggary could be no more for him than it was for others who were more valuable members of society, and, with that, he went to sleep like a good citizen, and the next day started for Quincy where he arrived August 7.[16]

This is typical of his highly elaborate and artificial nonchalance, so unattractively draped over the nervous tension and the sense of personal affront. What is sometimes an ingenious technique for telling a complicated kind of truth about himself—combining highly personal with highly impersonal perspectives—is at other times, and quite as often, a self-indulgent posing which seems to regard itself as exempt from the obligation to tell any kind of truth, much more the other obligations to his readers.

Justice Holmes made a good comment on this insistent and unreal posing in Adams.

> When I happened to fall in with him on the street he could be delightful, but when I called at his house and he was posing to himself as the old cardinal he would turn everything to dust and ashes. After a tiresome day's work one didn't care to have one's powers of resistance taxed by discourse of that sort, so I called rarely.[17]

And Santayana tells of their friend, Ward Thoron, taking him to see Adams in Washington.

> 'So you are trying to teach philosophy at Harvard,' Mr Adams said, somewhat in the gentle but sad tone we knew in Professor Norton, 'I once tried to teach history there, but it can't be done. It isn't really possible to teach anything. . . .'
> Still both Mr Adams' house and that of Ward's new family were luxurious. I got the impression that, if most things were illusions, having money and spending money were great realities.[18]

Here one applauds Santayana, but in the third volume of the same work he represents himself in essentially the same posture and gesture that he had criticised in Adams. When he wanted to stay at Oxford, a friend of his proposed to get him a tutorship.

> Oh no! I had never wanted to teach. I had nothing to *teach*. I wished only to learn, to be always the student, never the professor. And with being eternally the student went the idea of being free to move, to pass from one town and one country to another.[19]

This constant demand for social and intellectual freedom, and a freedom so absolute as to be almost empty, lies behind the lives of all the aesthetes.

But worst of all is the constant threat of vulgarity. Perhaps this idea is put into our minds by an irritated reaction to their insistence on refinement and elegance, but once there it lodges and grows. The worst case is Berenson, so reluctant to have it mentioned at I Tatti that he earned money as an art-expert (though he in fact earned £20,000 a year from Duveen between 1910 and 1936) and so secretive about both that (even to his wife) and his Jewishness. When facts of such size are kept buried, in an establishment of that exquisiteness, an ugly smell breathes upward from the cellars. But Berenson was a perfect Henry James character (if only James had written *that* novel), and there is a vulgarity too in the long drawn-out, delicately hinted-at, revelation of something wrong with, say, Gilbert Osmond's life. To other people, such a life could never begin to seem distinguished, and a big revelation would be unnecessary. James and Berenson thought an imperious elegance of gesture, however artificial, could carry moral authority in despite of every other personal trait. There is a vulgarity too in all the manoeuvrings of Henry Adams' persona: his anonymous novels, and third-person autobiography, and manuscript-circulated poems, and privately published treatises. For a man who insisted on 'seeing through' the verdicts of history, he remained distressingly concerned with the verdicts of this week. For a man who saw through the world so early, he remained painfully interested in aspects of it less disillusioned men disregard.

As one would deduce from their liking for Thackeray, the aesthetes' taste in contemporary art stopped short of the modern. Berenson was very philistine about Picasso and Joyce. James preferred Hugh Walpole's fiction (and Oliver Onions' and Compton Mackenzie's) to D. H. Lawrence's. They all disliked the reckless experimentation and self-revelation of modern art. But the most interesting case is Santayana. During the First World War he was invited to a weekend at Garsington, where Lady Ottoline Morell often entertained some of the brilliant younger people in the arts. There he met Lytton Strachey, whom he summarizes as 'obscene', and Siegfried Sassoon, of whom he remarks, 'He seemed to be swimming socially on the crest of every wave and to be universally well-informed, with moral chaos and bitterness underneath.' [20] These comments (particularly the Strachey details) and all his remarks about Garsington, are strikingly like those Lawrence makes in his portrait of Garsington in *Women in Love*. (We have seen Santayana's ability to see and feel like James and like Adams; perhaps this is another example of the same talent.) But the realization of how easily he might have met Lawrence at Garsington reminds one that such an encounter was unthinkable. Santayana's life was largely shaped by a determination to avoid such encounters. He in fact refused all re-invitations to Garsington. It was the *old* Oxford, the *old* England he loved, he says. It was precisely Lawrence—that passionate commitment to the exploration of life—naked contemporary personal experience—that he was refusing to meet.

In all these ways, the aesthetes command less than total deference and attention. They are, nevertheless, a significant force in American literary culture today; much the most significant part of the New England heritage. They are, for instance, the America out of which T. S. Eliot comes; the sensibility which found the modern ugliness in twentieth-century London was trained in doing the same in nineteenth-century Boston; the vision of all Western Christianity and culture drowned in a rising tide of barbarism is modelled on the vision of Boston's decay. But also quite directly, and in themselves, the four aesthetes today act on the education of American students, particularly in the Ivy League schools. *The Education of Henry Adams* and *Character and Opinion in the United States* are important books even in undergraduate courses at schools like Amherst and Wellesley. Henry James is everywhere established as a great American novelist and a great American intelligence. The aesthetes' habits of irony and indirection, in style, of role-playing and myth-making, in thought, have become parts of the most high-powered American literary mind. Their horror of naïveté, their insistence on irony and disillusionment, make it hard for literary Americans to appreciate any such 'innocent' insights as, for instance, Salinger is concerned with.*

* See Appendix C.

They enjoy this effectiveness because they are all impressive writers, and they are impressive because their individual talents found a favourable tradition to work in. In them the Boston tradition achieved probably its most brilliant successes. But it did so by a kind of suicide, since their version of that tradition contradicted the older version in very important ways. They rejected the whole idea of the responsible society. Are we then to conclude that this idea was so mistaken that only by rejecting it could writers create something really alive? If not, if this idea and this tradition were valid ways to approach literature, why didn't Boston in its period of full vigour produce equally brilliant writers? What went wrong?

Chapter Eight

WHAT WENT WRONG?

By THIS QUESTION we imply more than the failure of New England to produce many brilliant writers. We imply that the level of literary work in most genres was significantly low. That as we follow Boston's literary record chronologically through the century, we more and more clearly discern that these writers' talents were being not fostered but suppressed, deformed. And that when we come to the aesthetes the impression is clinched, because we see talents released and gaining energy by a rejection of the Boston tradition.

That the artistic record does read in this way, we must, in a book of this length, assume to be generally agreed in advance; and if we focus again on the literature, presumably we can assume so. Despite attempts to find in the Schoolroom Poets enough rich ambiguities and metaphysical puns to win them a place in the anthologies, most critics today believe, or act as if they believe, that the literary efforts of nineteenth-century Boston were by and large misdirected. This judgment may be sometimes softened by the formula 'Their taste was not ours', but if pressed, most critics will admit that 'their taste', unlike that of, say, Pope's world, was as a whole bad taste.

There are as many variations as one would expect between particular writers in the Boston tradition, but what they all have in common—

what they all agree makes a good poetic subject, and a good poetic style, the feelings and facts to expatiate on, the feelings and facts to pass over, the tone to take with one's audience—all this was by and large unhelpful to them. And what is so interesting is that 'all this' is exactly the work of the culture they belonged to; which, as I have tried to point out, not only set out to establish a city of 'culture', but even accorded literature the highest position within that culture, devoting much time, money, enthusiasm, and indeed imagination, to the encouragement of writers. I have also tried to prove that this attempt was not as a whole a feeble or insignificant thing. And yet Boston's verse and prose were thinner, sparser, duller than London's, although a writer's place in London must have been much less important, much less secure, much poorer in encouragement, reward, prestige.

It is sometimes argued that the quality of work done in New England was worse than that done in contemporary Britain simply because the larger population was statistically bound to produce more men of the highest talent. This cannot be refuted; we can only offer an alternative explanation in the hope that it will carry more conviction. Our case is that such talent as there was in Boston did not write in the proper traditions, and thus could have done better work than it did; and the difficulty with such a case is that the only obvious test of talent *is* the work it produces. If that is brilliant, we say the talent is brilliant. If that is not, how can one say what the talent would have done and been under other circumstances? Well, it is possible to distinguish, even among bad books, which are the work of the interesting minds. But our answer must be mostly that one *can* judge whether actual circumstances were favourable—the most important circumstance being the literary traditions of the time—and how much difference that must have made. Many aspects of a work of literature derive from the tradition within which the individual writer is working, and after reading several examples of a particular genre we come to know (in some cases more clearly than in others) which merits to expect from the next such work. Some traditions produce more successes than others, even from the same writer, and the culture which makes successful traditions available to its writers we call favourable to its literary talent.

That is what we mean by saying that the writers of an unfavourable culture 'could have done better work', and in that sense we say that Boston was largely unfavourable to its writers.

There were of course exceptions, men whose talent triumphed over their conditions, and a few words must be said about them to align them with the general proposition. The aesthetes broke with the conditions; they left Boston, refused to serve the community into which they were born; and their success as writers owes a great deal to (though it also suffers a great deal from) that break. Their sense of form, of tone, of literary tradition, was developed in defiance of 'what the community expects of you', and exactly this gave them their energy.

A greater problem is posed by the New England Renaissance; is not this a literary triumph, and produced exactly by the conditions here described? (Poe, Melville, Whitman, also creep into these discussions, on various pretexts, which boil down to the similarity of the conditions under which they too worked. But what we mean by Boston conditions is not just what the city shared with the rest of America, but the peculiar concentration and institutionalization of them there. Their operation is more observable there, and both halves of the paradox—good conditions and bad work—are more sharply opposed.) Hawthorne is the hardest author to discuss under this heading, because of his grossly exaggerated reputation today; * but it is interesting that his admirers try to dissociate him from the Boston community, stressing his essential solitariness and his scorn for his neighbour writers; and we can go so far towards agreement with them as to say that if 'the Boston author' could have been excised from Hawthorne early enough, we would have had a much better writer. Thoreau withdrew from the Boston community, and his achievement clearly owes much, in many ways, to that act of virtue. He did not allow those conditions to work on him with any concentrated force.

In Emerson's case we must discriminate; he lived long enough to let us distinguish between periods in the Boston community he belonged to, and between the effects on him of belonging to

---

* I have made some remarks on Hawthorne in *Re-Appraisals*, which explain why I don't discuss him at more length here.

this community. What we have called the Ticknor period there was for him the time of early Transcendentalism, *The Dial,* and all his most interesting work. He lived and wrote then in opposition to Boston institutionalism; Concord was the intelligentsia of Boston; but such opposition is one of the artist's traditional modes of belonging to his society, and Emerson (contrast Thoreau) fully appreciated and 'belonged to' his. In many ways he benefited from so doing; it was a culture as favourable as not to his talent. But in the Norton period, with the establishment of the *Atlantic,* and the emergence of James Fields as intellectual impresario, the Boston community became significantly different. Emerson, though a genuinely solitary man, had not that ebullient vitality which allows someone to maintain a posture of radical dissent from and independence of society without suffering in the richness of his experience. He achieved self-sufficiency through serenity, not vitality; so when Boston abandoned the simple hostility of Ticknor and Andrews Norton, and invited Emerson to join the *Atlantic* authors in the role of serene sage, he had no defences against the invitation. But this was not a climate favourable to his talent. He was accepted into Boston literary society as a man of supernatural purity of soul and loftiness of thought; he was asked for a succession of beautiful thoughts; he was kicked upstairs. It is thus that we have the Emerson of his last fifteen years, who wrote what justifies his angriest critics, and who does seem to have wandered around Boston in a state of bland, benign vagueness.

It is clear, in a hundred anecdotes by Norton, Howells, Wendell, Holmes, Lowell, how treacherous Boston's welcome to Emerson was. There was a general covert resentment and scorn beneath the deference of these men. They felt he was 'too good for this world'; that his saintliness—for which they sincerely deferred to him—was possible only to someone who closed his eyes to actuality. Here is Howells, for instance, talking of his loss of memory.

It is known how before the end the eclipse became total and from moment to moment the record inscribed upon his mind was erased. Some years before he died I sat between him and Mrs Rose Terry

Cooke, at an Atlantic Breakfast, where it was part of my editorial function to preside. When he was not asking me who she was, I could hear him asking her who I was. His great soul worked so independently of memory as we conceive it, and so powerfully and essentially, that one could not help wondering if, after all, our personal continuity, our identity hereafter, was necessarily trammeled up with our enduring knowledge of what happens here. His remembrance absolutely ceased with the event, and yet his character, his personality, his identity fully persisted.[1]

Howells is of all the Boston writers the one most simply marred by their heritage. The contrast between that third sentence, so maliciously vivid and funny, and the next, so falsely pious and inflated, is surely quite shocking. Or consider James Russell Lowell, reminiscing about Emerson's lectures. 'Cynics might say what they liked. Did our own imaginations transfigure dry remainder-biscuit into ambrosia? At any rate, he brought us *life*, which, on the whole, is no bad thing.' [2] We must not let the manner conceal from us that Lowell is here suggesting to his readers that dry remainder-biscuit was all Emerson had to offer; and whatever *life* may mean to us, the rest of that sentence tells us that it was not a precise or important term to Lowell. 'Was it all transcendentalism? magic-lantern pictures on mist? As you will. These, then, were what we wanted. But it was not so. The delight and the benefit were that he put us in communication with a larger style of thought. . . .' [3] Here again no credit is ultimately given to Emerson; they were put into communication with a 'larger style' during his discourse, but was it *his* style, and was it anything more than large? At the same time, Lowell portrays himself as being, and no doubt was, in a state of enthusiastic reverence before Emerson. The evil of this particular Boston mode was just that it allowed one to manufacture reverence quite un-selfcritically, and to mingle such reverence with quite vivid malice without concern for their compatibility. In another place, after detailing Emerson's absurd fumblings with his notes, '. . . but it was as if a creature from some fairer world had lost his way in our fogs, and it was *our* fault, not his.' [4] He insists on the generous posture even while his hand does the ungenerous deed. They did not really like Emerson, or indeed understand him, so far as

one can see. Naturally, therefore, there was no fruitful intercourse between Emerson and this society, and his work derived
no vitality from it. His failures more than his successes are to be
credited to the community he belonged to; Boston after 1850 was
a culture unfavourable to his talent.

It is the period after 1850 we take to be the sharpest test of the
Boston theory. Despite the changes beginning in the social and
economic community, the structure of high culture remained un-
altered till the end of the century, and the idea of the responsible
society only now took its full literary effect—when writers who
had been trained in that tradition were producing their mature
work.

But when we turn to that work, what do we find? All the
Indian Summer writers' careful attention to the craft and the
dignity of literature ended in a profusion of minor verse and
light essays, and all the major subjects they attempted yielded
even smaller artistic success. Who reads Longfellow's *Christus* or
Lowell's 'Cathedral'? They were most lively in the role of institutional or occasional performer. Oliver Wendell Holmes was the
ideal Harvard class poet. They were themselves when literature
was completely identified with, reduced to, its social functions.
The society behind this adjective 'social' was not the abstract
public; it was the Saturday Club of Boston authors and intellectuals; but the Saturday Club took a very social view.

Oliver Wendell Holmes was the star of that club. He often
remarked that he had been born exactly a hundred years after Dr
Johnson, and he courted the comparison; he was the nineteenth-
century Bostonian Johnson, and the Saturday Club was the
equivalent of Johnson's. His contemporaries agreed with him.
Tom Appleton, Boston's irreverent wit, told Mr and Mrs Fields
that the sayings and doings of that Club would be recorded,
discussed, appreciated, in time to come, just as Johnson's were. It
is clear now that that will not happen; and a principal reason is
that the mode of performance at the Club, and its relationship to
the larger public beyond, were so much less risky than those of
Johnson's day. People only pretended to get drunk, and used
euphemisms for swear-words, and their laughter was arroused by
puns, mispronounced French, and mock-Yankee dialect. The

only person in that circle who could have taken a place in Johnson's was Henry James Sr; and he deserved it by the energy, the dangerousness, indeed the brutality of his wit.

The rest were careful to be 'human', even 'boyish', and they paid the price, in their work as well as in their manners.

> His magic was not far to seek—
> He was so human!

So says Lowell in his ode on Agassiz, another star of the Club. It is one of Lowell's more interesting poems, expressive of the genuine admiration they all felt for Agassiz, who, like Fields but more impressively, had the qualities they admired so much more than their own uncomfortable intelligence: geniality, kindliness, good nature, good fellowship.

> Once more I see him at the table's head
> When Saturday her monthly banquet spread
>   To scholars, poets, wits,
> All choice, some famous, loving things, not names,
> And so without a twinge at others' fames.[5]

As Lowell said in a letter, 'It is better to be a good fellow than a good poet, and perhaps (I am not sure) I might have shown a pretty fair talent that way with proper encouragement.' [6] That is all too obviously the source of his feeling for Agassiz, who turns into Santa Claus as the poem proceeds.

> Ample and ruddy, the board's end he fills
> As he our fireside were, our light and heat,
> Centre where minds diverse and various skills,
> Find their warm nook and stretch unhampered feet.

This is self-indulgent fantasy language, which makes the subject unreal, but if we compare it with the language about Emerson, we see that the affection is real here, the fantasy expresses and soothes some powerful complex of real feelings. Agassiz was the guarantee that intellectual prowess, and friendship with intellectuals, need not bring with it sharpness of tone, coldness of temperament, eccentricity, unpleasantness, effeminacy.

> For he was masculine from head to heel
> A mortal, built upon the antique plan,
> Brimful of lusty blood as ever ran,
> And taking life as simply as a tree.

I have dwelt rather long upon Lowell, but he is representative of the others, and the clearest case of something going wrong in a man, and his knowing it. Holmes was simply not intelligent enough to know it, and indeed not sensitive enough for anything to go wrong. Under other conditions, he would presumably have had a less exaggerated opinion of himself, but one does not imagine him being a much better or a much different poet. But Lowell said, with the kind of honesty he did have, 'I feel that my life has been mainly wasted, that I have thrown away more than most men ever had,' and after his death Norton, with *his* kind of honesty, said this feeling was 'justified'.[7] Everyone who knew Lowell seems to have been struck with his abilities; and indeed his essays do show a very quick, lively mind—he *sees* everything —and a remarkable gift for phrasing. He is like the student who seizes a point before the teacher has made it, and rephrases it better; and never does anything more than that. The essays remain, like the poems, unreadable; in the end, neither the insights nor the phrases are really appropriated, achieved.

What is lurid in Lowell, because it blights so completely, is vivid enough in the others. I have called Howells marred, because much of his work, fiction and essays, is impressive in its way, while other parts, especially the autobiographical, are the reverse. Howells was the great liar of the group, and shows how that culture fostered literary lying. In the area of personal truths, he falsifies and distorts his own feelings again and again. Here he is, discussing Lowell.

> He had always so much of the boy in him that he liked to tease the over-serious and over-sincere. He liked to tease and he liked to mock, especially his juniors, if any touch of affectation, or any little exuberance of manner gave him the chance; when he once came to fetch us, and the young mistress of the house entered with a certain excessive elasticity, he sprang from his seat, and minced towards her, with a burlesque of her buoyant carriage—which made her laugh.[8]

Of course she had to laugh; this was Mrs Howells, newly married, and in a rather dependent relationship to Lowell; but if we imagine the scene fully, we must suspect that she and her husband felt some impulse to more than laughter; Lowell was more than, and less than, funny. But it seems clear too that Howells did not allow himself to acknowledge those impulses. He lied. He called Lowell's behavior boyishness.

The lies, the fakery, the frustration, the inner muddle, all added up to a radical betrayal of the kind of integrity a literary talent lives off. Perhaps the point can be made with two short lists of crucial late-Boston vocabulary; the first for the everyday virtues, the second for Sundays.

1. Sunshiny, cheerful, boyish, kindly; sweetness, frankness, fun and fancy, good fellow.

2. Noble, lofty, elevated, simple, majestic, sacred, strong, white.

That last word is quintessential Boston. Norton called Clough 'as white a soul as ever lived', and Howells described Longfellow (adapting an allegedly Norwegian phrase, 'the white Christ') as 'the white Mr Longfellow'. What these words do, we need hardly point out, is not only to dissociate sensibility, but to impose on each separate category of experience a bullying push towards evaluations which are in themselves exempt from any free play of intelligence or irony. This is a philistine vocabulary, hostile to any risky play of the critical intelligence.

We can illustrate both vocabularies, and the way they coexisted, from Mrs Fields' memories of the Hawthornes. On one of Hawthorne's last visits to the Fields, he said (boyishly, of course),

> Why has the good old custom of coming together to get drunk gone out? Think of the delight of drinking in pleasant company and then lying down to sleep a deep strong sleep.[9]

Of course they all had a hearty laugh at that, though such remarks were taken to be genuine signs of Hawthorne's broad-based masculinity. But immediately after his death, Mrs Fields received a letter from Mrs Hawthorne, which began,

I wish to speak to you Annie.

A person of more uniform majesty never wore mortal form.

In the most retired privacy it was the same as in the presence of men.

The sacred veil of his eyelids he scarcely lifted to himself—such an unviolated sanctuary as was his nature, I, his inmost wife, never conceived or knew.

So absolute a modesty was not before joined to so lofty a self-respect.

The letter continues in this vein for some time, each sentence beginning on a separate line, like verses of the Bible. One last sentence,

To me—himself—even to me who was himself in unity—he was to the last the holy of holies behind the seraphim.[10]

There are two opposite kinds of falsity there, the would-be devilish and the would-be angelic, and quite equally disastrous. A culture which teaches two of its inmost illuminati to use language in these ways is a bad culture.

Boston used language better in Ticknor's time. Here is an extract from a letter written by John Lowell to his son in 1811.

It is peculiarly your misfortune that a certain readiness in acquiring a superficial knowledge of subjects has given you a reputation with many of your friends of possessing talents, with which both you and I know you are not favoured. The necessity is therefore greater, to exert yourself to support an opinion which you are conscious is too flattering. The most prominent trait in your mind is the rapidity with which you comprehend a subject and acquire some plausible knowledge of it, unless this quality be equalled or excelled by your feeble power of retaining what you have thus learned. . . . Let me, my son, now advert to a danger at the very thought of which I tremble because I consider it the greatest to which you are exposed. It is the most prolific source of all other failings and even vices. You will already have anticipated that I allude to the habit of idleness. You have never been idle, and therefore can have no just conception of the degrading, powerful effects of this habit. But though you have not been idle, yet paradoxical as it may seem, you have not been studious. I have never yet been able to perceive in you till within the last three months, the smallest disposition to study for the sake of acquiring knowledge, or from a principle of duty.[11]

We recognize here something of Ticknor's stately fusion of the public and private. Vocabulary, sentence structure, general tone, all invite objective participation from the boy, encourage a free play of intelligence and feeling on the subject of the letter. The boy's relationship with his father is not put in jeopardy, and yet is quite seriously invoked. The moral issue is kept separate from the emotional one, and the intellectual zest of the writing establishes the subject on a third level, impersonal and open-ended, on which the son can join the father in equal discussion of his own future.

Then we compare this letter of 1883, by John Lowell's great-grandson Percival, the astronomer and travel-writer, then in Japan, to his friend Frederick J. Stimson, in Boston.

> Why were you absent from a river expedition the other day. Your humble servant, an amicus and two amicae gifted in the musical line, not to mention boatmen and retainers all of whom have to be remembered at least pecuniarily. After threading our way through the innumerable canals which render the half of Tokio a mass of islands, we got into the river and gradually against the tide succeeded in gaining a suburban tea-house. I carried my photographic apparatus but was balked of views. So the girls are lost to posterity. The Japanese are a deeply religious people. There was a more than usual fair at Asakusa, and as you know one of the main temples, to which one of the fair ones attempted to entice us. We did not entice much, but hauled up to a landing and allowed her to go. She departed to pray while we graciously waited for her. The other amica, who was too lazy to move, amused herself by asking amicus to secure for her some cockle shells which attracted her infantile mind. Her childish delight, surprize and ignorant cruelty to these crustaceai were a striking index of the geisha mind.[12]

This is not a perfect parallel, because inspired by so much less serious an occasion, but I should point out that the writer was twenty-eight, and that this was a conscious literary effort. He and Stimson both were training themselves to become writers (Lowell afterwards wrote *The Soul of the Far East,* and other works) and they criticised each other's style and structure in these letters. This was then a serious attempt at literariness in the contemporary mode, and by a man of some talent. What we therefore notice is the uneasy habit of jocularity, the self-conscious use of foreign and learned words, the lurches into pompous seriousness (the last sentence), the involuntary patronizingness, the inability to sustain any sort of tone. Public and private are here not fused, but confused.*

This change can of course be presented in terms larger than (if blunter than) the use of language; for instance, the ever-stiffening Puritanism of literary decorum is another result of the literary world's insecure grasp of the distinction between public and private. Thus Norton, discussing James Russell Lowell after his death,

> I cannot take my readers, however worthy of confidence they may be, within the inner circle of intimacy, of which the charm would suffer, were its sanctity violated and its seclusion disturbed. The poet may tell what he likes of his own emotions, but . . .[13]

It is easy to sympathize with, and even to admire, this shutting of the door against all mere gossip; but in point of fact one *must* trust one's readers; to exclude them from that intimacy is to subordinate literary values to social ones, and to stifle literature.

The same deterioration is visible in the gradual excommunicating of contemporary European literature, the gradual refining of a taste that only Kipling and Stevenson were innocuous enough not to offend. Pater, we have seen, was too strong for Norton's stomach, Tolstoy for Lowell's, Ibsen for Babbitt's. 'There are some tastes that deserve the cudgel,' Babbitt threateningly declared; but those tastes that did not, suffered a worse fate; they came to deserve not even attention.

Finally, it is visible in the attitude to contemporary science, which earlier Boston had so eagerly assimilated, at the Lowell Institute and elsewhere. James Russell Lowell said of science, 'I hate it. I hate it as a savage hates writing, because I fear it will hurt me somehow.' And he is again representative. The crucial case was the theory of evolution. Agassiz declared against Dar-

---

* Of course this is a contrast between eighteenth-century prose and nine-teenth-century, and one could find similar contrasts in British prose of the same dates. My argument is that whereas Boston's version of eighteenth-century prose was characteristically distinguished, its version of nineteenth-century prose—certain important kinds—was not, because the culture had deteriorated in between.

win, and Boston as a whole followed Agassiz. John Amory Lowell reviewed *The Origin of Species* unfavourably for *The Christian Examiner;* the Lowell Institute refused to have John Fiske lecture on evolution; Ticknor and Fields refused to publish the Scientific Series, which included Darwin, Huxley, Tyndall, Buckle, and Lecky. Instead, Appleton published it in New York, and Ferris Greenslet says this was the first step in Boston's losing its primacy in publishing. (Later there was a reconciliation with science, in the aesthetic manner of Percival Lowell's book on Mars, and Henry Adams' fantasies about dynamos. These queer gaudy confusions of literature and science are typical of the aesthetes' ways of dealing with the cultural problems their Boston inheritance brought them—their 'Transfiguration and Assumption'.)

In every sector of high culture, the abilities counted for less, and the disabilities counted for more, in the second part of the century. Ticknor, though a severer (or at least simpler) moralist than Norton, excluded less of contemporary European literature; Emerson, though closer to Calvinist Puritanism than Barrett Wendell, was less haunted and hampered by it.

Of course, external, non-literary causes contributed to this failure. In 1855, 50,000 Irish immigrants were living in Boston, a city of perhaps 150,000. Of the Irish work force, 50 per cent were undifferentiated 'labourers'; of the native work force, only 5 per cent were.[14] They took the lowest place in society; they lived degraded lives in terrible slums; they drove out of the textile mills the New England girls who had made capitalist industrialism seem a decent economic system; they took over the city's politics. By 1900, as we have said, 35 per cent of the city's population was foreign-born.

Outside New England, the balance of power in the country shifted rapidly to the West, in numbers of population, in representation in the Senate and House, in wealth of product and speculation.

And in the class and economy structure of the country as a whole, the ruling-class Bostonians were losing status even while they maintained or increased their fortunes. Before the Civil War, the biggest single gift to a college was the $50,000 Abbott

Lawrence gave to Harvard. (Amherst was founded on a total endowment of $50,000.) But after the war, Johns Hopkins was given $3,500,000, Stanford $24,000,000, Chicago $34,000,000. During the eighteen forties there were not twenty millionaires in the country,* but by 1892 there were four thousand, and not many of them in New England. By 1910 there were twenty millionaires in the Senate (which was called the Millionaires' Club) and 9 per cent of the families in the country owned 70 per cent of the wealth. The great educational foundations were receiving enormous single gifts: the General Education Board, in 1902, $46,000,000; the Carnegie Corporation, in 1911, $151,000,000; and the Commonwealth Fund, in 1918, $43,000,000.[15] New England had few fortunes of that size. It found itself unimportant, even in its own preserve of education; it *staffed* the new foundations. Throughout the country, the members of the old-family, college-educated class, who owned family businesses and had traditions of political leadership, who had followed New England's lead in national affairs, were unable to maintain their places under the new conditions. Their scruples, their reputations, their social standing, now hampered them in dealing with their rivals —the corrupters of legislatures, the buyers of franchises, the allies of bosses. Even in the small towns and the countryside, the civic leaders of the past, so powerful in New England—the lawyers, the preachers, the editors, the old families—were overshadowed in the national consciousness by the big cities, big business, and the big labour unions. That old class had lost status, as Richard Hofstadter puts it. It seemed to them, and to everyone else, that their day was over, and that the future belonged to their sworn enemies—a fear by no means wholly realized. This was no mood in which to build a vigorous culture in New England.[16]

But the relations between the different parts of a culture are much too complicated for us to explain a class's literary feebleness simply by reference to its economic or even its social decline. New England in the Gilded Age was a plutocratic society with democratic ideals, and therefore a deeply uneasy, unhappy, cul-

* These are Richard Hofstadter's figures. This one is challenged by William Miller in 'The Realm of Wealth', an essay in *The Reconstruction of American History*, ed. John Higham (London, 1962). He suggests forty.

ture. But the same could be said of Paris at that time, and yet the writers there responded very differently—in literary terms, very much more creatively—to that cultural situation. The same could be said of London. Men can write books of magnificent vitality about the phenomenon of exhaustion, and descriptions of ugliness that are in themselves beautiful, and wise analyses of folly. That was what New England signally failed to do.

It is striking that while several of the great culture prophets of nineteenth-century England, the theoreticians of the responsible society, had American disciples whom they not only trusted, but respected more than any of their countrymen, these disciples wrote so much less, and so much worse, on the subject than their British counterparts. This contrast is most strikingly true of Ruskin and Norton, but is true also in some measure of Carlyle and Emerson, and even of Leslie Stephen and Lowell. The Americans seem nowadays much thinner, more dated, less readable. In the case of the poets—the contrast between Tennyson and Longfellow, between Browning and Lowell—the difference is there but I think the comparison is less relevant to our argument. In the case of the cultural novel (restricting our purview to New England within America) there is no comparison to make, because there was no fiction to compare with that of Dickens, George Eliot, or even Mrs Gaskell.* But culture, its theory and its practice, its incorporation of religious, moral, sociological, aesthetic material, was exactly the centre of the New England philosophy, the focus of its interest in literature, for instance. New Englanders read the great British writers on the subject with more understanding, it often seemed, than Englishmen did. It was in New England that Carlyle received his first recognition; it was at Harvard that Ruskin's ideas of art and culture were first made into a university course. Emerson and Norton saw to that. Why then did they, and their friends, have so little to say on similar subjects which now seems worth reading? Where are their analyses, economic or so-

---

* I must make an exception there for Howells and John W. de Forest, who were cultural novelists in some sense, and who were certainly comparable with Mrs Gaskell. My generalization must be taken to use the term 'cultural novelist' to mean a writer whose novels form part of a tradition of culture-criticism, and a powerful aggressive tradition, like that of nineteenth-century England.

ciological, either of England or of America, to compare with *Culture and Anarchy* or *Unto This Last?* Emerson's generalizations were too broad and vague, Charles Francis Adams' railway investigations were too narrow and too particular, and in between, in the properly cultural area, in Matthew Arnold's territory, what do we have? Not very much.

Even in purely literary criticism there was a striking poverty for a culture so devoted to the appreciation of literature. What is there to compare with (there is nothing to rival) the work of Arnold and Stephen in England? Almost the best we can think of are Lowell's profoundly unsatisfactory essays. Norton, when he writes about Clough, for instance, confines himself to reciting the received opinions; not so much out of simple timidity as out of that hypertrophied sense of decorum, of the gulf between the public and the private domains. However, though he could be livelier on such subjects in his private letters and journals, and though he gave so much practical advice to contemporary writers, he seldom makes directly critical judgments even there, and when he does they are rarely interesting. Judgment was not part of the Boston literary tradition. It was the source of some of the resentment against Emerson (in Howells, for instance) that he did judge; that he thought Hawthorne's novels poor, and Holmes' poems insignificant, and all Lowell's serious work outweighed by one humorous poem. It would be hard work to make Emerson out a great critic—though he made many shrewd judgments—but he was interested in the activity. He cared about quality in literature; cared enough to jeopardise his amiability to his neighbours and clubmates. Moreover, he judged *contemporary* literature. Even when the Boston tradition took up the practice of criticism, under Irving Babbitt, contemporaries were what it handled worst. Most modern literature Babbitt had not read, and his critical grasp of what he had was rather like a bull's critical grasp of a red flag. All of which illustrates further how little free play of intelligence, in the putting together of experience and ideas and art, the Boston tradition then allowed.

Where we do find literary judgment, rudimentary in some ways, but assuming the full function of criticism, is in *The Dial*. Parrington says,

Transcendentalism may have run into follies, but foolish in its
critical judgment—blind to the gap between profession and reality
—it was not. It might be severe, but it was honest and intelligent,
and honest intelligent criticism America stood greatly in need of.[17]

This is of course directed at more than literary criticism, but the
Transcendentalist mind was profoundly and essentially literary
in its criticism of social matters; that criticism was always directed at the quality of individual life in the persons involved.
When Lowell's *Poems* came out in 1844, Margaret Fuller
wrote,

> His interest in the moral questions of the day has supplied the want
> of vitality in himself; his great facility of versification has enabled
> him to fill the ear with a copious stream of pleasant sound. But his
> verse is stereotyped; his thoughts sound no depths, and posterity will
> not remember him.[18]

This, for its force as well as its truth, is the kind of criticism
which Lowell needed to get, and which Boston even more needed
to have in circulation. Margaret Fuller's taste was not to be
depended on, and her analyses were not always illuminating, but
she *criticised* the literature of her time, she put it in relation with
some of the major ideas, and she talked freely of personal experience. If she had lived, or if other people had developed her
beginnings, Boston might have had what it so much needed. But
after 1850 it became clear that would not happen. Brook Farm
was particularly productive of critical editors—John Sullivan
Dwight and George William Curtis are two of the most famous
—and American intellectual life would have been much poorer
without them, but they were not literary critics.

In Matthew Arnold's essay 'The Function of Criticism at the
Present Time', he declares that the function of criticism is always
to master the ideas of the age and render them available to the
great creative artists who follow. He prophesies that this is about
to happen in his own England. The essay is one of his most
stimulating theoretically, but when one thinks of its practical
application, one is at first inclined to judge it an unfortunate
prophecy. No great creative period in poetry followed on 1864,

nor did any successful poetry thereafter have much to do with the critical thought of the times. But we are misled by Arnold's emphasis on verse. As soon as we think of the novel, which was of course the main stream of British literature in the nineteenth century, we see how right Arnold was. It was just because of Carlyle's work in *Sartor Resartus* and *Past and Present* that Dickens was able to write *Hard Times,* Kingsley *Alton Locke,* Disraeli and Mrs Gaskell their novels. It was just because Southey and Owen, Coleridge and Cobbett, Macaulay and Spencer, had hammered out exactly the ideas and alternatives, the connections and examples, the crucial *vocabulary,* that grasp the essential drama of industrialism in England, that the novelists were able to write books which still stir us and move us today. They went to the heart of the biggest problem—of the *experience*—of their day. The crisis John Stuart Mill describes in his autobiography is the crisis of Louisa Gradgrind in *Hard Times;* his solution was, as Carlyle had said, to close his Byron and open his Goethe; only he followed Arnold's emendation, and opened his Wordsworth. The ideas, the art, the experience of that culture, drew strength from each other, flourished symbiotically; but in New England, where were the ideas, where were the novels, and what was the quality of the experience? And, to pass from the rhetorical to the real question, why?

There are two conventional answers to that question. The first is that of the literary scholar, and it is to the effect that America was such a new, materialistic, unsettled country that men of culture in it felt themselves isolated and enfeebled and had no energy for creative thought. This is still the cry of the American intellectual. But in the case of nineteenth-century New England, it is plainly not true. With those cultural institutions, with those powerful families who recognized every kind of cultural responsibility, with that full response from readers and listeners in every community, the writers of New England were as 'rooted' as writers anywhere have ever been. New England was isolated in America, true; but the isolation that cripples is surely the personal, or domestic kind. If one has a band of brothers-in-arms, and access to the printing presses, and a reading public, to be faced with overwhelming odds is surely only a stimulus. Certainly they were more rooted in their society than their British equivalents were, while they were fighting so brilliantly against the same enemies. Ruskin was far more a dangling man socially than Norton. Ruskin went literally mad in his isolation. The New England writers taught at Harvard, lectured for the Lowell Institute, visited the Perkins Institute, were on the board of the Athenaeum or of the Hospital, and wrote for the local publication, the *Atlantic* or *The North American Review*. If Arnold may be said to have found a semi-similar place for himself in British society, at Oxford and working as a school inspector, Carlyle, Ruskin, Morris, Dickens, George Eliot, emphatically did not. It was the British who were the more displaced, and in a more dislocated society.

The other is the answer of the historians proper, who imply that the Bostonians were inherently feeble, or alien (Puritan), and could not adapt themselves to or assimilate American reality. Thus it is customary, when discussing the failure of Yankee reformers to win immigrant votes, to blame this failure simply on the former; to explain that the immigrants wanted kindness, and didn't understand democratic politics, and 'naturally' resented the educated accents of these candidates. 'Of course' they preferred the ward boss, and the Yankees 'failed to understand' this, and so on. There is no question of the immigrants sharing the blame; they are placed in a special protected category a priori, absolved from normal adult responsibility. This is perhaps the only reasonable attitude in some cases; but surely not in all.

Even Hofstadter and Handlin take this tone. Handlin, after describing how the immigrants destroyed the Yankee culture, says,

> Indeed it was the immigrant who proved most capable of resisting the later efforts to cram American culture into an artificially developed strait-jacket. In the half-century after 1870, the development of American society produced forces that sought to impose an official orderly pattern upon the chaos of folk culture, to define what was good music, good art, good literature, and to exclude from the canons of good taste that which did not fit.[19]

Here we surely recognize the voice of the anti-intellectual tendency in that eternal struggle in the American mind. How does

Professor Handlin expect the life of the mind to proceed except by defining what is good music, good art, and good literature, and by excluding from the canon what does not fit, and by imposing order on chaos? To make this process sound like political oppression or social snobbery is one of the most familiar of anti-intellectual manoeuvres.

It is not the only one familiar among scholars of American history. Merle Curti, after *telling* us how men at the frontier refused to have schools in their communities, and established a set of social conventions which compelled men with educated voices or minds to conceal them, goes on to imply that these facts are myths invented by the East. Moreover,

> Educated men frequently expected deference and respect. To the democratic frontiersman this was still further occasion for resentment, for, in the words of a keen observer, Judge James Hall, the pioneer would not be 'patronized or high-hatted'.[20]

Between being patronized and meeting someone who expects respect there is surely a crucial difference, and the word 'democratic' rocks badly between the resentment against education (is *that* what 'democratic' means?) and the tough, hearty manliness of the sentence's end. Curti is again whisking away an inconvenient fact under an ideological conjuror's cloak.

And thus, after giving the details of railway construction in the Gilded Age, the historians say, 'However, by fair means or foul, the railroads got built.' What they mean is, 'By these foul means the railroads got built.' Thus Charles and Mary Beard, after describing the party machines in the Gilded Age, say, 'No doubt the scene was far from pleasing to aesthetes, and there were occasional outbursts of moral indignation against the party bosses, but . . .'[21] when it was only to aesthetes a spectacle *could* be pleasing which made politics and serious social action seem impossible to decent men. And finally Arthur Schlesinger Jr, discussing Hawthorne's membership in the Democratic Party, says that the novelist's 'quiet sense of sin and his hatred of human pride immunized him against the claims of Whig conservatism to moral or political superiority. . . . The current of his sympathies . . . ran clear and strong with the plain, solid, common life of the people.'[22] Which would be the sheerest sentimentalism even if, as is not true, Hawthorne had had any such motives.

What we seem to recognize in all these writers is a radical confusion of thought and value. They cannot, apparently, afford to feel themselves condemning or blaming the socially inferior, or to identify themselves, however obliquely, with the more privileged class; to do that would involve assuming a moral monocle and a drawl; and to avoid it they will falsify their feelings and the facts. This is a very American confusion, resulting from a centrally American and democratic dilemma.* It is a good deal because the Bostonians approached this dilemma differently from the rest of the nation that we are interested in them, and perhaps it is also for that reason that the historians misrepresent them. They did not, at their best, merely inherit anything; much less Puritan or Bourbon values. Their inheriting was a complex and difficult act of self-formation, and their values were those of Matthew Arnold and his tradition, not John Cotton and his, or Lord Eldon and his. It was with cultural values in Arnold's sense that they tried to solve the problems of democracy and industrialism. In their early period, they did not wholly fail; how and why they did in the end we have already indicated; and why this failure was accompanied by a failure in literature also remains now to be explained.

* See Appendix B for a discussion of another kind of intellectual confusion deriving from the same democratic dilemma.

Chapter Nine

THE PROBLEM OF
CULTURE AGAIN

FIRST OF ALL, let us repeat that the phenomenon
we are seeking to account for is a literary one, a
failure in literary standards, purposes, and performances, and that therefore its explanation
must be literary. Behind it lies the whole range
of intellectual interests we call high culture, and
behind (around) that, all we call culture. The
connections between the three are vital. But we
cannot proceed predictively from either high
culture or culture to the literary in casual explanation, because literature can derive from,
writers can react to, a cultural situation, in many
different ways; ways so different as to cover between them every kind of literary enterprise and
achievement.

Thus we reject propositions like that of Hayakawa and Jones about Oliver Wendell Holmes:
'The true weakness of Holmes was not that he
failed to understand Emerson or Wendell Phillips; his true weakness was that he failed to
understand Boston,' by which they mean the
workings of nineteenth-century capitalism there.[1]
Perhaps we should not say we think this untrue,
because the quarrel is so much over the order
and relation of truths; but the ideology of our
particular comments and general explanation
will be quite different. Holmes could have 'mis-
understood' Boston much more completely than

he did; could have ignored it quite complacently, or accepted it quite whole-heartedly, or fought against changing it quite furiously; and still not written such feeble verse and prose as he did. The anthologies are full of men who have combined political-economic stupidity—or villainy—with literary power and intelligence. So we say that Holmes' true weakness (though it was more a group than an individual weakness) *was* that he did not understand Emerson.

He failed to understand in Emerson for instance the function of that solitariness and independence so important in the early years at Concord. To Holmes, to all his Boston, the literary life was centrally a matter of clubs and sociability; there was no need for gestures of radical independence; indeed there was no room for them, because the only useful and truthful gestures were those which expressed social participation and co-operation. The taste for solitude looked 'Romantic' in the sentimental sense. 'The poets' was for Holmes a term of contempt as often as of praise; he meant Romantics—people who took their own emotions seriously enough to reject society's moralizing or ridiculing comments as irrelevant. Holmes and his Boston had no sympathy with that.

But to the Bostonians, it was not only the Romantics who seemed anti-social; the eighteenth-century writers too had paid inadequate tribute to society. Thus, Norton wrote to Leslie Stephen in 1887,

> I wonder whether you would agree with me that the set of men of letters, and their kindred, whom we have known, is a good deal the best that the world has seen; not the greatest, perhaps, but the pleasantest to live with, the best intentioned and honestest. Froude for instance is a moral contemporary of Warburton rather than of the men of today,—interesting as a survival.* But there are no such liars as Pope, or cynics as Swift, or vulgarians as Gay, or sycophants as Young, or mockers as Sterne,—indeed, you and I find it uncommonly difficult to pick our own friends to pieces.[2]

On this the best comment is finally the first one that occurs—that there were no such *writers* among them, either (at least, among

---

* Norton's quarrel with Froude was over the latter's publication of intimate papers of the Carlyles' after their death—that is, over Froude's *freedom*.

the Americans) and that their being the pleasantest to live with
has something to do with their being not the greatest. The social
amenability of Howells and Lowell—not to mention Twain—
was got in part exchange for their talent.

Among the Englishmen of Norton's acquaintance there were
some whose writing was not inferior to that of the eighteenth
century—Dickens, George Eliot, his great friend Ruskin. Ruskin's prose, in *Praeterita* and his letters, will bear comparison
with Swift's and Sterne's; but Ruskin, as we have seen Norton
tell him, was not pleasant to live with in the relevant sense.
There was no-one like him in New England. Longfellow told Mr
and Mrs Fields, after a visit to England, that,

> it was one of the most surprising things in the world to see the
> quiet, gentlemanly way in which Ruskin gave vent to his extreme
> opinions. It seems to be no effort to him, but as if it were a matter
> of course that everyone should give expression to the faith that is
> in him in the same unvarnished way as he does himself, not looking
> for agreement, but for conversation and discussion.[3]

What we glimpse here is surely the kind of freedom and vitality
American intellectual life needed and lacked; but we see also
that that lack was not to be blamed on American society as a
whole, or its lack of established social conventions. Ruskin's freedom was not awarded him by established British conventions; he
paid for it by the bitterest isolation and personal suffering. The
lack must be blamed on Longfellow himself, and Emerson, and
Norton, and Lowell: on Boston literary society.

In Boston, social amenity was priced so high that several other
virtues suffered a discount. Thus Howells, exclaiming over his
first enchanted evenings with Lowell, Fields, Holmes, and the
rest, says he had heard of British authors who were quite fierce
with readers who invaded their privacy—who claimed to want no
part in literary sociabilities—who lived by and to themselves.
'But our gentler and honester celebrities did not forbid approach.'[4] Gentler, honester, and feebler; guaranteed harmless at
the tea-table and in book form. These pastel qualities shaded off
into the white serenity and moral purity of the great soul; an
ideal in perceptible opposition to that of artistic freedom, though
this was disguised by their taking Emerson or Wordsworth as the

poet-type. They used the word 'genius', in opposition to 'talent', to serve this purpose. Emerson said, after hearing Dickens read, 'I am afraid he has too much talent for his genius; it is a fearful locomotive to which he is bound and can never be free from it nor set at rest'; [5] and Norton said of Lowell, '. . . in everything his genius was superior to his gifts and master of his acquisitions.' [6] Thus social amenity, sanctity, and genius, were all blossoms on the same bough.

The aesthetes renounced this vocabulary, with all its presuppositions, and this bourgeois kind of social amenity, when they renounced the responsible society. They accepted the immorality of the artist and the luxury of high civilization; they were not interested in plain living and high thinking. The rich, the sophisticated, the aristocratic, were the people Berenson and Santayana sought out. Corruption and evil fascinated Adams and James. Their social amenity was of the kind that included such things in the social perspective importantly, appreciated them with discrimination, consulted them with relish; and deprecated any attempt to build a more morally consistent scheme. If Ruskin's freedom and vitality of intellectual life were what New England lacked, we may say that Henry Adams rediscovered the freedom, but not the vitality, since he renounced the effort to seriously praise or blame society. But he had made a significant act of courage at which the pure Bostonians failed.

The pure Bostonians did not take enough risks. That much seems clear. But what were these risks they needed and refused to take? Presumably we are not asking that they actually 'lie like Pope' or mock like Sterne, and so on; or that they get really drunk at the Saturday Club, or tell Emerson really dirty stories. No, but surely the risks every nineteenth-century writer did need to take had to do with the new modes of self-exploration and self-affirmation introduced by Romanticism.

In *Culture and Society*, Raymond Williams offers us three characteristics by which to recognize the Romantic artist. The first is his lack of any direct relation with his readers, and of any sense that he belongs in some fixed place in society; the market relationship has replaced the patron relationship. The second is his contempt for the public's taste and judgment, which leaves the artist responsible to himself alone or to a few elect and isolated readers. The third is his being an agent of the revolution for life, carrying everywhere with him relationship and love. Beneath and within all these, I would like to add, the Romantic artist cuts himself off from participation in society's values, makes an opposition between the social and the sincere, and feels it his vocation to discover the other, truer, more deeply personal values. If we accept this as the distinguishing nature of serious Romanticism, then we see writers like Dostoevski and D. H. Lawrence as Romantic; and any other writer who ruthlessly explores the self, and passionately affirms it against conventional social values. We also see that, apart from the Transcendentalists, no Boston writer was Romantic.

It was Carlyle's great achievement, which made him so important on both sides of the Atlantic, to show how one could return from, and indeed through, the dangerous personalism and antisocial feeling of the Romantics to affirmations of the basic decencies on which the whole structure of society is built. Duty to God and duty to one's fellow-man were rediscovered in despite of Byronism, and somehow through Byronism; and turned out to be, formulated this way, full of a new power which transcended the mere worldly conformities of the eighteenth century. Society, the time-old idea of living together with one's fellow-men, could be believed in again, though one continued to hate 'society'. Sensitive people continued to hate 'the world' in the eighteenth-century sense, but they began to employ their rational and moral faculties in analysis of exactly what was wrong with it, and in prescription of exactly what would cure it, in order to create, in the imagination, the world as God intended it to be—which usually meant, in practice, the world as it used to be before the Industrial Revolution. It was a major inspiration of the tradition of culture-prophets, from Burke and Cobbett on, to discover some more real community to affirm, which one could put in opposition to the more actual community one denied: 'culture' and 'civilization', as Coleridge and Arnold use the terms.

Perhaps one should say that this effort was made in response to the Industrial Revolution rather than to Romanticism. But the two are inextricably intertwined as cultural forces; the explosive effects of the Industrial Revolution, changing society continually, and so tragically, made the inner disturbance and revolt of the Romantics continually *the* contemporary mood. It was therefore an enormous problem of nineteenth-century thought in the West to normalize the forces of Romanticism, to give them free acknowledgment and expression of a kind that would also amount to creative social participation. It was the distinguishing mark, and also the glory, of Britain, that there the enterprise took the form of this tradition of culture criticism. In France, for instance, the best talents seem to have remained more purely and antisocially Romantic. (I only suggest this, and it is perhaps very naive.) Baudelaire and Rimbaud sign no social contract, however 'cultural'; which is why they so shocked the Anglo-Saxons as irresponsible as well as immoral. The socially constructive expressions of Romanticism in France tended to be less vivid and less solid aesthetically, perhaps; the Catholicism of Chateaubriand, for instance, and the pastoralism of George Sand, seem less impressive now than Flaubert and Rimbaud.

What then do we discover of this kind in Bostonian literature? Emerson set out along lines parallel to Carlyle's. He withdrew from Boston society—into that privacy Holmes failed to understand—but not out of sentimentality or embitterment. His Transcendentalism was an attempt to normalize the Romantic impulses to solitude, self-exploration, anti-social self-affirmation, an attempt to live these through but to come back from them into a higher and deeper kind of community. It was because Thoreau's solitary musings never brought him back into social participation that Emerson was disappointed in him. 'Pounding beans is good to the end of pounding empires one of these days: but if, at the end of years, it is still only beans.' [7] Emerson was not such a materialist as he is sometimes taken for, on the evidence of passages like that. His scorn for beans is in the name of critical social participation, not in the name of Napoleonism. Thoreau seemed to him too simply Romantic.

But once we leave the Transcendentalists, whom do we find who had any understanding of this double problem? The Bostonians understood the need to preserve the social structure, but who was willing to also live through a Romantic emotion—as opposed to a Romantic sentiment? Their version of the responsible society was significantly different from the parent version in England, because it derived from and expressed no passionate dissatisfaction with all nineteenth-century social arrangements, no forceful demand for something absolutely different. That is the way Norton's 'culture' differs from Ruskin's, and even Emerson's from Carlyle's. The Bostonians remained in many ways eighteenth-century, and got no nearer to being Romantic than Gray and Collins did. Any more wholesale commitment to Romantic emotions dismayed them.

Lowell is again a good case to examine, because he so clearly 'knew' what the issues were. In his essays on Thoreau and Rousseau we find a considerable range of sympathetic understanding, counteracted by a self-defensive disapproval, and all corrupted into resentment and malice. Thoreau had 'so high a conceit of himself', and he suspected other people's worldly success, only because he, Thoreau, had failed; and his sojourn at Walden was like going back to flint and steel when one has a matchbox in one's pocket which one knows very well how to use at a pinch. And when Lowell is not being malicious, he is being philistine; Thoreau 'had not a healthy mind or he would not be so fond of prescribing for others', and he had no humour, which implies that he was a sorry logician. What Lowell resents most is Thoreau's disregard for the position assigned him by society as a writer; and his disregard for the duties of that position—to be humorous and cheerful and heart-warming. A cold and wintry sensibility, he calls him. But a disregard for the position assigned the writer by society *is* Romanticism; it is a quite cardinal article of that creed and trait of that temperament. Rejecting that independence, one rejected the whole corpus of dangers and duties that constituted the contemporary writer's fate.[8]

The Boston writers did reject it. This is unmistakably clear of Lowell's period; one of the stock figures of fun of that literature was the man who took his own emotions tragically; we find him in much of Twain, in Holmes, and in the Blighted Being joke of Aldrich's *Story of a Bad Boy*. Ticknor's period cannot be summed up so clearly. The choice was not so obligatory then; it could be evaded; men like Ticknor could be unaffectedly and

vigorously eighteenth-century. That is why we don't feel the ignominious muddle and muddying of feeling, the diminution of
mind, in the writers of that time. They had not rejected their
fate. On the other hand, they had not accepted it, and that is
why we so rarely get anything of the first quality even in that
early period.

Emerson and Thoreau accepted the full challenge of their vocation; and consequently, in their work one feels oneself in contact with minds that are full alive; again and again one comes
across passages in which both thought and language are working
at the highest pitch. The same is not true even of Ticknor, much
less of Prescott, or any other of their contemporaries. Nevertheless, in the first part of the century, the lack of great writers can
seem accidental, or necessary only because of the smallness of the
population, the youth of the country, various external factors.
One finds few talents warped or cramped from within. (Perhaps
the first example of that is Hawthorne.) In the second part of the
century, that lack seems necessary because of the mistreatment of
what talent there was. The New England version of the responsible society prevented literary people from thinking about or
writing about the feelings that mattered most to them and to
their audience. Consequently they wrote about things that did
not matter much; and were either light-weight, like Holmes, or
pompous, like Lowell. Their use of language revealed that they
had no habit of honesty. Their wit, their gaiety, their irresponsibility, all bore the marks of the timid and flabby mind.

Boston, to put the same thing another way, excluded from its
literature the telling of deeply personal truths; those truths
which reveal the non-social self, or the non-social aspects of relationships and states of being, aspects so painful or so obscure as
to be useless even detrimental to consider in the conduct of
one's social (which here includes much of 'moral') life. Since
1800 these truths are what fiction at least has had to deal with, to
be really significant. These are what French, German, Russian,
British, novelists and story-writers dealt with during the century.
They are what appeared in character-analyses like George Eliot's,
and in melodrama like Dostoevski, and in a theatrical mode, in

Dickens. There is no New England fiction that is comparable. There aren't even any New England autobiographies to put beside those of Ruskin, Mill, or Newman. It is notable how much less well Ferris Greenslet wrote in his autobiography than he did in the essay on Ticknor—when he was in the tradition of Arnold and George Eliot. And it is prose about personal matters, by the Hawthornes and by Percival Lowell, that seems so inferior to the eighteenth-century equivalent in Boston. Literary scholarship, as we have seen in Wendell's case, and Norton's, refused to discuss personal matters. Personal truths Boston decorum forbade; and thereby it forbade significant fiction.

The case of the culture-criticism essay is even more striking. At first sight this seems to have nothing to do with the telling of personal truths, and *Hard Times,* for instance, is an exception to my generalization about significant fiction in the nineteenth-century. But there is a sufficiently vital connection between the two modes, in fiction and the essay, to explain the exception. The culture-criticism essay derived from Romanticism, too. It expressed a rejection of actual society, and a search for some ideal alternative in which the self would have free and perfect expression, though it harnessed those drives to rational and moral analysis. It and the novel were both ways—nothing else was—of dealing with the crucial experience of the era; the first with public experience, the second with private. Both faced the possibility of there being something terribly wrong with the fundamental entity—society or the individual. The connection, however we define it, seems demonstrated in the case of Boston. The failure in the two categories was so dramatic and so equal. There was so much material available to the Bostonians for culture-critical analysis: in the contrast between their own way of life and that of the rest of America, or in the contest between their loyalties to American democracy and their loyalties to British intellectual life. They should at least have been able to write analyses of England that would challenge comparison with those of Carlyle and Ruskin. They did none of these things, because they rejected the full fate of the writer in their times.

And with this we return to Dr Leavis—for he is the great

194   *The Problem of Boston*

modern representative of that tradition of culture-criticism in England—and to the question we started from in Chapter One: why should a society which resembles so much in its structure the kind of social structure he recommends differ so much in its literary product from the kind of literature he recommends? Dr Leavis's work has been one long attempt to normalize the disruptive forces of Romanticism in literature, by setting up his own version of the culture/civilization split, and by demonstrating in himself the only kind of social-moral responsibility the modern literary sensibility can take seriously. Over and over again he has eloquently insisted, as in what was quoted in Chapter I, on the need to integrate modern knowledge, on the culturally destructive forces at work in modern society, and the literary man's duty to battle against them, to conserve the values of the past, to re-create, insofar as is possible, a responsible society. (All the duties nineteenth-century Boston undertook, and, in considerable measure, discharged.)

He has often been accused of indifference to purely aesthetic questions, so much has he insisted on the cultural and moral values and functions of art. 'The possibilities of education specifically directed against such appeals as those made by the journalist, the middle man, the bestseller, the cinema, and advertising,' Mrs Leavis says in *Fiction and the Reading Public,* should be explained to young people with literary sensibility. They 'may even be fired with a missionary spirit'; the job of an English teacher could be a vocation. That was written in 1932, and the thirty years since have amply proved it true. Young people trained in literature by Dr Leavis have gone into the teaching of English—and the writing of criticism, and the writing of poems and novels—fired with exactly that missionary spirit. They have fought for culture against civilization; which has meant, in practice, against mechanization, against scientism, against mass-entertainments, against mass-democracy, against cultural fragmentation; against all the things Boston fought against, and for the responsible society.

The opening of *Reading and Discrimination* will remind us in more detail of that feeling of responsibility on which Leavis and his tradition insist.

The quality of a man's life nowdays depends largely on the quality of what he reads.* As it stands, that is an assertion which requires much elucidation and discussion, but only a few suggestions can be made here. Take the case of a man—factory-hand or millionaire—whose work is uninteresting and unsatisfying; his life does not start until the day's work is over, and his idea of how he should use his leisure, i.e. what kind of life he should lead, will be formed by the printed word, aided by the cinema. Unless he is an exceptional person, he will resort to novel or newspaper as a soporific; he reads uncritically, off his guard, so long as it holds his interest, and thus he unconsciously takes over the writer's attitude to life. In time he will become incapable of thinking or feeling for himself; he will live at second-hand . . .

The section of Mrs Leavis's book from which I quoted is entitled 'Living at the Novelist's Expense', and the idea behind both arguments is that the leaders of culture must act on their responsibility to improve the quality of reading, and consequently the quality of life, of their society. We are to contrast the modern state of affairs, Leavis says, with that of the eighteenth century, which, as we have seen, is his emblem of the high level of culture produced by a responsible society. But we have tried to prove that nineteenth-century Boston is at least as striking an example of that. The careful attention, morally and socially responsible, paid there to everything published and written, checking its effects on the readers, and to every kind of institution, checking its effect on the community, was much closer to the kind of thing Leavis wants than anything the eighteenth century did.

That he did not pick nineteenth-century Boston as his emblem is presumably just because its literature is so unexciting. That, in turn, is because the Boston system of social responsibility amounted to shutting off part of the nineteenth-century writer's sources of serious inspiration; to a degree that would not have occurred in the eighteenth century (the sources of literary inspiration then being somewhat different) even if the system had been applied as thoroughly then. Now I am not suggesting that what Dr Leavis wants, or what he would involuntarily get if he had his way, is a similar shutting off of the sources of literary vitality today. I am suggesting that he takes it for granted in his

---

* Here, as so often, Leavis starts from Arnold.

theory of culture that this serious 'irresponsibility' in a writer, this nineteenth-century soul-disturbance, this Romantic rebellion, is (somewhere, somehow) always there in the significant modern artist, is an irreplaceable credential of the serious writer and thinker today.* (I am making the difference between art before 1800 and art since, our art, a black and white contrast for the sake of clarity, but it is really one between two shades of the same colour. In no era, presumably, have writers been a characteristically serene and superficial group; and since 1800 they have not all been profound and stormy. All I claim is that the Romantic Revolution did take place, and that its effects persist.) Dr Leavis assumes that we know, when he speaks of 'a responsible culture', that he does not mean nineteenth-century Boston, even though nothing logically excludes that, because the writers and thinkers of that culture refused their full vocation, and so are not to be taken seriously.

Once we realize this assumption, Dr Leavis's theory becomes more interesting and more satisfying. Most people who complain of his 'moralism', for instance, have failed to realize the sympathy with 'immoralism' (the need to defy every conventional moral and social code) which precedes and underlies that. Modern literature can only be significant when it includes some powerful aspiration towards freedom as well as towards order, when it has defied social legality and risked real suffering in the exploration of what I called personal truths. It cannot therefore be merely a part of society's culture, or easily a part of high culture's humanism. It is more resistant than the art of the past to that kind of assimilation. If the writer himself attempts that assimilation, as nineteenth-century Boston writers did, he is likely to produce non-literature. In modern times, it is the work of the critic (Dr Leavis's criticism is a great example of it) to build a bridge between the work of art and the social structure—to give it its cultural meaning—however laborious and paradoxical the effort. This bridge-building is central to modern humanism—more central than the creative work itself, which must be allowed a freedom that includes anti-humanist initiatives.

* Isn't it because C. P. Snow does not seem to him disturbed in the right way that he is so angry at Snow's being taken seriously as a novelist?

It is perhaps clearer in Dr Leavis's choice of authors to discuss than in his choice of terms for the discussion, how fully he accepts the need for that freedom in modern literature. His enthusiasms, for D. H. Lawrence and Henry James, for the late Yeats and the early Eliot, involve accepting a great variety of self-disengagements from society by the artist, some energetic repudiations and some bland evasions of all social involvement. Indeed, his taste seems biased in favour of writers like Conrad and Hawthorne, who have a profound experience of social isolation (not entirely involuntary) beneath their theory of social participation. But his taste for James is the most significant, and in the short run, surprising. James is not, in any obvious sense, a poet of the responsible society, nor did he accept the full Romantic challenge to explore personal truths. But like the other aesthetes, he did inherit the freedom (if not the vitality) of modern art, through his apprenticeship to the great artists of nineteenth-century Europe; he broke the old bonds of social limitation, which the pure Bostonians failed to do; like Thoreau, for once, and unlike Lowell, his friend, he refused to accept society's definition of his scope and function as an artist. His own theory of that function was as ambitious as Proust's and his success in realizing it certainly made him what Dr Leavis says he is, a very important modern artist. However, I have argued elsewhere—differing with Dr Leavis—that James's fiction suffers from a conflict between his aspiration to elegance of gesture, and his concern for profounder values; that concern being too often mortified—in its expression and in its operation—by an inappropriate epigrammaticism and nervous flounces of style. And this failure seems to me connected with his not risking that passionate exploration of the self or the anti-self, society, which amounts to vitality in modern art, and which marks the really great men. The aesthetes did not risk that, and consequently all fell short of greatness; their creed thinned down their experience, their representation, and their understanding of too much of life.* Dr Leavis does not feel this to be true of James; and if we

---

* It is interesting that Santayana had such a strong reaction against Whitman, that very passionate explorer of the self, and Romantic. Irving Singer, in his introduction to *Essays in Literary Criticism by George Santayana* (New

ask what it is that wins his admiration so completely, we must surely answer that it is James's freedom, that energy of aesthetic invention and device which escapes every bondage to other kinds of truth and value, and makes art a realm in itself.

The need to build a humanism out of modern high culture, to interconnect the different parts of our total culture, to create some harmonious, unifying, articulating language by means of which every interest in society can be related—this need is as great as Dr Leavis has taught us. But the values he proclaims are so important because of the lion forever struggling with this unicorn; I mean the rebellious distrust of society, the appetite for a perfect freedom and self-assertion. The lion without the unicorn we see ravaging the streets in a thousand nightmare expressions of hatred and disgust at life; modern literature leaves us in no need of a reminder against trusting that. The unicorn without the lion we must go back to the works of James Russell Lowell to find; but once we have found it, we shall realize we want always a literature that displays the full heraldic crest, the

York, 1956) finds that the failure really to appreciate Romanticism was Santayana's great weakness as a literary critic. Mr Singer's and Santayana's idea of Romanticism differs somewhat from mine, putting the major stresses on different features of that complex entity. But Romanticism was after all an entity. That overwhelming preference for 'classical' qualities in literature, for form, reason, order, ideality, was a refusal of Romanticism (and therefore of his own period in literature) in my sense as well as in his. In fact, of course, no-one can simply refuse his own period, and especially no mind so complex and responsive as Santayana's, but he did in some sense try to.

Obviously in some connection with this dislike for Whitman is Santayana's disregard for truth-telling in literature. Mr Singer argues that the weakness of Santayana's theory of idealization, his whole theory of art, is that 'it seems to minimize the importance of truth. Idealizations do not tell us how things are, but how they ought to be, or how the "heart's desire" would like them to be. If aesthetic excellence is primarily determined by idealization, art is treated as wish fulfilment more than anything else. As long as we concern ourselves with the artist's idealization, we are not especially interested in what he tells us about the world.' This very much answers to my sense of all the aesthetes' work, in detail and in practice as well as in theory. They assume a complete freedom of the imagination, a complete transcendence of the mind, giving it the right to transform completely what is being talked about into a vivid pattern, whether frankly aesthetic or ostensibly historical, philosophical, scientific. Henry James's characters and events, in his late work, have disturbingly little independent reality—independent of their creator's hypertrophied patterns.

fierceness of the one animal supplementing the mild chastity of the other.

Defending his calling as man of letters, Lowell once said, 'I believe that the study of imaginative literature tends to sanity of mind, and to keep the Caliban of common sense, a very useful monster in his proper place, from making himself king over us.' [9] It is of course Ariel who represents imaginative literature here; for Prospero we have to turn to someone like Lowell himself, able to see further than, to balance against each other, both his servants. Imagination has become a mythical spirit, common sense a monster, and the royal human mind itself is dislocated, dispersed, inert, and cowed. It is itself subject to an alien 'social' discipline. In the Agassiz ode, Lowell describes those minds that have slipped the bridle of social usefulness and amenability.

> In some the genius is a thing apart,
> A pillared hermit of the brain,
> Hoarding with incommunicable art,
> Its intellectual gain. . . .
>
> Their nice adjustment, part to part,
> Were shaken from its serviceable mood
> By unpremeditated stirs of heart
> Or jar of human neighbourhood. . . .
>   Dazed by the social glow they cannot share.

Then he turns to Agassiz.

> His nature brooked no lonely lair,
> But basked and burgeoned in copartnery,
> Companionship and open-windowed glee.
>   He knew, for he had tried,
> Those speculative heights that lure
> The unpracticed foot, impatient of a guide,
>   Tow'rd ether too attenuately pure
> For sweet unconscious breath, though dear to pride
>   But better loved the foothold sure
> Of paths that wind by old abodes of men
> Who hope at last the churchyard's peace secure,
> And follow time-worn rules, that them suffice,
> Learned from their sires, traditionally wise, . . .
> His mind, too brave to look on Truth askance,

> No more those habitudes of faith could share,
> But, tinged with sweetness of the old Swiss manse,
> Lingered around them still and fain would share.

There could surely be no more eloquent 'expression'—that is, betrayal—in every detail of its language, as well as in its statements, of the aspiration to 'sweet unconscious breath' and 'the church yard's peace secure'. There could surely be no praise of a mind 'too brave to look on Truth askance' itself more eloquent of intellectual cowardice and deathwardness. The challenge most obviously evaded is of course the question of religious faith, but the more important failure, in its effect on strictly literary success, in this poem and elsewhere, is the rejection of Romanticism: the refusal to take part in the exploration of the crucial experience of the era and in the development of the crucial new modes and forms, the refusal to learn from those who *had* taken part. When this was rejected, even the extraordinarily favourable attitude of society, expressed in so many ways, could not bring writers to the point of successful creation. And as we read the literature of Boston in the nineteenth century, that act of cowardice is what we gradually discern, on the part of a whole literary community. That surely is the solution of our problem.

APPENDIX A

The passage from Norton's journal I reproduce here seems to me an interesting case of his power to voice the mood of his times—by that phrase I mean of course the mood of his contemporary Boston intellectuals—and at a time before his contemporaries fully realized they felt it. This was written in 1874, and if we compare it with what Barrett Wendell had to say on the same subject in 1900, we see how far in advance Norton was. It is one of the earliest expressions of these attitudes, but in even the most recent and contemporary versions—for these attitudes remain orthodox today—there is little change in the thinking.

Emerson was the greatest talker in the ship's company. He talked with all men, and yet was fresh and zealous for talk at night. His serene sweetness, the pure whiteness of his soul, the reflection of his soul in his face, were never more apparent to me; but never before in intercourse with him had I been so impressed with the limits of his mind. . . . His optimism becomes a bigotry, and, though of nobler type than the common American conceit of the preeminence of American things as they are, has hardly less of the quality of fatalism. To him this is the best of all possible worlds, and the best of all possible times. He refuses to believe in disorder or evil. . . . He is the most innocent, the most inexperienced of men who had lived in and reflected on the world; he is also the most cheerful and the most hopeful. . . .

He was born nearly with the century, and his soul received its bent from the innocent America of before 1830. He breathed in the confident, sweet, morning spirit of a time when America believed that the Fourth of July, the Declaration of Independence, the common school, and the four year Presidential term, were finalities in political science and social happiness; of a time when society was simple, and comparatively innocent; when our institutions and our progress were the wonder of de Tocqueville and the Old World, and the delight of ourselves; when there were Peace Societies, and it seemed to the youth uninstructed by the past as if the Millennium were really not so very far off. His philosophy was of necessity one of hope; the gospel of prosperity; and it was settled so far as its influence on thought, action, and character were concerned, before General Jackson was chosen President and we had entered on the new and less child-like epoch of our modern democracy. . . .

But such inveterate and persistent optimism, though it may show only its pleasant side in such a character as Emerson's, is a dangerous doctrine for a people. It degenerates into fatalistic indifference to moral considerations, and to personal responsibilities; it is at the root of much of the irrational sentimentalism in our American politics, of much of our national disregard of honour in our public men, of much of our unwillingness to accept hard truths, and of much of the common tendency to disregard the distinctions between right and wrong, and to excuse guilt on the plea of good intentions or good nature.[1]

This is Norton's thinking and writing at its best; his mind is fully engaged by the problem. It is unfortunate that he did so little writing on such topics, and never published what he did. It is unfortunate, too, that the profound dissatisfaction with American society, expressed in the first and third paragraphs, never inspired in him full-scale rational and moral analysis like Ruskin's or Carlyle's, never *energized* his theory of the responsible society. In Boston intellectuals that dissatisfaction only fed a pessimism as fatalistic as that opposite optimism he complains of in Emerson.

The second paragraph is equally interesting, for the way it foreshadows so much modern emphasis on disillusionment and achieving a 'new and less child-like' mood, to suit our new and less child-like epoch. Americans sometimes seem to cherish a personal grudge against their country for having let them in, as they suppose, for more 'innocence' than other people. *Norton's* tone, as he discusses that early American history, is surely in part resentful. Of course it is also loving and nostalgic, with the nostalgia which presumably nourished his interest in the twelfth century—another child-like epoch and age of faith—and the interest of Adams, Berenson, and even T. S. Eliot, in medieval culture.

American intellectuals have made for themselves (I must confess its modern manifestations seem to me often self-indulgent) a myth (I don't mean to imply that it is simply mistaken) that the whole nation is and has been obsessed with innocence: with a 'remembered' candour and cleanness forever forbidden the adult mind, but forever more beautiful than adult experience. I would suggest that the nostalgia of later-nineteenth-century Boston for early-nineteenth-century Boston was one of the most powerful sources of this obsession. The myth is usually represented in much larger terms—larger periods of time, larger aspirations, larger features of the mind involved—and it is usually implied that the aspiration is *felt* by 'America', 'the people', and *interpreted* by the intellectuals. I would suggest that it is quite as much something *felt* by the intellectuals and *imputed* to the people.

APPENDIX B

One of the interests of this study for me lay in the realization of how often Americans ignore part of their history. Their idea of the meaning of 'America' and 'the American' (and very important those concepts are to them) survives by omitting all reference to the history of nineteenth-century Boston, or by calling that the Europeanized part of America, or by calling it the Puritan heritage. They choose out of the complex factuality of American history certain highly coloured elements to call 'American'; no doubt Englishmen do this to *their* history, but the Americans' proceeding seems more arbitrary and dangerous, because what they choose are the elements unfavourable to themselves as readers. They abstract an American *idea* or principle which is fully realized in comparatively few individuals or events, but which marks the American out as sharply different from every other nationality. It is a neat irony that the characteristic failing of the American mind they so often present us with is 'a tendency to abstraction'.

A good example of this is Stanley Elkins' book on slavery, which was 'read in manuscript' (which presumably amounts to some kind of sponsorship) by a host of distinguished scholars from a variety of intellectual disciplines, including Lionel Trilling, Bruno Bettelheim, Marvin Meyers, Richard Hofstadter, David Riesman, C. Vann Woodward, and others. This book is interesting also because it seems to express a reaction against the historiographical patterns of Turner and his followers—whose admiration for Jacksonism and the Western frontiersman of course left them with little sympathy for Eastern-seaboard types —without redeeming Boston from its long neglect. This new version of 'the American man' admits a few Bostonians, or rather Transcendentalists, to the title, but only the better to condemn them. In this kind of history, 'the American man' remains much what Turner described, and is even more sharply opposed to 'the European man'; but the historian's feelings about the two abstractions are reversed.

Mr Elkins puts 'slavery in America' in opposition to simple slavery; his principal contrast is with slavery in South America, which was managed by 'the European mind'. Slavery was condemned everywhere in the nineteenth century, but,

> the simple and harsh moral purity of our own anti-slavery movement, from the 1830s on, gave it a quality which set it apart from the others . . . every phase of the movement combined to produce in our abolitionists that peculiar quality of abstraction which was, and has remained, uniquely American. For them, the question was *all* moral; it must be contemplated in terms untouched by expediency, untarnished by society's organic compromises, uncorrupted by society itself.[1]

This is a representative statement of a general belief. Mr Elkins is however too much the historian to leave the word 'American' entirely metaphysical. Had he, the American, a past? Yes; two hundred years old, but he could now forget it. Had he once known institutions? Yes, but he could now ignore their meanings. It was 'now', in the nineteenth century, that America became 'America', the land of abstraction—and of anti-institutionalism, which was the other face of the same fact. Institutions, such as an established church and a body of legal tradition, are society's main ways of making morality *concrete;* they give moral issues a local habitation and a name, and therewith a susceptibility to compromise and manoeuvre and management. In the nineteenth century, in the vigour of an expanding capitalist economy, institutions were no longer so economically and socially necessary, but without them the moral life of the community suffered badly. 'Now' the church fell into a thousand parts; the bar had no central focus of tradition and vested power, like the Temple and Inns of Court in England; the great trading families of the East were losing out to new petty industrialists; even the political parties lost their institutional structure as they were democratized. Individuals decided moral questions on their own. Institutional structures seemed no longer necessary, and the thought of the time praised only perfect individual freedom.

Mr Elkins sympathizes with this vigorous development (or claims to), only asking, 'Might there not have been (in spite of everything) a price? Where, for instance, in such a setting, were art and learning to find their occupation?' He quotes Hawthorne ('the lonely Hawthorne') saying in a preface that no-one without trying it could conceive the difficulty of writing a romance about a country where there was no shadow, no antiquity, no mystery, no picturesque and gloomy wrong, and so on.[2] He quotes James on Hawthorne, and explains that the 'things' James so valued in England were the signs, agents, and products of social institutions, of continuing institutions upon which one could count for mooring posts, for points of view, for centers of force. Institutions with power produce the things not only upon which one leans but also against which one pushes. Without them one is in a vacuum. The lack of them, moreover, removes the thinker not only from the places where power resides but also from the very *idea* of power and how it is used. Power itself is transformed into an abstraction. This, in Emerson's time, says R. P. Blackmur, 'intensified the general heresy that the arts and learning can be divorced from the power and resources of society without danger to both'.[3]

Emerson and Transcendentalism are in some sense the villains of this drama, for Mr Elkins, because they were so anti-institutional. By the eighteen thirties, he says, the closest thing to an intellectual community in the United States consisted of men with no concrete commitment to the social system at all. They were men who had no close commitment to any of society's institutions. They were therefore 'men without responsibility', for all their moral afflatus and lofty idealism. He cites Emerson, Thoreau, Ripley, Margaret Fuller, Alcott, Parker, and Channing. They were the glorifiers of self-reliance and naturally also leading abolitionists.

Wisdom was not available for the solution of the slavery problem in America, Mr Elkins believes.

> What makes 'wisdom' possible? What are the daily conditions which enable the men of thought and feeling in a society to function responsibly? If a society's institutional resources are to remain grounded in reality, if they are to be at hand in a form appropriate to the problems of the day, what are the prerequisites? [4]

Mr Elkins is of course sure that the answer lies in the institutions and their traditions. But Emerson's only answers to such questions were individual. Wisdom's support, for him, was individual character. Transcendentalism was in fact quite unable to 'transcend' its age; far from revolting against the age, Transcendentalism embodied in aggravated form certain of its most remarkable features—its anti-institutionalism, its individual perfectionism, its abstraction, its social guilt and reforming zeal.

This is a treatment of American history the reverse of what we are used to, in important ways. The great American qualities— free enterprise, idealism, individualism, democracy of judgment —are here shown leading straight to social disaster. There is truth in the indictment, and Mr Elkins makes some interesting suggestions of what other things the abolitionists might have done, which would have been more socially wise. But when one turns to the larger historical implications, one is bound to protest. Why is so much that is American omitted from this theory of America? If the omission of Boston was unsatisfactory in Turner's theory, in Mr Elkins' theory—where the sympathies are the opposite—the omission is perverse. Is he determined to find no wisdom in America?

Concord was not the only intellectual community in America in the eighteen thirties, unless one defines 'intellectual' a priori as implying anti-institutionalism. The Boston community to which Ticknor, Everett, Webster, Prescott, belonged, had its claims to be called intellectual; and their attitude to politics in general, and to slavery in particular, *was* institutional; to say nothing of that of other communities. Moreover, Concord was Concord in reaction against, and in relation to, Boston. They were two sides in a debate over the good life, which taken as a whole offered a considerable variety of vigorous alternative ideas. No community was ever so full of institutions as Boston; I realize these were not the national institutions Mr Elkins chose to discuss, but were they not institutions? No-one ever had more 'things to 'push against' than Emerson. If we are to estimate the Transcendentalists, we must at least take them in their social context, and not abstract them.

But both these are perhaps quibbles (though there are other such objections one would make) in relation to Mr Elkins' argument on the abolition movement itself, the basic propositions of which are left untouched by what I have said. It is his making them archetypally 'American' which is really to be objected to, his assimilation of all American history and present psychology to this pattern. For instance, after discussing reform movements 'in America', and the role of the intellectual in a reform situation 'in America', he conjures up a pure American in contrast with a pure European. (This reminds us of James, and much of this book's thinking shows how the aesthetes have influenced contemporary scholarship.)

> The morally implacable American has always been seen by the European as somehow unpredictable and dangerous. On the other hand, the European, to that same American, has immemorially evoked suspicions of cynicism, expediency, and corruption. This is because, between ourselves and the Europeans, the most basic conceptions of morality and sin, of 'the good' and 'the bad'—have traditionally lain poles apart. All such conceptions have inevitably been formulated, in our culture, from the viewpoint of the individual looking outward; the individual in America has historically insisted upon his right to define sin for himself. The complex life of Europe, lived out century after century in the same place, has never been able to afford this. There, it has traditionally been regarded as much too dangerous to intrust the definition of iniquity to inspired itinerant preachers and young men on the make. Too much has been at stake; it is through the eyes of society that such attempts have been seen; it is society's voice that has articulated them; it is within society's institutions that such formulations have been set down, conserved, and woven into the ancient fabric of custom. Between America and Europe a staggering range of cultural differences rests upon this single point; the meaning of 'sin'.[5]

It is clear that nothing could be more abstract than this (have there been no Protestants in Europe—no Englishmen, no Miltons?); and I use the word 'abstract' in Mr Elkins' sense, of a simple and harsh purity. It is surely just because so much has been strenuously mythified—and much else ignored—in making these generalizations, that they are so full of emotional potential (and vice versa—the one feeding the other, in an intellectual vicious circle). What has been ignored is, for example, the Boston community in the nineteenth century, a major piece of American history for intellectuals; a piece that is their truly usable past. And the emotional potential in differentiating America so much from the rest of the world, and categorizing it with such pseudo-descriptive words as 'abstraction' and 'idealism' and 'innocence', really so full of anger and contempt, is surely very dangerous. Isn't this exactly what is wrong with being 'abstract'? And isn't it the *habit* of writers like Mr Elkins to be abstract in this way?

The habit derives, I would suggest, from that sense the American intellectual has of being at a disadvantage in his own society. This seems to me a rationalization, in the proper sense, of that feeling, and therefore an inadequate way to deal with it. It names and rearranges a complex system of emotional drives without accurately understanding them or their interconnections, and thus sets up new and still more dangerous drives.

It is clear from the list of the book's sponsors, how many intellectual disciplines in America come together over this concept of 'the American innocence'. It is clear also in Mr Elkins' rich and confident use of language that he knows he is expressing not some specialized learning, but a wisdom. Indeed, one notices how often all educated Americans comment on political, social, or intellectual events with a phrase like 'in this country' or 'in America', with a depth of feeling and a range of meanings (mostly bitter) far beyond the Englishman's use of his equivalents. It is an essential and habitual part of their intellectual procedure to set America in separation from, in opposition to, the rest of the world, and indeed themselves.

Mr Elkins is representative in this. So it is all the more disturbing that, among other things, his appreciation of institutions should go together with such a depreciation of all moral enthusiasm, all zeal. His respect for Europe is based on assumptions a European can hardly share or like. 'People who have thus lived with sin for centuries have become intimately acquainted with it,' he says, 'shock does not come to them so easily; their methods of dealing with sin do not appear as callous to themselves as to the innocent.'[6] But is that necessarily an advantage, one is bound to ask? This is not to dispute the whole point about the abolitionists, or indeed some wider application of that point as a criticism of much American moralism. But the issue is not wholly one-sided; Mr Elkins—and he is again representative—seems to regard any moral enthusiasm as abstract, and wants to empty the terms 'good' and 'bad' of any absoluteness. This would amount to crippling our vocabulary, our language, our mind.

But the really important issue is this rejection of history. By simplifying the past down into a drama in which they have always been the victims (because they have never had social power) but also the villains (because they have never wanted it) educated Americans surely create for themselves a sort of cultural neurosis. Isn't the theory of the nation's obsession with innocence a major obsession itself today? Doesn't the way out lie through some broader and more inclusive version of American history?

APPENDIX C

The connection between the four aesthetes and an important tendency in modern taste—perhaps the most important, in literary studies—has been remarked often enough. For instance, Yvor Winters, in *The Anatomy of Nonsense*, discusses a group of four writers at length, of whom Henry Adams is the first, and the other three are modern poets, Wallace Stevens, T. S. Eliot, and John Crowe Ransom. There is of course something Mandarin in the manner of those three which makes it easy to connect them quite superficially with the Boston aesthetes. But the connection Winters is making goes deeper than that, and he groups Adams also with Pound and Joyce—'those who have found the dissolving mind the normal mind'. It is the modern revolt against all that Winters means by 'reason' of which he makes Adams the sponsor, and Pound and Joyce were leaders of that revolt. They, too, were aesthetes and exiles, and just as essentially so as the Bostonians; their manner was not Mandarin, but it expressed just as profound an alienation as Adams', just as decisive a rejection of the responsible society, which is the root of the matter. Pound and Eliot stood as far back from contemporary American society as Adams and Santayana did. Ernest Samuels, in *Henry Adams; the Major Phase*, tells a story which neatly ties together all these people; the story of a book on education projected by Faber and Faber in 1940, to be written by Pound, Eliot, and Santayana together. This project was suggested by Pound, who had read in Santayana's autobiography that anecdote of Henry Adams' asserting the impossibility of all teaching (retold here on p. 160) and was highly delighted by it. He thought he, Eliot, and Santayana, the three literary exiles, could together say something important about national education. The Adams anecdote, he declared, writing to Santayana, should be in the opening pages, if not the opening paragraph, of this book; which was to 'save further generations from the horrors of past education'. We are told no more about the book, but its 'aesthetic' character, in our sense, seems clear.*

Winters' main point is explicit in his title, 'Henry Adams or the Creation of Confusion', and it is clear that the 'complexity' of modernist American writers, in thought as well as style, has found some inspiration in Adams and James. But their debt is a good deal more than that. It is also the delight in the fictional uses of 'point of view' which modern literature and criticism owes them. Adams' *Education* (a literary experiment which he thought only Henry James would really understand) is one of the great festivals of 'point of view' and 'the untrustworthy narrator'. And in *Mont-Saint-Michel* he created a picture of the thirteenth century which helped make it, for Eliot and others, the Golden Age that modern society needed to remember. In three or four ways, Adams' work has been at the source of the modern literary tradition, and when to his work we add James's, and the aesthetic idealism of Santayana and Berenson, we have a body of taste

---

* Eliot of course worked his way back, from and through his alienation, to his own idea of the responsible society—it is another of his great distinctions.

which has been, in an inconspicuous way, very influential.

Among strictly contemporary writers, Robert Lowell is the major representative of that taste, that sensibility, and an ample proof of its continuing power to inspire. It was from the hands of T. S. Eliot, not directly from the four aesthetes, that he received their tradition, and so he inherited also that modernist melodrama, that Gothicism of the imagination which the twentieth century grafted on to the *fin-de-siècle* stock. But Lowell's sense of his aesthete forbears is clear enough; it is there in his poems on Santayana and Ford Madox Ford. And in his plays adapting Hawthorne and Melville, the two nineteenth-century writers canonized by twentieth-century taste, we see another aspect of his debt to those forbears. Hawthorne and Melville were two writers who could seem worthy precursors of this modern sensibility, because they had been ill-at-east in the old Boston, unable to believe in the whole enterprise of the responsible society. They saw through the city's optimism, and foretold the decay of its self-confidence, and this has seemed like wisdom to men in the aesthetic tradition. The death-pangs of the Boston enterprise have reverberated in Lowell's imagination (and in other people's) with tragic dignity, with intellectual authority, with contemporary relevance. Its life-rhythms have had no twentieth-century resonances.

The aesthetes themselves, as I have pointed out, held back from the reckless experimentalism of the modern artist, in aesthetic techniques, and in personal life-styles. Berenson even looked askance at Bloomsbury. But their successors of the next generation were able to take part in that experimentalism (in the Paris of the twenties, for example) without having to give up their sense of quite other, grandly Olympian, values in 'art'. They were sustained in that experimentalism, in fact, by their belief (so central to this aestheticism) that all experience is equally fleeting, equally ignoble, and that only art can give it dignity. It is in this idealism—not strictly a belief, often, but a powerful tendency of taste—that the heritage of the aesthetes has survived most generally into modern literature. We have heard Berenson on this theme (in the quotations from *Aesthetics and History*) and Santayana's theory seems to be essentially the same.

'Life as it flows is so much time wasted, and nothing can ever be recovered or truly possessed save under the form of eternity, which is also the form of art.' Wallace Stevens' poetry may be said to express this theory, and this feeling, fairly directly; but even T. S. Eliot and Robert Lowell, who in the world of dogma might well deny it, show the emotional and nervous equivalent importantly; in their insistence on the unsatisfactoriness of all experience, on its categorical need to be ennobled—by art or by religion. To be ennobled means sometimes only to be enamelled, and always art of this kind keeps a character of something to be applied to life, of a substance antithetically different from mere experience.

That remark of Santayana's comes from his essay on Proust, and this is symbolic, for Proust's is the one kind of great modern fiction (apart from James's own) which one can see the aesthetes' taste and teaching lead to. Santayana and Berenson did in fact appreciate Proust; and James and Adams, nervous as they were of decadence in that form, must surely have loved the early volumes, while one does not see them particularly loving Lawrence, Kafka, Dostoevski. The best thing one can say for the fine parts of Adams' two late books is that they are Proustian. They are more Proustian than they are Jamesian. (Adams and Proust are parallel, presumably, in developing one side of Ruskin's rich heritage.) Proust *saved* experience, through memory; saved life, through art. He showed both the poverties and ignominies of being, and the riches and beauties of imagining.

And if Proust is their novelist, presumably Yeats is their poet —the Yeats of the mask theory and the autobiography, the poet of Byzantium. In Yeats as in Proust we see the implementation of aesthetic strategies taking over a whole life, reaching deep into the total personality, and dominating the other, the social and moral, faculties; and yet resulting in work we must call unequivocally splendid. This is the triumph of the aesthetes, the triumph of art over life, insofar as that phrase can have any respectable meaning.

Perhaps no one uses that phrase today, but that taste is very much alive. One need only consult the lists of Dissertation Abstracts, and of Work in Progress, to see how largely the taste of young students of modern literature has turned to Yeats, to Proust, to James, to Stevens, to Eliot, to Faulkner, and in nineteenth-century literature to Hawthorne and Melville.* If Frost and Twain are bigger names just now, it is largely because of the pendulum motion of taste—even the greatest enthusiast gets tired of hearing other people recite his hero's virtues, and the dissertations on those first writers are now innumerable as well as unreadable. Besides, Frost and Twain are often discussed as if they were Yeats and James.

This is a set of preferences and evaluations which derives from the aesthetes' taste, and in the scholarly books about James and Adams themselves, one finds their kind of aesthetic idealism taken for granted as literary dogma. For instance, in *The Mind and Art of Henry Adams*, J. C. Levenson tells us that 'Henry Adams offers his fellow Americans the richest and most challenging image of what they are, what they have been, and what they may become'. The tone is of a prophetic urgency, but mixed with aesthetic mystery, all concentrated in the word 'image'. Adams can do all this because 'he defied laws he thought of as absolute and universal. Making history into art . . . he won a victory over oblivion'. We should notice the use of 'art' here, which obviously means more than that Adams wrote history well. Just how much more it means we can guess from another phrase nearby, '. . . for the man deeply committed, art virtually becomes life.' This is 'art' in the largest sense, and with the largest value. Mr. Levenson's book is a very rich example of the contem-

---

* These are the writers who need to be explained, whose works constitute a hermetic world, to which only the literary man has the key; by virtue of his long study, by virtue of his general sensitiveness, by virtue above all of his *imagination*, which here means being at ease with irony, hyperbole, metaphor, myth—all the non-literal ways of telling the truth. These writers constitute a world of meaning to which only the literary intellectual has access— or so he may plausibly tell himself; so it is natural they should be the special kingdom of our literary intellectuals, who may plausibly describe themselves as being, in the general community, under constant imputation of impotence—of having no special kingdom, and no special truths to tell. This is of course a factor of some importance in keeping the taste of the aesthetes alive and meaningful today; and by no casual coincidence. The aesthetes' taste was *formed* in self-assertive reaction against a community which they felt had no longer a place for them. Naturally it is well adapted to serve the same function for literary men today.

porary triumph of the aesthetes' taste and theory. On every page
it celebrates the power of the mind (the literary mind—indeed,
literary techniques is what it often amounts to) to transform and
transcend matter. 'Henry Adams' quarter taint of Maryland
blood may be an unrewarding datum of biology, but it is a
fruitful metaphor.' And that—it is implied—is what matters.

That sentence contains, in its shape and tone as well as its
idea, the germ of this whole body of taste. It could have been
written by Adams himself; and the same could be said of many of
Levenson's sentences. It identifies a more than personal voice,
and an important one. Time and again one hears in Adams'
prose tones which characterize (exaggeratedly, in particular
cases, but still expressing a *general* and dangerous eccentricity)
the best literary mind in America today. For instance, the insistence on the casualness, the playfulness, the experimentalism, of
life-acts which obviously could not in reality be so casual; insisting that he wrote *Esther* to make an experiment with British and
American opinion, and with himself; or insisting that he wrote
his nine-volume history of the United States 'to see whether one
could fix for a familiar moment a necessary sequence of human
movement'. The mind so aggressively asserts its freedom, its
transcendence—against all probability, in this case; in other
cases, against the dignity of fact and experience. It is no wonder
this mind is not disturbed by Hawthorne's 'experiments with
himself'.

For all its subtlety, its energy, its range, this mind seems to me
to allow itself liberties which amount to delusions of grandeur,
and to draw on energies which amount to a hatred of life—a
hatred of the thinkers' own sources and conditions. Perhaps the
best explanation and demonstration of what I mean is this extraordinary letter from Henry Adams to Henry James in 1903.
(*Selected Letters*, ed. Newton Arvin, New York, 1951, pp.
239–240.)

Paris, 18 November 1903

Although you, like most men of toil, hate to be bored, I can hardly
pass over your last work without boring you to the extent of a letter.
We have reached a time of solar antiquity when nothing matters, but

still we feel what used to be called the law of gravitation, mass, or attraction, and obey it.

More than ever, after devouring your William Story, I feel how difficult a job was imposed on you. It is a *tour de force,* of course, but that you knew from the first. Whether you have succeeded or not, I cannot say, because it all spreads itself out as though I had written it, and I feel where you are walking on firm ground, and where you are on thin ice, as though I were in your place. Verily I believe I wrote it. Except your specialty of style, it is me.

The painful truth is that all of my New England generation, counting the half century, 1820–1870, were in actual fact only one mind and nature; the individual was a facet of Boston. We knew each other to the last nervous centre, and feared each other's knowledge. We looked through each other like microscopes. There was absolutely nothing in us that we did not understand merely by looking in the eye. There was hardly a difference even in depth, for Harvard College and Unitarianism kept us all shallow. We knew nothing—no! but really nothing! of the world. One cannot exaggerate the profundity of ignorance of Story in becoming a sculptor, or Sumner in becoming a statesman, or Emerson in becoming a philosopher. Story and Sumner, Emerson and Alcott, Lowell and Longfellow, Hillard, Winthrop, Motley, Prescott, and all the rest, were the same mind,—and so, poor worm!—was I!

Type bourgeois-bostonien! A type quite as good as another, but more uniform. What you say of Story is at bottom exactly what you would say of Lowell, Motley, and Sumner, barring degrees of egotism. You cannot help smiling at them, but you smile at us all equally. God knows that we knew our want of knowledge! the self-distrust become introspection—nervous self-consciousness—irritable dislike of America, and antipathy to Boston. *Auch ich war in Arcadien geboren.*

So you have written not Story's life, but your own and mine—pure autobiography,—the more keen for what is beneath, implied, intelligible only to me, and half a dozen other people still living; like Frank Boott: who knew our Boston, London and Rome in the fifties and sixties. You make me curl up, like a trodden-on worm. Improvised Europeans, we were, and—Lord God!—how thin! No, but it is too cruel! Long ago,—at least thirty years ago,—I discovered it, and have painfully held my tongue about it. You strip us, gently and kindly, like a surgeon, and I feel your knife in my ribs.

No one else will ever know it. You have been extremely tactful. The essential superficiality of Story and all the rest, you have made painfully clear to us, but not, I think, to the family or the public. After all the greatest men are weak. Morley's Gladstone is hardly thicker than your Story. Let us pray!

The complex of attitudes Adams expresses here, to himself, to Boston, to America, is very interesting; he shows quite sharply the power of nineteenth-century Boston as an idea, an influence, a way of life, and the passion with which the aesthetes repudiated that idea; and he expresses quite disturbingly a repudiation of him*self* and of his times, which is inseparable from his cultural theory. Clearly, he is telling the truth, in some sense, there. But in another sense—and this is equally interesting—he is not.

James wrote back that he had meant no such thing, and anyone who reads his book will see that James was right. This letter is an early, vivid, example of that habit of ascribing insidious intentions, unavowed or even unconscious, to books which insidiously affect oneself—that habit so characteristic of the American literary mind today. It is also a very vivid human document, its combination of emotional upset and intellectual composure almost insane. It is sane enough personally, perhaps, because of the clear control exerted by the mind and will, the element of play and pose in what is said. This is a cultural insanity here, affecting the communal mental habits this voice confidently participates in—the habits we have called aestheticism. And when that voice becomes and remains a high culture's symbol of sensitivity, of personal distinction, of a kind of disillusioned wisdom (isn't it recognizably the voice of Ralph Touchett in *The Portrait of a Lady*, and of Mr Compson in *The Sound and the Fury*, to name but two?) then surely something is wrong with that high culture?

FOOTNOTES

CHAPTER ONE

1. Samuel Eliot Morison: *One Boy's Boston 1887–1901* (Boston, 1962), p. 68.
2. M. A. de Wolfe Howe, ed.: *Barrett Wendell and His Letters* (Boston, 1924), pp. 145, 146.
3. Henry Adams: *History of the United States*, Vol. I (New York, 1889), pp. 20–25.
4. William Dean Howells: *Literary Friends and Acquaintances* (New York, 1900), p. 68.
5. William Charvat: *Literary Publishing in America 1790–1850* (Philadelphia, 1959), p. 23.
6. The details in this and the following paragraph were taken from Samuel Eliot Morison: *Three Centuries of Harvard* (Boston, 1936).
7. Oscar Handlin: 'Immigration in American Life: A Reappraisal', in H. S. Commager, ed.: *Immigration and American History* (Minneapolis, 1961).
8. Quoted in Richard Hofstadter: *Anti-Intellectualism in American Life* (New York, 1962), p. 157. The account of John Quincy Adams' message to Congress comes from there, too.
9. Merle Curti: *The Growth of American Thought*, second edition (New York, 1951), p. 469.
10. Marius Bewley: 'Cooper and Bryant', in Perry Miller, ed.: *Major Writers of America* (New York, 1962), p. 282.
11. Q. D. Leavis: *Fiction and the Reading Public* (London, 1932), p. 201.
12. F. R. Leavis: *Mass Civilization and Minority Culture* (Cambridge, England, 1930), p. 4.
13. Quoted in F. R. Leavis: *Education and the University* (London, 1943), p. 24.
14. Irving Howe: 'This Age of Conformity', *A World More Attractive* (New York, 1963), p. 278 and *passim*.
15. Quoted in Van Wyck Brooks: *The Writer in America* (New York, 1953), p. 35.

CHAPTER TWO

1. The remarks by Godkin and James are quoted in the "Civil War" section of Ferris Greenslet: *The Lowells and Their Seven Worlds* (Boston, 1946); and that by Holmes is reported and discussed in S. Hayakawa and H. M. Jones: *Oliver Wendell Holmes* (New York, 1939).
2. Edward Everett Hale: *A New England Boyhood* (Boston, 1893 and 1900), p. xxiii.
3. Josiah Quincy, *The History of the Boston Athenaeum* (Cambridge, Mass., 1851), pp. 39, 40, quoted in Curti, *op. cit.*, p. 227.
4. Hale, *op. cit.*, p. 19.
5. Edward Everett Hale: *James Russell Lowell and His Friends* (Boston, 1898), p. 55.

6. Quoted in Oscar Handlin: *Boston's Immigrants* (Cambridge, Mass., 1959), p. 1.

7. Charles Dickens: *American Notes* (London, 1843), Ch. 3. All the quotations from this work in this chapter come from Chapter 3.

8. These details and most of those in the next four paragraphs are taken from Handlin, *Boston's Immigrants*.

9. Dickens, *op. cit.*

10. The details about the Perkins Institute are mostly taken from Harry Best: *Blindness and the Blind in the United States* (New York, 1934).

11. These details are taken mostly from *Massachusetts General Hospital: A Memorial and Historical Volume* (Boston, 1921).

12. My authority for these details is *The Athenaeum Centenary* (Boston, 1907).

13. *Ibid.*

14. These details, and those of the next two paragraphs, are taken mostly from Harriette Knight Smith: *The History of the Lowell Institute* (Boston, 1898).

15. My authority for the assertions of this and the next paragraph is Greenslet, *The Lowells and Their Seven Worlds*.

16. Noel G. Annan: 'The Intellectual Aristocracy', in J. H. Plumb, ed.: *Studies in Social History* (London, 1955), pp. 243–287.

17. Curti, *op. cit.*, p. 522.

18. Henry Adams: *The Education of Henry Adams* (Boston, 1918), p. 420.

19. Taken from Michael Kraus: *The United States to 1865* (Ann Arbor, 1959).

20. Adams, *The Education of Henry Adams*, p. 211.

21. Richard Hofstadter: *The Age of Reform* (New York, 1955), Ch. 4, *passim*.

CHAPTER THREE

1. Newton Arvin: *Longfellow* (Boston, 1963), pp. 7, 21.

2. Annie Fields: *Authors and Friends* (Boston, 1897), p. 17.

3. Curti, *op. cit.*, p. 218.

4. M. A. de Wolfe Howe: *American Bookmen* (New York, 1898), p. 25 and *passim*.

5. E. Wilder Spaulding: *Ambassadors Ordinary and Extraordinary* (Washington, 1961), *passim*.

6. My authority for this and the next two paragraphs is Frank Luther Mott: *A History of American Magazines*, 3 vols. (Cambridge, Mass., 1938).

7. D. H. Lawrence: *St Mawr* (New York, 1925), p. 28.

8. Hale: *James Russell Lowell and His Friends*, p. 135.

9. Hofstadter: *Anti-Intellectualism in American Life*, Ch. 7, *passim*.

10. Adams: *History of the United States*, Vol. I, pp. 76–110.

11. Howells, *op. cit.*, p. 115.

12. Hale, *James Russell Lowell and His Friends*, p. 22.

13. Howells, *op. cit.*, pp. 179, 146.

14. Ferris Greenslet: *Thomas Bailey Aldrich* (Boston, 1908), p. 81.

15. Mott, *op. cit.*, for this and the next three paragraphs.

16. Hale, *James Russell Lowell and His Friends*, p. 106.

17. Smith, *op. cit.*, *passim*.

18. My authority on Fields is W. S. Tryon: *Parnassus Corner* (Boston, 1963).

CHAPTER FOUR

1. Reported in D. B. Tyack: *Gentleman of Letters: George Ticknor* (Harvard thesis, 1958). The address can be found in J. S. Buckminster, *Works,* Vol. II (Boston, 1839), pp. 339–365.
2. Hale, *A New England Boyhood,* p. 160.
3. The facts about Ticknor in this paragraph, and in the rest of the chapter are derived from his *Life, Letters, and Journal,* 2 vols. (Boston, 1878), ed. Anna Ticknor, unless otherwise identified.
4. Ticknor's *Letters,* II, p. 433.
5. Ticknor's *Letters,* I, p. 169.
6. Ticknor's *Letters,* I, p. 27.
7. Ticknor's *Letters,* I, p. 357.
8. A. La Piana: *Dante's American Pilgrimage* (New Haven, 1948).
9. There is a discussion of this in Tyack, *op. cit.*
10. Hale, *James Russell Lowell and His Friends,* p. 106.
11. Ticknor's *Letters,* I, p. 258.
12. These comments are reported in Tyack, *op. cit.*
13. Ticknor's *Letters,* I, p. 182.
14. Marius Bewley: 'Cooper and Bryant', in *Major Writers of America,* pp. 284–285.
15. Quoted in William L. Hedges: 'Washington Irving', in *Major Writers of America,* p. 182.
16. Ticknor's *Letters,* II, p. 50.
17. Ticknor's *Letters,* II, p. 75.
18. Greenslet, *The Lowells and Their Seven Worlds,* p. 164.

CHAPTER FIVE

1. 'Boston', *Encyclopaedia Britannica,* eleventh edition.
2. Hofstadter, *Anti-Intellectualism in American Life,* p. 400.
3. *Ibid.,* p. 173.
4. Hofstadter: *The American Political Tradition* (New York, 1954), p. 162.
5. Quoted in Hofstadter, *The Age of Reform,* Ch. 4, section 1.
6. The facts in this and the next five paragraphs are taken mostly from M. A. de Wolfe Howe: *The Boston Symphony Orchestra* (Boston, 1931).
7. The quotations and facts here, and in the next two paragraphs, come from Morris Carter: *Isabella Stewart Gardner and Fenway Court* (Boston, 1925).
8. The facts in this paragraph are taken from M. A. de Wolfe Howe: *The Atlantic Monthly* (Boston, 1919).
9. Howells, *op. cit.,* p. 37.
10. *Ibid.,* p. 136.
11. Ellery Sedgwick: *The Happy Profession* (Boston, 1946), p. 175.
12. Barrett Wendell: *A Literary History of America* (New York, 1900), p. 342.
13. *Ibid.,* p. 152.

CHAPTER SIX

1. Unless otherwise identified, the facts about Norton are all derived from Sara Norton and M. A. de Wolfe Howe, ed.: *The Letters of Charles Eliot Norton,* 2 vols. (Boston, 1913).
2. Ferris Greenslet, ed.: *The Life, Letters, and Journal of George Ticknor*

(Boston, 1909), p. x.

3. John Jay Chapman: *Memories and Milestones* (New York, 1915), p. 132.

4. George Santayana: *Persons and Places* (New York, 1944; later published as *The Backgrounds of My Life*, Vol. I of the 3-vol. *Persons and Places*), p. 154.

5. Barrett Wendell: 'Mr Lowell as a Teacher', *Stelligeri, and Other Essays Concerning America* (New York, 1893), p. 206.

6. Adams, *The Education of Henry Adams*, Ch. 4, *passim*.

7. Edmund Wilson: *Patriotic Gore* (New York, 1962), Ch. 16.

8. *The Letters of Charles Eliot Norton*, I, p. 368.

9. *Ibid.*, II, p. 10.

10. F. Manchester and O. Shepard, ed.: *Irving Babbitt, Man and Teacher* (New York, 1941), p. 44.

11. *The Letters of Charles Eliot Norton*, I, p. 297; II, pp. 15, 122.

12. Charles Eliot Norton: 'James Russell Lowell', *Harper's Magazine*, May, 1893.

13. *Ibid.*

CHAPTER SEVEN

1. Quoted in Sylvia Sprigge: *Bernhard Berenson* (Boston, 1960), p. 107.

2. B. Berenson: *Sketch for a Self-Portrait* (New York, 1949), p. 70.

3. Quoted in Sprigge, *op. cit.*, p. 216.

4. George Santayana: *Character and Opinion in the United States* (New York, 1920), p. 105.

5. Santayana, *ibid.*, p. 109.

6. Santayana, *Persons and Places*, p. 137.

7. Henry James: *The Bostonians* (London, 1886), Ch. 3.

8. Santayana: *My Host the World* (New York, 1953; Vol. III of *Persons and Places*), p. 33.

9. Henry Adams, *The Education of Henry Adams*, p. 70.

10. *Ibid.*, p. 6.

11. R. S. Moore: *Constance Fenimore Woolson* (New York, 1963), pp. 31–32.

12. Iris Origo: 'Bernhard Berenson', *The Cornhill*, Spring, 1960.

13. George Santayana: *The Middle Span* (New York, 1945; Vol. II of *Persons and Places*), p. 129.

14. George Santayana: *The Genteel Tradition at Bay* (New York, 1931), p. 56.

15. *Ibid.*, p. 58.

16. Adams, *The Education of Henry Adams*, p. 337.

17. H. D. Cater, ed.: *Henry Adams and His Friends* (New York, 1947), p. lxx.

18. Santayana, *Persons and Places*, p. 234.

19. Santayana, *My Host the World*, p. 97.

20. *Ibid.*, p. 95.

CHAPTER EIGHT

1. Howells, *op. cit.* p. 133.

2. James Russell Lowell: *My Study Windows* (Boston, 1871), p. 379.

3. A continuation of the preceding.

4. A letter to Norton, quoted in M. A. de Wolfe Howe, ed.: *Memories of a Hostess* (Boston, 1922), p. 92.

5. James Russell Lowell: 'Agassiz', *Poetical Works* (Boston, 1892), Vol. IV, p. 101.
6. Quoted in Ferris Greenslet: *James Russell Lowell* (Boston, 1905), p. 169.
7. Norton, 'James Russell Lowell'.
8. Howells, *op. cit.*, p. 217.
9. Howe, ed.: *Memories of a Hostess*, p. 63.
10. *Ibid.*, pp. 70–72.
11. Reproduced in Greenslet, *The Lowells and Their Seven Worlds*, p. 219.
12. *Ibid.*, p. 350.
13. Norton, 'James Russell Lowell'.
14. Figures taken from Handlin, *Boston's Immigrants*.
15. See the last chapter of Hofstadter's *Anti-Intellectualism in American Life*.
16. Hofstadter, *The Age of Reform*, Ch. 4, section 1.
17. V. Parrington: *Main Currents in American Thought*, Vol. II, p. 385.
18. Margaret Fuller: 'American Literature', in Perry Miller, ed.: *Margaret Fuller: American Romantic* (New York, 1963), p. 239.
19. Handlin, 'Immigration in American Life', p. 22.
20. Curti, *op. cit.*, p. 268.
21. C. A. and M. R. Beard: *The Rise of American Civilization* (New York, 1927), Vol. II, p. 397.
22. A. M. Schlesinger: *The Age of Jackson* (Boston, 1950), p. 374.

CHAPTER NINE

1. Hayakawa and Jones, *op. cit.*, p. xv.
2. *The Letters of Charles Eliot Norton*, II, p. 181.
3. Fields, *op. cit.*, p. 55.
4. Howells, *op. cit.*, p. 32.
5. Fields, *op. cit.*, p. 74.
6. Norton, 'James Russell Lowell'.
7. Ralph Waldo Emerson: 'Thoreau', *Lectures and Biographical Sketches* (Boston, 1894), pp. 447–448.
8. James Russell Lowell: 'Thoreau', *Literary Works*, Vol. I (Boston, 1890).
9. James Russell Lowell, a lecture, published in the Harvard *Crimson*, and quoted in Greenslet, *James Russell Lowell*, p. 125.

APPENDIX A.

1. *The Letters of Charles Eliot Norton*, I, p. 503.

APPENDIX B.

1. Stanley Elkins: *Slavery: A Problem in American Institutional and Intellectual Life* (Chicago, 1959), p. 27.
2. *Ibid.*, Part 2, *passim*.
3. *Ibid.*, Part 4, *passim*.
4. *Ibid.*, p. 140.
5. *Ibid.*, p. 161.
6. *Ibid.*, p. 162.

INDEX

DATE DUE